CSR in Practice

Also by Andrew Kakabadse and Nada Kakabadse

GOVERNANCE, STRATEGY AND POLICY: Seven Critical Essays (*editors*)

THE GEOPOLITICS OF GOVERNANCE

SMART SOURCING: International Best Practice

INTIMACY: An International Survey of the Sex Lives of People at Work

WORKING IN ORGANISATIONS, 2ND EDITION

ESSENCE OF LEADERSHIP

CSR in Practice

Delving Deep

Edited by

Andrew Kakabadse

and

Nada Kakabadse

First published in 2007 by
PALGRAVE MACMILLAN
Houndmills, Basingstoke, Hampshire RG21 6XS and
175 Fifth Avenue, New York, N.Y. 10010
Companies and representatives throughout the world.

PALGRAVE MACMILLAN is the global academic imprint of the Palgrave
Macmillan division of St. Martin's Press, LLC and of Palgrave Macmillan Ltd.
Macmillan® is a registered trademark in the United States, United Kingdom
and other countries. Palgrave is a registered trademark in the European
Union and other countries.

ISBN-13: 978–0–230–01368–1 hardback
ISBN-10: 0–230–01368–6 hardback

This book is printed on paper suitable for recycling and made from fully
managed and sustained forest sources.

A catalogue record for this book is available from the British Library.

Library of Congress Cataloging-in-Publication Data

CSR in practice: delving deep / edited by Andrew Kakabadse and
Nada Kakabadse.
    p. cm.
Includes bibliographical references and index.
ISBN-13: 978–0–230–01368–1
ISBN-10: 0–230–01368–6
1. Social responsibility of business. I. Kakabadse, Andrew.
II. Kakabadse, Nada.

HD60.C78 2007
658.4′08—dc22   2006050503

10 9 8 7 6 5 4 3 2 1
16 15 14 13 12 11 10 09 08 07

Printed and bound in Great Britain by
Antony Rowe Ltd, Chippenham and Eastbourne

Contents

List of Figures

List of Tables

Notes on Contributors

Kerry Elliott, Postgraduate Researcher, Northampton Business School, University of Northampton, UK.

Andrew P. Kakabadse, Professor of International Management Development, School of Management, Cranfield University, UK.

Nada K. Kakabadse, Professor in Management and Business Research, Northampton Business School, University of Northampton, UK.

Antje Kaspurz, Postgraduate Researcher, Northampton Business School, University of Northampton, UK.

Reeves Knyght, Director, Wingate House, Melbourne, Australia.

Richard Middleton, Postgraduate Researcher, Northampton Business School, University of Northampton, UK.

Cécile Rozuel, PhD Researcher, School of Management, University of Surrey, UK.

Foreword

According to a recent McKinsey Global CEO Survey of 4000 executives in 116 countries, 84% of those questioned believe that the old mantra that 'the business of business is business' no longer describes the reality of a company's role and responsibility in society.[1] These same senior managers recognise the increasing risk and exposure of their companies to reputation damage and the destruction of shareholder value where economic, social, political and environmental impacts are not properly understood and managed. From climate change to job losses and off-shoring, from pensions and healthcare to access to emerging markets, from human rights and supply chains to ethical consumers, make no mistake, business in society issues are increasingly strategic for top management.

Nevertheless, perhaps the most noteworthy finding of the survey was that while 70% saw 'some' or 'substantial' room for improvement in managing business in society issues in their companies, when questioned on the tactics most often used versus what would be likely to be most effective, there was a significant disparity. While companies favoured traditional measures such as communicating through the media and public relations, lobbying of regulators and governments, CEO speeches and CSR reporting, top leaders believed that increasing transparency and information on the risks of products and processes, developing and implementing internal policies on corporate responsibility and engaging stakeholders would deliver far better results. Put simply by senior executives' own admission, there is a significant disjoint between their strategies and the realities of a complex, globalised world.

This sets the context and explains the significance of *CSR in Practice: Delving Deep* as an important contribution in helping companies to seriously understand, develop strategies and manage the risks (and opportunities) of an operating environment that is changing fast as a result of the pressures and realities of globalisation and shifts in stakeholder expectation on the role and responsibility of business in society.

As the editors point out in their first chapter, myriad different terms and definitions surround these issues including stakeholder management, corporate citizenship, CSR or any number of other nuances. Call it what you will, but theory and practice have quickly moved from the 'what' to the 'how'.

While corporate responsibility essentially emerged from a philanthropic desire to give something back to a 'bolt-on', quasi-corporate function in its own right, companies are increasingly looking at how they can integrate corporate responsibility into strategy and operations across the organisation to achieve long terms business success. From my own experience with leading companies, it seems that the Communications Director's words in the introduction ring true, 'change is taking place ... "CSR hype" is coming to an end'.

The book employs a broad lens in understanding the challenges and opportunities of integrating corporate responsibility in and across companies. This includes an exploration of strategic issues, business functions, industry sectors and stakeholder groups involved in the debate and practice of corporate responsibility across a range of different national cultures and geographies. From the role of investment brokers and insider trading in the finance industry to public and private healthcare delivery in the UK and France to supply chain and corporate governance in the boardroom, the breadth and depth of analysis is impressive.

This is complemented by a powerful thematic framework that takes managers through a learning journey. Each chapter begins with a key strategic consideration and concludes with concrete takeaways to help managers support corporate responsibility implementation. The book's starting point emphasises on understanding what you are talking about with regard to corporate responsibility, the different issues, stakeholders, terms, etc. The next steps are to understand the importance of reflecting on current practice, considering the broader picture and then proceeding to act. The journey correctly concludes with the importance of considering the 'context' in terms of the interaction between organisations, individuals and national and regional cultures amidst the complex economic, social, political and environmental forces of globalisation. These all have an enormous impact in shaping the understanding of the role of business in society and the different approaches to corporate responsibility adopted by companies as well as identifying and understanding critical success factors.

As I sit here having just finished the book, it strikes me that the real strength of the publication is that the editors' and authors' ability to bridge theory and practice in a way that is enlightening and enormously, well ... practical! This is no mean feat at a time when business and academia seem to be moving further apart. As Winston Churchill once wrote, 'there is nothing like the practical value of a good theory'.[2] At the same time, there is nothing quite like the theoretical value of understanding good practice. To my mind, *CSR in Practice: Delving Deep* achieves both admirably.

This success is perhaps unsurprising given Andrew and Nada Kakabadse's leadership of the project that underpins this book. Not only is their world-class thought leadership and extensive track record evident in this book, their energy and commitment to work in partnership with business executives to solve real world problems through research, knowledge development and learning comes shining through.

I strongly recommend this book to business executives grappling with the magnitude of the real world challenges of integrating corporate responsibility into core activities. However, I would have no hesitation in also recommending it to a wider audience including representatives from civil society organisations, policy-making and government. Its practically grounded approach to identifying future areas in need of research also makes it highly relevant to an academic audience, particularly as it goes a long way to bridging what Nonaka describes as the boundaries between implicit and explicit managerial knowledge.[3]

Peter Lacy
Executive Director
European Academy of Business in Society

Notes

1. McKinsey (2006), 'Global survey of business executives', *The McKinsey Quarterly*, January, 1–10.
2. There is some dispute about whether Churchill or Kurt Lewin – the father of action research – first used this quote. While acknowledging both possibilities, perhaps out of a residual romantic attachment to British history, I hope the reader will forgive me for going with the former!
3. Nonaka, I. (1994), 'A dynamic theory of organizational knowledge creation', *Organization Science*, 5(1): February, 14–37.

Acknowledgements

Our deepest thanks to all those who took part in the studies reported in this book. Your views, challenges and practices have provided for invaluable learning to many.

Our sincere gratitude to Severstal, the Russian Steel company that sponsored many of the inquiries reported in this book. Your concern for people and community is acknowledged and admired. Alexey Mordashov, Vadim Makhov, Vadim Shvetsov, Anatoly Kruchinin, Mikhail Noskov, Dmitry Afanasyev, Dmitry Kouptsov are but a few of those from Severstal who sincerely encouraged us to research and delve deep. We, the editors, are truly thankful.

Finally, particular thanks go to Sheena Darby and Alison Cain whose patience, perseverance and good humour have been distinctly instrumental in the production of this book. Organising meetings and interviews, dealing with changes to programmes and last minute rescheduling of appointments, you persevered with all that and the transcription of numerous tapes and draft after draft of copy – all with a smile, good humour, fortitude and a sensitive touch. This book is as much a tribute to both of you and the care and concern you displayed to all those involved.

Introduction

Andrew P. Kakabadse and Nada K. Kakabadse

> Change is taking place!
> — A corporate communications director

Not our words, us the editors that is, but the words of an experienced corporate communications director of a well known global company. Her background was impeccable from the corporate social responsibility (CSR) point of view, political lobbying, media and communications supported by seven years' experience of working for a well-known NGO.

> Yes, change is taking place, she re-affirmed. Despite all the frustrations with the term CSR, I do believe that companies, the watchdogs (press, media and stock exchanges) and shareholders are taking note.

The lady in question was attending a workshop exploring the role of CSR in the boardroom. Most of the attendees had started the day with positive comment about CSR but by the time of the mid-morning coffee break, their true sentiments began to show, namely that CSR was a nice topic of conversation but in reality that meant bolstering corporate image – as long as the company looked good, that was all that was needed!

However, one voice stood out and that was the lady corporate communications director.

> We have gone beyond making the annual report look good. I think CSR is beginning to take hold.

She was convincing. Her theme was that the phase of 'CSR hype' was now coming to an end, despite frustration with the term.

> Although CSR means anything to anybody, the CSR movement has become serious and should be treated as such.

> We do not need to know more about what CSR could be. What we need to know is how to make it work!

Her next words stuck in our minds.

> We are not delving deep enough – we need to understand what happens in practice and develop the action steps about making CSR work! We are here today to find out about CSR in practice.

The 'here today' referred to the workshop and from those comments emerged this book and title – CSR in Practice: Delving Deep.

> Is CSR still corporate hype? – maybe.
> Are most becoming more sincere about CSR? – probably.
> Do we know enough about really making CSR work? – probably not.

This book explores what CSR means to the various members of the executive community and as a result, how CSR can be more efficiently and effectively adopted. Driven by the phrase 'delving deep', a number of case studies were initiated to inquire into CSR application. The case studies reported in this book stand alone, with each occupying a separate chapter and each having its own literature analysis. The cases range from examination of CSR policy development to the operational reality of how CSR really works 'on the ground'. In so doing, issues and questions are raised which, although addressed, require more intense, quantitative examination in order to emerge with definitive statements about CSR practice and the pit falls to avoid. Therefore, throughout, mention is made of the need for further research.

From seven separate inquiries, four considerations for effective CSR adoption are identified. First, CSR is broad, not because academicians wish to complicate but because the topic itself is complex. The term corporate social responsibility is a meeting point of philosophy, sociology, the organisation and strategic literatures, micro economics and even the psychologies of behaviour and cognition. So, *theme 1; at least know what you are talking about*, and in order to do that, an appreciation of the spread of interpretations is helpful. In response, the opening chapter of this book overviews the literature drawing attention to the contrasting meanings of CSR. Inevitably, Chapter 1 does focus on the old favourite debate between stakeholder and shareholder. However, also examined is the historical development of varied CSR meanings and through so doing the CSR interpretations likely to arise in the future, are discussed. Included in the chapter are the varying clusters of meanings from academician, corporate and NGO/governmental sources. Through such comparison, the question posed is, can such tension be positively harnessed? The chapter concludes affirmatively, emphasising 'leverage power' and that through mature reflection of one's own and the organisation's values and expectations, businesses and governments can exhibit more responsible conduct towards society.

From that analysis emerges *theme 2; reflect on what you are doing and would like to do*. The term 'reflection' implies singularity, namely what I do or should do. The 'I' focus is interpreted at two levels, the individual and the organisation, captured in the next two chapters. In both chapters, case study examination delves deep into the reality of CSR pursuit. Chapter 2 explores how a CSR award winning and particularly well-known food processing multinational corporation (MNC) has adopted CSR. As the MNC is large, the study focused on one of its divisions and, in turn, only on one product, vanilla. The study traces CSR application right from strategic conception and through the vanilla supply chain to the farmers who grow this fragile plant. The mind-set of a well-intended CSR oriented corporate centre is contrasted against farmers living on the edge of poverty in Madagascar, fundamentally ignorant of the term CSR. The learning to draw from Chapter 2 is 'follow through'. By all means be considered, concerned and be well intended in terms of CSR but support that with organisational discipline. Needed are protocols of follow through, capturing exactly what is happening at each point of the supply chain and thus ensuring for consistent pursuit of CSR strategy. In this sense, CSR is treated as simply one aspect of strategy adoption. The company in question, 'lovely' and socially conscious as it is, did not enforce follow through protocol adoption. So what happened – well what was intended did not happen! The 'good guys' at the top were, through their inaction, allowing social inequity to continue. Not reported in this chapter is that certain of the senior management were informed of the findings of the study and their collective reaction was,

> We have the dilemma of every business when markets mature, the management of costs. By implication, when the going gets tough, cost determines the nature of CSR pursuit.

Maybe, but also maybe not. Cost discipline and CSR pursuit are not a dilemma but more of a continuous tension. The balance between attention to costs and social enactment is dynamic. No perfect point of balance can ever be found. As change happens, be informed! Through being informed, disciplined responsibility can be pushed 'down the line'. Informed responsibility requires measurement and through that emerges a confidence that strategic intentions are transformed into operational reality through consistent, disciplined application. The combination of measurement and consistent application allows senior and middle management to reach meaningful decisions on how to address the dilemma of controlling costs but also on being responsive to social needs. Be lax on measurement and very shortly application becomes inconsistent, ultimately ineffective and the age old excuse of, 'I did not know that was happening', becomes a way of being.

From reflection and being informed then comes action, or do something irrespective of the discomfort that arises. From the multinational world of food processing, Chapter 3 captures life at a local French hospital. The study highlights the meanings of care adopted for patients and for community. France, as most Western nations, is rethinking its national health policy with the current, seeming inevitable transfer of responsibilities from the state to the private sector. As with most local hospitals, French or not, the pressure to remain 'in budget' and the danger of being 'closed down', for purposes of rationalisation, are ever present. What emerges from the study is, in many ways, an informed populace who in their own way are making a 'pretty good job' of facing up to the pressures of healthcare delivery. However, differences of view of care and internal organisational barriers require leadership and robust dialogue in order to pull together a more cohesive vision and pursuit of healthcare. As the chapter shows, the need for better leadership is appreciated. What is required is leadership will to act. The desire to change in the French hospital was there. The drive to improve and the strength of character to raise the difficult question(s) did not emerge as forthcoming. Thus, if one side of reflection is recognising what are the necessary organisational disciplines to ensure for action, the other side is the courage to stand up, speak the truth and do what is considered as right. As shown in both cases, easy to say, far more demanding to apply.

From what 'I' do, the book moves onto the pluralist view of 'we'. The book takes the reader from reflect to recognise! Thus, *theme 3, recognise what is happening around you, look at the broader picture and do not accept today's reality as normal.* Review what is considered as normal. Just because that is the way 'things' have been done, does not mean to say that life should so continue into the future. Thus, from single organisational case studies, attention is given in the next three chapters to the much broader influence of the norms and values predominating communities and whole sectors. Examination is undertaken of the powerful demographic influences that provide shape to the world in which we live. On a sector basis, Chapter 4 examines CSR in the world of investment banking and particularly through the 'lens' of the investment broker. Investment banking is a bit of a 'sensitive world'. Bankers seem to have been reluctant to draw open the curtain on just what really happens in pulling together multi-billion dollar deals. Well, inquiry unfolds a world driven by personal gain. How the deal is initiated; how it is structured; how it is executed, emerge as the results of the endeavour of one person or a small group, each time differently configured according to the demands of each new deal. The telling factor is the commission arising from each deal. The more brokers do for themselves, the more they keep in terms of financial gain. So, one interesting dilemma emerges between making money with, at times, little regard for anyone else and the need to nurture a network of relationships critical to attracting the next deal. In a world driven by concern for self and the size of one's own financial reward, what of CSR? Precious little attention is given to CSR but when there is, that is the result of the wishes of a particular client or through a requirement from top management to protect the reputation of the bank.

From banking back to health but this time an examination of the United Kingdom's private healthcare industry. Chapter 5 explores the views of care but from the threefold perspective of consultant surgeons, hospital managers and patients. Contentious health issues, such as infertility treatment, cosmetic surgery and the termination of pregnancy provide the setting for analysis of one aspect of CSR, namely the ethical considerations involved in the reaching and exercising of decisions in circumstances of 'those who can pay, benefit'. The inquiry shows that doctors care most for their patients, patients care most for themselves and managers care most for their hospital. Certainly, no 'earth shattering' result, except for the fact that the moral 'ownership' of care is switching hands. On the one hand, doctors in private healthcare do not emerge as a community working to make money for themselves. Saying no to medical procedures that are, in the doctor's eyes, not in the best interest of the patient and thus losing a 'client', is a conscious and exercised option. Managers, on the other hand, are more concerned with meeting the financial goals of their hospital. Patients want what they want and try to get what they want at times to their own detriment. The fact that the three respondent groups adopt contrasting moral platforms to determine their decision-making behaviour is not the issue. What is, is the ethical determination of medical practice through the Hippocratic oath. Doctors, as guardians of the oath, are identified as its passive champions. All the doctors seem able to do in today's world of focused marketing and information freely available on an unpoliced web, is to refuse to proceed with surgery despite patient protest and hospital employer displeasure. The ethics of medicine are emerging as, 'what I (the doctor) cannot or will not do'. The healthcare organisation is the stronger influence, promoting its interests and that of shareholders, not necessarily at the expense of patients but more likely with them as lesser on the list of stakeholder priorities. Economic value add uncomfortable balances against patient welfare with doctors less able to proactively champion the healthcare rights of the patient.

From healthcare to financial markets, particularly capital markets, equities, 'liquid' money, the funding source of the 'big deals'. Chapter 6 delves into the world of insider trading but holds one parallel with Chapter 5, that of ethical consideration. Analysis of the Vienna, London and New York stock exchanges indicates that insider trading is alive and well. The only difference across the three sites is that the Austrians are more open about insider trading, whilst the British and Americans took longer to 'open up'. Although the term is extensively used, questioned is just what is insider trading? – and what transpires seems to be the very essence of working in capital markets. Insider trading is the holding of some form of 'insider', privileged knowledge of possible mergers, acquisitions, larger financial transaction or whatever, for the purpose of financial gain. The structuring of financial deals, as shown in Chapter 4, is strongly determined by each person's network of relationship ties. Thus, insider trading is knowledge and personal connection. Interestingly, the study respondents asked us, the researchers, questions. What is the difference between research (a must in financial deal making) and insider trading? Further, how many forms of so-called insider trading go unpunished? For example, having the knowledge not to proceed with a deal but punish those that do, are both forms of insider trading but one is penalised and the other not. What about the reality of living in a networked community, particularly a small one as Austria, where probably a 'secret' has a shelf life of about 30 seconds? The view put forward is that insider trading is here to stay, as research, networking, gossip, long- established 'philos' ties are the very essence of financial dealings. Hence, if networking and financial deals are so interlinked, what is all the fuss about? Not much is the answer of those interviewed but attention should focus on the large firm. The study respondents discussed the influence of the 'global corporation', determining market shape and swing and offer the view that stamping out insider trading is tackling only one, and at that, less important problem. Their view is that the global corporation can do much more harm to communities than can insider deals.

And so to Chapter 7, the study of boardroom behaviour. What role, if any, does CSR really play in the ultimate strategic forum – the boardroom? Chapter 7 introduces the fourth and final theme of this book, *theme 4; so with all this insight what are you really minded to do?* American, British and Continental European board members' views of the role of CSR in the boardroom surfaces a critical division between the Anglo-American shareholder world of philanthropy and the stakeholder world of the firm as an agent of the community. The bridging of these worlds remains a challenge. What is interesting is the orientation of UK public agencies. Despite the UK being a foremost champion of the 'marketisation of government', UK public agency board members profess a strong stakeholder philosophy and as a result, confess to deliberately walking away from private sector employment.

As a consequence of being informed (theme 1), reflecting on current practice (theme 2), considering the broader picture (theme 3) and then proceeding to act (theme 4) one final consideration remains, that of context. As each context is considered as unique, the manner of adoption of the four themes will vary with each new circumstance. One form of context is that of the organisation and the challenges it faces due to its position on the economic life cycle. Another form of context is the deeply held values that determine people's mind-set and behaviour. At the country and regional level, distinct aggregates of values are detected, highlighting three CSR platforms, those of social community, environment and corporate ethics (Figure 0.1). Through such scoping, stakeholder management, corporate philanthropy and citizenship are contrasted and compared in the various chapters of this text. Philanthropic good is but one form of CSR; there are others which are discussed at length.

Thus, from operation and measurement to policy determination, this text of CSR highlights certain of the realities of social responsibility application in the world of today. It should be noted that gaining access to the various sites described was no easy matter. The reluctance to open up and relay 'what is really happening here' was a common experience. However, once in, amazing insight emerged about the nature of organisation and markets and the reality of CSR adoption.

The evidence suggests that the CSR movement (if there is such a thing) is taking hold. Visible responsibility to community, in whatever

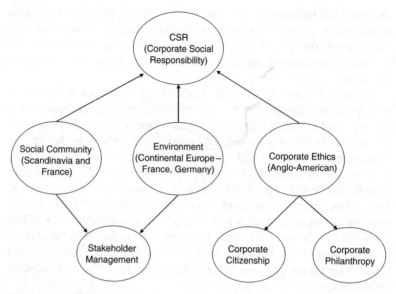

Figure 0.1   CSR Platforms

shape, is likely to be required by investors, stock exchanges, government and their codes of conduct and legislation. The message to take from this book is, be CSR positive, in whatever shape that takes, but couple intent with the adoption of strategic, leadership and managerial skills which lead to disciplined application.

1
Corporate Social Responsibility: Contrast of Meanings and Intents

Andrew P. Kakabadse, Nada K. Kakabadse and Cécile Rozuel

Introduction

Business and societal ethical dilemmas have been matters of concern for at least a century and probably ever since the pursuit of 'self-interest' began to determine the nature of wellbeing of communities (Berenbeim, 2000). However, the debate on the relationships between business and society (i.e. what these are and what they ought to be) only hit the headlines some 25 years ago. Scholars of diverse backgrounds, ranging from philosophy to sociology to management science, began to ponder on the duties of business organisation in relation to its nature and role within society (Bowie, 2000). Corporate social responsibility (CSR) gained further recognition as a result of certain corporations collapsing due to legal and/or ethical misconduct which, in turn, nurtured a sentiment that 'business excess' could be alleviated by adopting a 'socially responsible' attitude. Yet, despite citizen outrage and governmental pressure, in certain quarters, it is considered that CSR and sustainable development are expressions in common usage but in reality little significant change has taken place in terms of practice (Matten *et al.*, 2003; Kakabadse *et al.*, 2005). Undoubtedly, society's expectation of business responsiveness to societal concerns has increased more or less in parallel with the power that corporations have gained but somehow the debate seems confused when it comes to agree on plans of actions (Carroll, 1999; Lantos, 2001).

Thus, this chapter aims to understand the reasons behind affording greater CSR attention through reviewing the progress that has been made and the promises that are still to be realised. In so doing, this chapter will first review the concept of CSR since the 1950s in conjunction with social events which may have pushed the discussion in one particular direction or another. The key elements recurrent in the CSR literature will be examined in order to provide a clearer picture of the nature and shape of CSR. Additionally, the chapter will examine the concepts of shareholder and stakeholder and accompanying derivative theories. Finally, the chapter will highlight areas of interesting challenge in terms of CSR research in order to alleviate the tension between assertion and praxis, which seemingly is the state of play today.

History of CSR

Emergence of corporate obligation to society

Adam Smith's opus, *The Wealth of Nations* (1991), still remains the landmark of modern capitalism (Smith, 1991). Smith's proposition is that when business is free to pursue profit and efficiency, it eventually benefits 'the common good', serving both its interests and those of society (Lantos, 2001). Smith's thesis spawned the moral philosophy of free market economics which Milton Friedman (1970) championed through his adoption of the neoclassical position by explaining that profitability is the ultimate social responsibility of business if pursued in an ethical way and in obedience to the law. Adopting agency theory, Friedman (1970) explained that the social responsibilities of business are nonexistent as the prime task of the firm is to best utilise the resources of the principals that it ultimately serves (Lantos, 2001; Moir, 2001).

Neoclassical economics, more commonly known as the 'shareholder model', has been questioned for over half a century particularly with Bowen's (1953) introduction of the idea of the 'social responsibilities' of business. Doubt as to the sustainability of shareholder value pursuit arose among scholars due to the growing discrepancies between liberal assumptions concerning wealth creation and its distribution and socioeconomic reality (Takala, 1999). Society's emerging disillusionment with the liberal economic model was evident when moral compromise stood side by side with business success, especially in the United States where rampant consumerism led to an outcry against immoral business practice (Carroll, 1999; Lantos, 2001; Thévenet, 2003). Thus, a core idea arose that businesses could and should be reasonably expected to serve society in a way that goes beyond its obligation to shareholders. It should, however, not be forgotten that there have always been entrepreneurs (sometimes referred to as 'industrials') who understood that providing decent wages and other social and material benefits to employees and their family was a proper and additional way to behave to realising obvious economic advantage (Juholin, 2004). Both the United States and Continental Europe spawned their share of 'Christian value driven' businessmen who believed that supporting their workforce in various ways beyond mere wages was necessary for the enhancement of social morality. Yet the very same act by others, for instance the building of houses close to the factory, was not out of concern for their employees' welfare nor to comply with moral or religious demands but rather because having employees next to the factory would make them easier to control, be more productive and reduce costs. Thus began the practice of providing housing and other facilities, which were often the property of the enterprise owner, for the purposes of utilising such resources for gain as well as for generating sufficiently sound living conditions. Establishing whether business involvement in societal concerns consisted of pure human decency or a mere cost/benefit analysis, historically was not and continues to not be clear today.

Despite such haze, the 1960s and 1970s brought a significant expansion of academic interest to the CSR field. Corporate social responsibility was examined and discussed in depth, resulting with the emergence of CSR models and debate on the interrelationship between business ethics and corporate social responsiveness (Carroll, 1999). Thus, a spread of themes became the focus of research in the 1980s, notably corporate social performance (CSP) and models of stakeholder management (Davis, 1960). Since the 1990s, CSR has also been used as 'the base point', or as an element of other related concepts, to explore how CSR applies to the public sector since public organisations have turned into more network type entities alongside the private sector (Scholl, 2001). There is also ample discussion of the 'business case' for CSR, on behalf of multinational corporations (MNCs) and for small to medium-sized enterprises (SMEs). Frederick (1978/1994; 1986; 1998) provided clarity by identifying four different 'waves' of CSR since the 1950s which illustrate a shift of concern from an almost ontological debate on the purpose of business (CSR1 – corporate social responsibility) to a very practical and managerial view of the corporations' social duties in the mid-1970s (CSR2 – corporate social responsiveness), moving back by the mid-1980s to discussing the essential normative dimension of CSR effort to improve business-society relationships (CSR3 – corporate social rectitude) and finally, challenging the truthfulness of the taken-for-granted view of the business-centred world (CSR4 – cosmos, science and religion). That latter stage of reflection remains at the edge of current

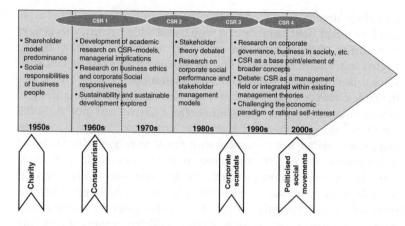

Figure 1.1   Evolution of CSR research since the 1950s.
Source: Adapted from Kakabadse *et al.* (2005).

CSR talks. In capturing these developments, Figure 1.1 summarises the evolution of CSR research and development since the 1950s.

Although being a key part of the debate on businesses' role in society, the concept of CSR is still questioned by some with regard to its relevance to economic survival. As Matthew Bishop, business editor of *The Economist*, recently argued, CSR-oriented programmes implemented by companies are little more than mere attempts to keep civil pressure at bay rather than an acknowledgement that business people should respond to stakeholders' as much as shareholders' concerns (Salls, 2004). Moreover, Bishop claims that society's outcries about some companies' decisions actually impede the development of an economic system which has proved to be globally beneficial over the past decades (Salls, 2004).

This view is shared by some scholars and business people but not without being challenged. As more evidence has shed light on the positive relationship between CSR programmes and (long-term) economic performance (Roman *et al.*, 1999; Post *et al.*, 2002; Margolis and Walsh, 2003; McAdam and Leonard, 2003), it is increasingly becoming expected that the proponents of the 'shareholder model' will develop a deeper understanding of CSR in the coming years and will integrate a wider range of concerns into core business strategy (Thévenet, 2003), particularly as the shareholder-focused model is not as predominant in Asia or certain European countries as it is in the United States (Emiliani, 2001). Further to the ever greater prominence of CSR has also come the realisation that the level and intensity of CSR adoption depends on the society in question. In the United States, philanthropy has a long tradition whilst European companies display a societal communal and wealth redistribution perspective through the payment of substantially greater taxes (Juholin, 2004). Such contrasts emphasise the point that the role of business within society is influenced by context, resulting in different nations embracing different 'enterprise philosophies'. Scandinavian countries and France, to a certain extent, perceive the firm as a member of the social community. Further, Continental Europe, particularly Germany and to a certain extent also France, analyses business activity in relation to the environment (not only the natural but also the social and the moral). In contrast, the Anglo-American view projects the enterprise as being at the heart of its economic wellbeing, placing inordinate emphasis on corporate conduct (Langlois and Schlegelmilch, 1990). Hence, the legitimate expectations any society may hold about business will depend on the social and moral lens through which the corporation is examined adding to the already growing myriad of meanings of CSR.

Spread of meanings

As shown, the debate on the relationship between business and society has been on going for decades with no consensus emerging on commonly accepted definitions of CSR (Carroll, 1991; Jones, 1995; 1999; McWilliams and Siegel, 2001; Garriga and Melé, 2004). Various interpretations have included varying moral philosophies, translations and adaptations to cultural context and efforts to provide a workable framework for 'real life' managers, all contributing to making the term sound familiar. Discussed issues pertain to CRS (Amnesty International UK, 2003), sustainable development, business ethics, corporate social contract, corporate (social) accountability, business in society, corporate citizenship and corporate governance (Kakabadse and Morsing, 2006). This variety of themes demonstrates the richness of the concept itself as well as the criticality of research spread (Carroll, 1999; Ougaard and Nielsen, 2002) which though lacking 'common ground', many have asserted undermines the legitimacy, credibility and value of research on the social and environmental responsibilities of business towards society (Angelidis and Ibrahim, 1993; Lantos, 2001; Ougaard and Nielsen, 2002; van Marrewijk, 2003). Table 1.1 highlights a collection of definitions of CSR from academic research stretching over the past 50 years. These definitions are drawn from a variety of theoretical perspectives ranging from agency theory, legitimacy theory, political economy, stakeholder theory and corporate governance frameworks.

Similarly, Table 1.2 presents interpretations of CSR by representatives from the business community. In turn, Table 1.3 introduces definitions produced by governmental institutions and non-governmental associations. As can be seen from both Tables 1.2 and 1.3, the meanings attached to CSR are more practical or managerialist in scope. It is noticeable that the more practice-driven definitions tend to be influenced by each stakeholder's position with regard to business processes or, as in the case of government, more associated with sustainability.

Table 1.1   Meanings of CSR: Academia

Author	Definition
Bowen (1953)	[CSR] refers to the obligations of business to pursue those policies, to make those decisions or to follow those lines of action which are desirable in terms of the objectives and values of our society.
Frederick (1960)	Social responsibility in the final analysis implies a public posture toward society's economic and human resources and a willingness to see that those resources are used for broad social ends and not simply for the narrowly circumscribed interests of private persons and firms.
Friedman (1962)	There is one, and only one, social responsibility of business – to use its resources and engage in activities designed to increase its profits so long as it stays within the rules of the game which is to say, engage in open and free competition without deception or fraud.
Davis and Blomstrom (1966)	Social responsibility refers to a person's obligation to consider the effects of their decisions and actions on the whole social system.
Andrews (1973)	CSR is a balance between voluntary restraint of profit maximisation, sensitivity to the social costs of economic activity and to the opportunity to focus corporate power on objectives that are possible but sometimes less economically attractive than socially desirable.
Arrow (1973)	Firms 'ought to' maximise profit according to their social obligation to do so since business profit represents the net contribution that the firm makes to the social good. On this basis, profits should be as large as possible and only be limited by law and ethical codes.

Continued

Table 1.1 Continued

Author	Definition
Sethi (1975)	Social responsibility implies bringing corporate behaviour up to a level where it is congruent with the prevailing social norms, values and expectations of performance.
Carroll (1979)	The social responsibility of business encompasses the economic, legal, ethical and discretionary expectations that society has of organisations at a given point in time.
Jones (1980)	Corporate social responsibility is the notion that corporations have an obligation to constituent groups in society other than stockholders and beyond that prescribed by law and union contract.
Wood (1991)	The basic idea of corporate social responsibility is that business and society are inter-woven rather than distinct entities.
Bloom and Gundlach (2000)	CSR is the obligation of the firm to its stakeholders – people and groups – who can affect or who are affected by corporate policies and practices. These obligations go beyond legal requirements and the company's duties to its shareholders. The fulfillment of these obligations is intended to minimise any harm and maximise the long-run beneficial impact of the firm on society.
Baker (2003)	CSR is about how companies manage business processes to produce an overall positive impact on society.
van Marrewijk (2003)	CSR is associated with the communion aspect of people and organisations, whilst corporate sustainability (CS) is associated with the agency principle. Therefore CSR relates to phenomena such as transparency, stakeholder dialogue and sustainability reporting, while CS focuses on value creation, environmental management, environmental friendly production systems, human capital management and so forth.
Crowther and Rayman-Bacchus (2004)	CSR in its broadest definition is concerned with what is – or should be – the relationship between the global corporation, governments and individual citizens whilst in its more local context it is concerned with the relationship between a corporation and its local society in which it resides or operates, or with the relationship between a corporation and its stakeholders.

Source: Adapted from Kakabadse *et al.* (2005).

Table 1.2 Meaning of CSR: the business community

Organisation	Definition
Adidas Group (2005)	We are dedicated to socially responsible, safe and environmentally sustainable practices in the company and its supply chain and to enhancing the value of our brands by: guaranteeing the ideals of the company for the consumer and for those making our products; strengthening our image and reputation; making the supply chain more effective and helping to provide a long-term future for sport.
Danisco (2005)	We will [achieve corporate social accountability] by being holistic, transparent and open to dialogue with our stakeholders – and by respecting and responding to the values and concerns of the communities in which we operate. In our dialogue with our stakeholders, we highlight: environmental ethics; business integrity and social issues; product safety; safety; health; environment and quality.
Danone (1974)	The corporate social responsibility statement contains five concrete recommendations: (i) scale workforces to meet actual needs but limit job insecurity and the negative effects of lay offs; (ii) develop and apply compensation policies that provide incentives consistent with the business conditions and environment of each company; (iii) develop personal potential and encourage contributions from managers and all staff members, helping them to better achieve both their own aspirations and the goals of the business; (iv) work in partnership with employees for better working conditions and greater business efficiency; and (v) open and improve lines of communication with employees and their representatives.

National Express Group (2005)	Adding to the quality of life of the communities we serve by providing mobility and delivering social, economic and environmental benefits. Public transport reduces congestion, pollution and reduces accident levels on roads. Our companies are part of the fabric of society – we make a real contribution to people's lives whether it be in providing services to our customers or offering employment opportunities. We are aware of the responsibility and commitment that this role brings and endeavor to provide the best possible level of service to all our stakeholders.
Novo Nordisk (2003)	Social responsibility for Novo Nordisk is about caring for people. This applies to our employees and the people whose healthcare needs we serve. It also considers the impact of our business on the global society and the local community. As such, social responsibility is more than a virtue – it is a business imperative.
Sony Corporation of America (2005)	Our philanthropic efforts reflect the diverse interests of our key businesses and focus on several distinct areas: arts and education; arts and culture; health and human services; civic and community out-reach; education and volunteerism. Each operating company has its own philanthropic priorities and unique resources from product donations to recordings and screenings that benefit a multitude of causes.
Tesco (2005)	Our core values 'no one tries harder for customers' and 'treat people how we like to be treated' characterise our approach to corporate responsibility. We believe we can achieve most when we work together on practical things that make a difference. 'Every little help' can become a great deal when everyone pulls in the same direction.
Unilever (2003)	We define social responsibility as the impact or interaction we have with society in three distinct areas: (1) voluntary contributions; (2) impact of (business's direct) operations; and (3) impact through the value chain.

Source: Adapted from Kakabadse *et al.* (2005).

Table 1.3 Meaning of CSR: sphere of civil society and government

Organisation	Definition
Amnesty International UK (2003)	Companies [have] to recognise that their ability to continue to provide goods and services and to create financial wealth will depend on their acceptability to an international society which increasingly regards protection of human rights as a condition of the corporate licence to operate.
The Corporate Responsibility Coalition (CORE, 2003)	As an 'organ of society', companies have a responsibility to safeguard human rights within their direct sphere of operations as well as within their wider spheres of influence.
CSR Europe (2003)	Corporate social responsibility is the way in which a company manages and improves its social and environmental impact to generate value for both its shareholders and its stakeholders by innovating its strategy, organisation and operations.
Enterprise Europe (2002)	There is an emphasis on the need for businesses to take into account the social, economic and environmental impacts of their actions – the so-called triple bottom line.
The European Union (Euroabstracts, 2003)	CSR is a concept whereby companies integrate social and environmental concerns in their business operations and in their interaction with their stakeholders on a voluntary basis.
Novethic (2003)	Linked to the application by corporations of the sustainable development principle, the concept of CSR integrates three dimensions: an economic dimension (efficiency, profitability); a social dimension (social responsibility); and an environmental dimension (environmental

Organisation for Economic Co-operation and Development (OECD, 2003)	responsibility). To respect these principles, corporations must pay more attention to all the stakeholders [...] which inform on the expectations of civil society and the business environment.
	Corporate responsibility involves the 'fit' businesses develop with the societies in which they operate. [...] The function of business in society is to yield adequate returns to owners of capital by identifying and developing promising investment opportunities and, in the process, to provide jobs and to produce goods and services that consumers want to buy. However, corporate responsibility goes beyond this core function. Businesses are expected to obey the various laws which are applicable to them and often have to respond to societal expectations that are not written down as formal law.
UK government gateway to Corporate Social Responsibility (2005)	CSR is the business contribution to our sustainable development goals. Essentially it is about how business takes account of its economic, social and environmental impacts in the way it operates – maximising the benefits and minimising the downsides. Specifically, we see CSR as the voluntary actions that business can take over and above compliance with minimum legal requirements to address both its own competitive interests and the interests of wider society.
World Business Council for Sustainable Development (WBCSD, 2003)	Corporate social responsibility is business' commitment to contribute to sustainable economic development working with employees, their families, the local community and society at large to improve their quality of life.

Source: Adapted from Kakabadse *et al.* (2005).

Recent research has attempted to review the concept of CSR in order to establish some sort of typology of the various theories and sub-theories in circulation, such as that of Jones (1980), Klonoski (1991) – see Figure 1.2, Meznar *et al.* (1991), Dobson (1999) – see Table 1.4 and the most comprehensive one so far proposed by Garriga and Melé (2004) – see Table 1.5. The three typologies highlighted offer a broad variance of interpretation of the CSR literature but make no claim that they are representative of the field.

The framework introduced in Table 1.4 focuses on the morality of business purpose and posits that profit maximisation has inherent moral value. The idea of a 'marketplace of morality' supposes that the market system regulates corporate behaviour in so far as corporations voluntarily work together with civil society in order to take opportunity of the 'synergies' created (Dobson, 1999). In addition, its proponents state that ethical rules are still needed as marketplace morality requires that preconditions be fulfilled, including the equitable balancing of power and transparent communication.

The morality of market approach holds that markets are not 'evil' as traditional CSR thinking portrays (Matten *et al.*, 2003). In fact, certain commentators perceive markets as 'virtuous' (Maitland, 1997) in so far as being virtuous is rewarded by market mechanisms. Maitland (1997) separates the 'pessimists' from the 'optimists' regarding the relations of

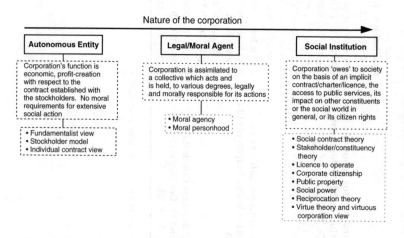

Figure 1.2   Typology of the character of the corporation.
Source: Compiled from Klonoski (1991).

Table 1.4 Typology based on the morality of profit maximisation

Position	Based on	Critique
Profit maximisation as morally neutral	Financial economics is justified by the 'invisible hand' and the moral neutrality of decisions based on pure market mechanisms.	The pursuit of profit maximisation is a decision taken within a metaphysical (hence moral) context.
Profit maximisation as immoral	The view of profit seeking as potentially incompatible with the pursuit of virtue.	The shareholder view does not exclude stakeholder concerns if this positively affects equity market value (market translates moral values into business language).
Profit maximisation as moral	The definition of a 'marketplace of morality' through a consensual dialogue between civil society and business actors.	There are in fact information asymmetry, imbalance of power, and no perfect market conditions.

Source: Compiled from Dobson (1999).

the market with virtue and explains that adopting an optimistic view (i.e. considering that virtue does not induce a dichotomy between personal interest and public interest) allows the market to be seen as reinforcing morality (Farmer, 1964; Ferraro *et al.*, 2005). Indeed, virtues such as trustworthiness, self-control, sympathy or fairness are desirable for social cohesion and act as 'a source of private advantage in the marketplace' (Maitland, 1997: 23). In 'real' imperfect markets, such dispositions will be pursued first as a means to personal benefit and then as ends in themselves, as inter-personal relationships between economic actors develop and flourish. Given that reputation and community support are an integral part of business prosperity, Maitland (1997) concludes that self-interest and virtue mutually reinforce each other to provide a sound basis for social morality.

Although profit maximisation provides an interesting view of the ethics of the market, making it attractive to practitioners and CSR sceptics, it is limited in at least two levels. First, it is possible to find practical examples to illustrate the veracity of the pessimist view as well as the optimist standpoint. Indeed, it is probable that every one of us knows someone who embeds self-interest with virtuous conduct as well as someone who would pursue one's interest no matter the consequences on others. As Maitland (1997: 20) puts it, 'social co-operation makes everyone better off than they would be if everyone pursued his narrow self-interest; but each individual stands to benefit most if he is selfish while everyone else is virtuous'. It is not to deny that the market cannot sanction immoral behaviour and reward moral action, but a number of writers have concluded that market morality is not sufficient and, in fact, cannot act as the guardian of social ethics (Maitland, 1997; Baker, 2003; van Marrewijk, 2003).

Second, 'marketplace of morality' reinforces the view that markets are the core of society placing business activities, which are regulated through market mechanisms, as central in our social world. Such perspective, dominant in current social thinking and research, places substantial emphasis on only one part of our social world and consequently grants that part excessive importance in comparison with others (Ferraro *et al.*, 2005). It is one thing to accept that markets are not bad or amoral, it is quite another one to instate them as the moral safeguard of society.

In keeping with the managerialist and market perspective, others have viewed the CSR concept as an aspect of Total Quality Management (TQM) (Wheeler and Sillanpää, 1998; McAdam and Leonard, 2003). The weakness in the argument is that TQM needs an 'ethical anchor' to combine normative demands and instrumental expectations in order to achieve 'sustainable performance through valuing people and the environment' (McAdam and Leonard, 2003: 38). However, that view has been more ignored as quality, and in particular TQM, have become mainstreamed references in companies. As such, McAdam and Leonard (2003) have proposed that CSR be integrated into organisations more efficiently and rapidly by being added to existing quality benchmark processes.

Still from a market and managerialist perspective, Hess *et al.* (2002) differentiated 'corporate social initiatives' (CSIs) from corporate philanthropy through attachment to the organisation's core competences and core values. The authors emphasise three main drivers behind CSI programmes: 'the competitive advantage factor' in that CSI helps strengthen corporate reputation and develop international expansion; 'the new moral marketplace factor' referring to the pressure companies feel, either through social reporting or peer pressure that would drive them to behave according to higher moral standards and 'the competitive advantage of private firms factor' suggesting that given their position in the marketplace, firms may hold a competitive advantage over governments to implement social or environmental programmes (Hess *et al.*, 2002). The Hess *et al.* (2002) view acknowledges the supremacy of marketisation asserting a shift of responsibility from government to private firms due to weaknesses within the political system (Ougaard and Nielsen, 2002; Wiedermann-Goiran *et al.*, 2002).

Even more challenging and providing a refreshing insight into the CSR debate, is the Margolis and Walsh (2003) review of existing research on the social responsibilities of business and the 'contractarian view of the firm'. They conclude that the most critical questions have been left un-addressed. They explain that scholars and managers have focused on trying either to reconcile two opposing views of the socioeconomic world or to discredit the opposite camp. As a result, no research has examined whether, how and under which condition a firm's social activities could benefit society (Margolis and Walsh, 2003). The authors stress that in order to respond efficiently to society's needs, scholars and practitioners should not try to address the dilemma of whether CSR is good or bad for business. Rather they should adopt a pragmatic approach which aims to 'craft a purpose and role for the firm that builds internal coherence among competing and incommensurable objectives, duties and concerns' (Margolis and Walsh, 2003: 284). The added advantage is that through being more practice-oriented, a support framework for managers to analyse and face the necessary trade-offs they ought to make, is provided (Margolis and Walsh, 2003).

Partly as a mechanism for escaping from the 'rhetoric' of CSR but principally to put into practice codes of ethics, codes of conduct, audit principles and standards, the 'balanced scorecard' and ISO, management systems (including the future ISO 26000 on social responsibility) have been introduced as frameworks of measurement. The Global Reporting Initiative (GRI – an initiative started by the Coalition for Environmentally Responsible Economies – CERES – and now working independently and in collaboration with the UN environment programme) and the UN Global Compact (initiated by UN Secretary-General Kofi Annan and involving corporations, NGOs and international agencies) have also gained popularity in recent years and nourished promise of improved control on multinational corporations. The London Stock Exchange uses the GRI, amongst other indicators (such as Business in the Community and FTSE4Good index) to evaluate corporations' social responsibility, known as the corporate responsibility exchange (CRE). Other organisations and institutions have developed more focused standards of measurement, such as the Dow Jones Sustainability World Index (DJSI), the ILO's labor standards, the Social Accountability International's SA8000 standard on workplace regulation compliance or even the inspirational triple bottom line approach developed by SustainAbility's John Elkington (Kakabadse and Morsing, 2006).

Many have been either recently launched or are being refined but so far none have really emerged as 'the standard towards which measuring CSR or sustainability performance as tied up to long-term financial profitability' (Elkington, 1998: 20).

Meznar *et al.* (1991) built on the ideas of economic and social benefit to develop an enterprise strategy classification of CSR approaches, maintaining that long-term legitimacy requires the firm to balance both an economic surplus and social surplus and to develop an enterprise strategy to do so. Enterprise strategy is defined as 'how a firm attempts to add value to its environment in order to legitimise its existence and ensure its future' (Meznar *et al.*, 1991: 53). Hence, a corporation can exercise choice concerning which strategy it wishes to pursue, ranging from providing purely economic goods to benefit only economic stakeholders (i.e. shareholders), to providing purely social goods to benefit social stakeholders (as in the case of not-for-profit organisations). In between are a diversity of strategies that aim to satisfy, to varied extent, both economic and social stakeholders by either lowering or increasing net economic value and social goods (Meznar *et al.*, 1991). Such a perspective has an obvious appeal to practitioners since it 'talks' strategy and focuses on how to successfully design a CSR strategy which can be implemented, managed and monitored.

In similar vein, Klonoski's (1991) review pictures CSR as a spectrum along which theories range from the purely economic purpose of the firm to the most integrated stakeholder model. The argument is based around the question of whether the corporation has a 'social nature' or not. At one end of the spectrum, those who believe that corporation is a 'distinctive economic institution', conclude that claims from society that exceed legal requirements and entitlements, or beyond what can be reasonably expected from an individual entity, are illegitimate (Klonoski, 1991). At the other end of the spectrum are those who hold corporations as social creations and that this very nature has made them especially indebted to society. The linkages between the social nature of corporations and social responsibilities are various, ranging from a broad legal view to a spiritually or religiously inspired approach to social activities (Klonoski, 1991). In the middle are theories that perceive the corporation as a moral and legal person, in which case the extent of the responsibilities of the corporate agent depends on the definition of a person, in that if a person is primarily self-interested then the corporate agent will similarly be perceived as self-interested (Klonoski, 1991). This classification emphasises an important element of the CSR debate, that being the nature of business and the corporation. Introducing CSR theories as a continuum rather than that of contrasting positions is welcome in the sense of working towards a unifying framework to justify the nature of the tensions encompassed. However, Klonoski's (1991) continuum is, to a certain degree, quite normative and has limits in terms of concrete application of CSR plans and actions. Indeed, it helps determine why corporations have duties towards society but it says little about the specific obligations businesses ought to fulfil.

Additionally, in a recent extensive review, Garriga and Melé (2004) offer a further typology which assimilates the alternative positions captured in various CSR theories. They argue that the varying CSR approaches can be identified according to their focus on the corporation as wealth creator (instrumental theories), the economic and social responsibilities which accompany the power granted to business by society (political theories), the necessary survival conditions of business as dependent on society (integrative theories) or the ethics overarching business–society relationships (ethical theories). Garriga and Melé's (2004) account of CSR thinking and research is substantial, especially as their typology links the ideologies surrounding the corporation with practical CSR strategies. Parallels can be drawn between the CSR approaches quoted by Garriga and Melé (2004) and Klonoski (1991), though the former classification is less flexible than the latter since it uses closed categories rather than a continuum. However, it is possible to integrate instrumental theories which emphasise the autonomy of the corporation, the political, integrative and ethical theories which assume that corporations are social in nature and thus develop desired patterns of the firm's relationship with society (Table 1.5).

Table 1.5 Typology of the rationale of business responsibilities towards society

Types of theory	Approaches
Instrumental theories (focusing on achieving economic objectives through social activities)	Maximisation of shareholder value Strategies for competitive advantage: social investments in a competitive context, strategies based on the natural resource view of the firm and its dynamic capabilities, strategies for the bottom of the economic pyramid. Cause-related marketing
Political theories (focusing on a responsible use of business power in the political arena)	Corporate constitutionalism, Integrative social contract theory, Corporate citizenship.

Continued

Table 1.5 Continued

Types of theory	Approaches
Integrative theories (focusing on the integration of social demands)	Issues management Public responsibility Stakeholder management Corporate social performance
Ethical theories (focusing on the right thing to achieve for a good society)	Stakeholder normative theory Universal rights Sustainable development The common good

Source: Adapted from Garriga and Melé (2004).

Characteristics of CSR

CSR and Philanthropy

From the shareholder perspective, the concept of CSR and corporate philanthropy have often been combined as broad models of CSR (Carroll, 1991). However, both have alternate and specific meanings. Corporate philanthropy refers to the firm 'giving back' (financially) to society some of the wealth it has created thanks to society's inputs; in effect a 'charity principle' as an obligation for the wealthy to support the less fortunate (Mitnick, 1995). The 'charity principle' parallels that of 'stewardship' whereby the business acts as the guardian of 'society's resources'. By itself, philanthropy (or charity) doesn't necessarily mean that a firm develops a broader strategy to comprehensively assess its impact on society and to design plans, policies and tools to improve its overall performance towards society. Indeed, Carroll (1991) defines CSR as a pyramid made up of four layers (economic, legal, ethical and philanthropic) and clearly states that 'CSR includes philanthropic contributions but is not limited to them. In fact it would be argued here that philanthropy is highly desired and prized but, actually, less important than the other three categories of social responsibility' (Carroll, 1991: 42).

Arguing from an evolutionary developmental perspective, van Marrewijk and Werre (2003) suggest that CSR has progressed according to various organisational stages representing different levels of awareness of responsibilities to be exercised. These are:

Stage 1 – compliance-driven response, namely the recognition of providing welfare to society within the limits of regulation from the rightful authorities. Such enactment is motivated by perceived duty and obligation.

Stage 2 – profit-driven response, namely the organisation's recognition for integrating social, ethical and ecological aspects into business operations and decision making, providing such aspects contribute to the financial bottom line. The organisation is motivated to reduce risks or increase profits leading to an improved reputation in various markets.

Stage 3 – care-driven response, namely the organisation's balancing of economic, social and ecological concerns, motivated by the enhancing human potential and promoting social responsibility and care for the planet as important.

Stage 4 – systemic-driven response, namely the organisation's recognition of the search for well-balanced, functional solutions creating value in the economic, social and ecological realms of corporate performance in a synergistic manner with all relevant stakeholders. As such, CSR is recognised as an inevitable form of progress.

Stage 5 – holistically driven response, namely the organisation's recognition of an integrated and holistic approach that is embedded in every aspect of organisation activity aimed at contributing to the quality and continuation of life now and in the future. Stage 5 enactment is motivated by the recognition that each person and/or organisation has a universal responsibility towards all other beings.

Similarly, Vogl (2003) argues that four factors can be identified as contributing to the recent rise of the CSR agenda which drive corporate entities around the world to embark on socially responsible behaviours, namely the tightening of regulatory pressures, changing demographics, the pressure from nongovernmental organisations (NGOs) and the increased necessity for greater transparency. The value of Vogl's (2003) classification is that it incorporates and acknowledges the effect of NGOs such as Friends of the Earth (FoE), Greenpeace, Amnesty International, the World Wildlife Fund, the Council on Economic Priorities and many others who have been particularly important in promoting the CSR agenda. In similar vein, Harrison (1997) offers a level analysis concerning CSR impact, where the first basic level (tax payment, law observation, fair dealings) and the second organisational level (minimisation of negative effect, acting within the spirit of the law) refer to what respectable firms believe are their responsibilities to society. Level three (responsibility for a healthy society, asset alleviation of societal ills) refers to a more enlightened type of organisation that accepts responsibility for a healthy society and contributes to addressing problems in society in an active manner (Goodpaster, 1991).

Long term

As can be seen, elements of the classification of CSR incorporate long-term thinking and long-term effects. However, certain writers have promoted the exclusive view that CSR provides long-term economic and social gain that may not be easily financially measurable but nevertheless generates a valuable asset for the future (Davis, 1973; Carroll, 1999). On this basis, CSR is linked to the concept of sustainability, namely that business should not just pursue short-term profit but, in fact, a multitude of goals which combine to guarantee the firm's survival and prosperity in a changing environment. Adapting to a longer-term perspective is viewed by some as essential in a knowledge-based society where organisational assets are as intangible (reputation, technology, know-how, etc.) as they are tangible (financial resources, buildings and equipments, etc; Meznar *et al.*, 1991; Lantos, 2001).

Strategic positioning

The expression 'CSR strategy' captures an additional interpretation of social responsibility implementation whereby ethical issues are treated strategically as any other business operation, in contrast to those writers who view ethics as a particular consideration separated from financial bottom line concerns (Wood, 1991; Bloom and Gundlach, 2000). Many articles, corporate reports and websites support this view asserting that social and environmental concerns are and should be treated as integral parts of the enterprise, highlighting that the question is no longer 'whether' CSR is an imperative, but rather 'how' to make it effective (Smith, 2003). Discussion has focused on whether CSR should be embedded in the firm's strategy or whether CSR would be more effectively applied by being positioned as a new form of corporate function. However, irrespective of forms and functionality, CSR is increasingly being considered as a strategic option in order for the corporation not to lose corporate advantage or not to be seen to have just jumped onto the 'good intentions' bandwagon, but more to position itself as an informed and involved partner expressing true concern for human and environmental distress (Kaptein and Wempe, 2002). CSR strategic positioning is captured in the phrase, 'the business case' for CSR, intended to attract more organisations to be part of a social dialogue movement (Smith, 2003).

Beyond the law

From the 1970s, a number of writers considered that CSR required to be positioned 'beyond the narrow economic, technical and legal requirements of the firm' (Davis, 1973: 312; Carroll, 1999). In so doing, abiding by the law was positioned as not necessarily being socially responsible. CSR was and continues to be considered as, implicitly, an expression of voluntary effort by which the firm complies with ethical standards as opposed to purely economic or legal imperatives (Jones, 1980; Carroll, 1999). Johnson and Scholes (2001: 220) state that 'corporate social responsibility is concerned with the ways in which an organisation exceeds the minimum obligations to stakeholders specified through regulation and corporate governance'. However, debate has centred on whether CSR ought to be voluntary or compulsory by nature. Some argue that only the voluntary aspect of pursuing corporate social initiatives gives CSR its true meaning and value (Jones, 1980). Others maintain that companies would do little if they were not forced to address CSR obligations (Kilcullen and Kooistra, 1999; Scholl, 2001). But whichever viewpoint attracts, CSR is increasingly accepted as a strategic consideration.

Social contract

Explicitly or implicitly, CSR has been associated with the theme of 'social contract' or, alternatively, of 'licence to operate' (Frederick, 1987; Mitnick, 1995; Jones, 1999; Freeman, 2004). Social contract determination implies that society allows businesses to operate assuming that they operate according to particular desired social norms and, in turn, are transparent in their accountability for their actions. A narrow interpretation of that view is 'a corporation is defined as an entity created and empowered by a state charter to act as an individual. Such authorisation gives the corporation the right to own, buy and sell property, to enter into contracts, to sue and be sued and to have legal accountability for damages and debt, only to the limit of the stockholder's investment' (Nisberg, 1988: 74; Kilcullen and Kooistra, 1999). A broader interpretation is offered by Moir (2001) who argues that the social contract perspective enables a firm to act responsibly, not 'because it is in its commercial interest but because it is part of how society implicitly expects business to operate' (Moir, 2001: 19).

Power and legitimacy

As with the social contract theme, power has also been viewed as being at the core of the debate on CSR; 'the source of this responsibility is based on the power and influence that organisations have which leads them to cause, both directly and indirectly, moral effects in society' (L'Etang, 1995). Linked to power is legitimacy in that the exercise of legitimacy involves adopting behaviours which influence others' perceptions of legitimate and illegitimate action; hence negotiating legitimacy is an exercise of power. Wilson (2000: 13) explains that CSR is related to various layers of behaviour whose extremes are, on the one hand, 'the basic need to meet commonly accepted ethical principles of "good behaviour" ' and on the other hand, 'an insistence that corporations have a social responsibility to help solve social problems [...] they may have, in part, created and that most certainly will affect their performance'. Wilson (2000) defines CSR as a 'set of new rules' somewhere in between these two positions which specify society's ethical expectations and relate to the themes of legitimacy, governance, equity, the environment, employment, public-private sector relationships and ethics. The rule of legitimacy for Wilson implies that 'to earn and retain social legitimacy, the corporation must define its basic mission in terms of the social purpose it is designed to serve rather than as the maximisation of profit' (Wilson, 2000: 13).

Citing the work of Suchman (1995), Moir (2001) examines the reasons that make legitimacy a key issue for businesses and introduces alternative strategies that organisations can use to overcome 'legitimation threats'. Others agree but state that 'society grants legitimacy and power to business. In the long-run, those who do not use power in a manner which society considers responsible will tend to lose it' (Davis, 1973: 314; Wood, 1991). The 'iron law of responsibility' suggests that business is granted power and influence under specific conditions decreed by society and that the non-fulfilment of these obligations seriously challenge the business's economic, social and political position. Indeed, society ultimately has the power to decide on what is right and wrong, to monitor societal members' compliance with its judgements and to clamp down on those who do not follow the rules. In other words, 'the firm is meant for society; the society is not for the firm' (Takala, 1999: 742). Also, the firm should act as a 'public steward' (Chen, 1975; Takala, 1999) or as a citizen entitled to social responsibilities as is expected of any other citizen (Davis, 1975; Takala, 1999). This (re)balance of forces between society and business, by making the latter part of the former, echoes a CSR inspired philosophy. Especially in the for-profit sector, at a time when multinational corporations have a truly significant influence on politics and the world order, the power and legitimacy campaigners position the individual citizen as ultimately wielding social control (European Commission, 2004).

Context

Whatever characteristic or interpretation of CSR is adopted, one underlying theme re-occurs, namely the type and quality of relationship between the firm and its constituent stakeholders and the circumstances of that relationship, in effect the influence of context. One strongly held view is of CSR as a process rather than 'a set of outcomes' (Jones, 1980; Carroll, 1999). As the relationships between the constituents themselves and the environment changes, the responsibilities of constituents change as well. The view adopted is that CSR becomes 'an ongoing process' whereby relationship forming and adjusting to changing circumstances, as much through gaining developments in the external world, becomes a way of life (L'Etang, 1995). In this way, CSR is under continual review driven by cycles of dialogue between the firm and its stakeholders (Wheeler and Sillanpää, 1998). This does not mean that the concept of CSR is viewed as relative per se, in that everything can be justified. Fundamental notions of respect, dignity and care which lie at the core of any CSR discussion exist but how these are then enacted becomes an additional critical consideration (Singhapakdi *et al.*, 1996; Jones, 1999). The growing relevance and importance of CSR has given rise to the involvement of organisational theorists such as Giddens (1984) or Pettigrew (1987; Pettigrew *et al.*, 2002) in order that CSR research becomes 'more useful' (Athanasopoulou, 2005).

Stakeholder interpretation

The contrast to the marketisation principles underlying the Anglo-American philosophy is captured in the term stakeholder. Carroll (1991: 43) considers; 'there is a natural fit between the idea of corporate social responsibility and an organisation's stakeholders. ... The concept of stakeholder personalises social (or societal) responsibilities by delineating the specific groups or persons business should consider in its CSR orientation'. However, the concept of stakeholder did not develop consecutively with the concept of CSR, despite the fact that the explicit relationship defined by Carroll is widely accepted by CSR enthusiasts (Jones *et al.*, 2002). The reason for this lies in the critical difference between CSR and stakeholder. CSR aims to define 'what' responsibilities businesses ought to fulfil, whilst the stakeholder concept addresses the issue of 'whom' businesses are or should be accountable to.

Yet, the term stakeholder underplays the diversity of studies that have participated in building a sort of common ground, eventually labelled as 'stakeholder theory' (Scholl, 2001). Jones *et al.* (2002) list the principal theoretical fields which have contributed to the development of the stakeholder conceptual frameworks, which include CSR, corporate planning, systems theory and organisation theory. Each field has analysed the stakeholder concept based on a specific body of assumptions and through a specific lens, but to emerge with different conclusions on the role of stakeholders, and such breadth is sometimes referred to as 'pluralism' (Jones et al., 2002). Hummels (1998: 1407) also suggests that the various interpretations of the legitimate claim of stakeholder groups on organisational purpose emphasise the 'different [expected] distributions of benefits and burdens, of pleasures and pains, of values, rights and interests'.

Capturing the 'mix of meanings' accompanying stakeholder thinking, Wood (1991: 712) clearly suggests that different stakeholders are likely to develop different understandings of what CSR means, what they expect from the organisation in relation to CSR and how they assess CSR. To create a balanced outcome acceptable to the majority, if not all of the stakeholders, notwithstanding the possible differences in the value systems and ideological positions of the various actors, is viewed as a harsh but necessary task for managers (Wood, 1991; Szwajkowski, 2000). An even more necessary 'core competence' is to operate at the centre of 'a network of interrelated stakeholders in order to sustain and enhance [their] value-creating capacity' (Post et al., 2002: 7). A core assumption underlying stakeholder thinking is that the environment in which the enterprise operates has changed and the firm's relationships with its stakeholders have shifted from essentially transactional to truly relational with these relationships affecting, either positively or negatively, the creation of organisational wealth (Post et al., 2002; Simmons, 2004).

Despite strands being drawn together, researchers have not emerged with an agreement on the scope of stakeholder theory (Harrison and Freeman, 1999). Hillman et al. (2001) claim that 'although a unified stakeholder theory with general acceptance has yet to emerge among stakeholder researchers, ... there does appear to be some agreement regarding the general concepts embodied in stakeholder theory'. Referring to the work of Jones and Wicks (1999), these authors list four main statements at the core of the stakeholder theory (Hillman et al., 2001): '(a) the firm has relationships with constituent (stakeholder) groups; (b) the processes and outcomes associated with these relationships are of interest; (c) the interests of all legitimate stakeholders have value; and (d) the focus of stakeholder theory is on managerial decision-making'. Other stakeholder theorists provide two stakeholder platforms 'that to perform well, managers need to pay attention to a wide array of stakeholders and that managers have obligations to stakeholders which include, but extend beyond, shareholders' (Jones et al., 2002: 20).

The notion that businesses must deal with other constituents than just owners for their prosperity, if not survival, have been alluded to and studied for quite a while, although at times not labelled as CSR. Citing Eberstadt's research, Jones *et al.* (2002: 21) identify similar notions of CSR thinking in classical Greece and in medieval times. The 1920s and 1930s saw the first theoretical developments on the more extended role of business towards society, especially the work of Mary Parker Follett (1918). Her research acknowledged 'inter-connectedness' among various constituents participating in the business performance of the enterprise whilst Chester Barnard (1938) stated that corporations were not an end per se but a means to serve society (Morris, 1997; Jones *et al.*, 2002; Post *et al.*, 2002). In the 1960s, Eric Rhenman alone (1968, *Företagsdemokrati och företagsorganisation*) and together with Bengt Stymne (1965, *Företagsledning in en föränderlig värld*) emerged with an explicit outline of stakeholder theory (Rhenman and Stymne, 1965; Rhenman, 1968). These works rapidly spread throughout Scandinavia and the notion of a stakeholder framework became popular in university management teaching, in academic research and in company application in the region. The global emergence of the stakeholder concept, however, began more with the publication of *Strategic Management: A Stakeholder Approach* by Freeman (1983). In what has become a landmark in the stakeholder research field, Freeman (1983) defined the term stakeholder as 'any group or individual who can affect or is affected by the achieve-ment of the organisation's objectives' (Freeman, 1983: 32; Vinten, 2000: 378). The ultimate legitimacy of constituents' claim on organisational purpose lies with either legal, economic, social, moral, technological, ecological, political or power interests, thus far beyond the for-profit motive of stockholders, with stakeholding claims being either past, present or future oriented (Weiss, 2002). As a consequence, stakeholder man-agement implies 'allocating organisational resources in such a way as to take into account the impact of those allocations on various groups within and outside the firm' (Jones, 1999). Thus, the ultimate purpose of stakeholder management theory is to achieve a 'win-win' outcome for stakeholders, with time in mind, that being most probably in the medium to long-term (Carroll, 1991).

Stakeholder effects

Marketisation theorists have argued that adopting stakeholder thinking is not viable due to having to sacrifice sound business objectives (i.e. profit) in favour of morally acceptable (but supposedly economically unsustainable) social goals (Vinten, 2000). Stakeholder theorists reject such assertion. Whilst recognising the legitimate claim of shareholders, challenged is the idea that shareholders should be, either, the only claimants or those privileged over the interests of other legitimate claims (Hummels, 1998; Emiliani, 2001). Although adopting a narrow, more instrumentalist view of stakeholder theory, Clarkson (1995) considers that organisations which don't include their primary stakeholders' concerns within their strategy undermine their own long-term survival. As Jones and Wicks (1999: 209) stress, the stakeholder approach doesn't aim 'to shift the focus of firms away from marketplace success toward human decency but to come up with understandings of business in which these objectives are linked and mutually reinforcing'. Extensive research, over the past 30 years, in examining the link between social responsibility policies and financial performance has drawn general conclusion that a positive relationship does and is likely to exist between the two (Meznar *et al.*, 1991; Margolis and Walsh, 2003; Orlitzky *et al.*, 2003).

Nonetheless, the challenge of measuring CSR and financial performance proves complex particularly in terms of defining the causality between economic success and responsible behaviour (Ougaard and Nielsen, 2002; Margolis and Walsh, 2003). One reason has been definitional. Donaldson and Preston (1995) highlight that despite a variety of concepts lying at the core of stakeholder theory (descriptive, instrumental, normative and managerial), the literature seems to have focused on exploring only two dimensions; instrumental and normative. Instrumental stakeholder theory understands stakeholder management as an instrument to achieve expected outcomes, principally profitability. Normative stakeholder theory, in contrast, acknowledges the ethical legitimacy of stakeholders' claims on organisational purpose (Jones *et al.*, 2002). The instrumental aspect of the stakeholder theory can sometimes be considered 'primary' but the normative view of stakeholder theory is often considered critical (Hummels, 1998). In similar vein, Scholl (2001) distinguishes two strands in stakeholder research, namely the 'social science strand' that examines the instrumental rationale of stakeholder theory and the 'business ethics strand' which argues that each stakeholder holds an intrinsic value by him/herself and calls for ethical guiding standards for managers (Epstein and Roy, 2001).

Another reason for the difficulty in defining causality between economic performance and socially responsible behaviour is the perceived, relatively poor managerial application due to the vagueness of advice offered to help managers to 'pragmatically deal' with stakeholders. In order to get round the causality concern, certain normative stakeholder theorists have grounded their studies on the Kantian argument that; 'the goodness of an act is the intention which motivated it' (L'Etang, 1995; Pesqueux and Biefnot, 2002: 186). As instrumental stakeholder theory lacks the critical moral aspect that gives the stakeholder concept intrinsic value, certain authors have called for the creation of 'convergent' stakeholder theory, defined as 'theory that is simultaneously morally sound in its behavioural prescriptions and instrumentally viable in its economic outcomes' (Jones and Wicks, 1999; Jones *et al.*, 2002: 28). Being both normative and instrumental, convergent theory is being recognised as having a strong and explicit moral basis whilst conscious of the processes involved in means–end application (Pesqueux and Biefnot, 2002).

Additional to concerns over causality, a considered major 'flaw' of stakeholder thinking (L'Etang, 1995) is who are the stakeholders? If stakeholders are 'those individuals or groups who depend on the organisation to fulfil their own goals and on whom, in turn, the organisation depends' (Johnson and Scholes, 2001: 206), then any one organisation is concerned with a large number of people, if not everyone, since considerable numbers of people depend, either directly or indirectly, on any organisation's activity. If the organisation is accountable to all its stakeholders (i.e. everyone) rather than to one constituency (i.e. shareholders), then the notion of accountability becomes valueless because it is too broadly set and almost impossible to implement from a managerial point of view (Hummels, 1998; Vinten, 2000).

Thus, one strongly emergent viewpoint is that adopting a stakeholder approach helps managers understand the relationships of the organisation with its various constituencies but it does not provide them with the means to exercise the nature and quality of these relationships (Argenti, 1993; L'Etang, 1995; Hummels, 1998). In order to avoid misinterpretation and effectively work through a myriad of relationships, stakeholder analysis tools, such as stakeholder mapping, the power/interest matrix and the stakeholder moral responsibilities matrix, have been developed to provide a practical framework for managers to apply (Vinten, 2000; Weiss, 2002).

Further, to prevent the term stakeholder being too broadly inclusive, some authors have proposed sub-categories. The most widely used is the external/internal stakeholder framework (Johnson and Scholes, 2001: 206). Others prefer the primary/secondary stakeholder framework (Weiss, 2002: 34), while some separate voluntary from involuntary stakeholders (Post *et al.*, 2002) and yet others favour the social/non-social stakeholders categorisation (Wheeler and Sillanpää, 1998). Another interesting approach is that of Phillips (2001), who identifies 'intrinsic' or 'definitional' stakeholders and 'instrumental' stakeholders who affect the definitional stakeholders.

Yet, despite poor effectiveness of application and definitional challenges, stakeholder management is becoming a more fashionable concept. In turn, there is evidence that a greater number of managers recognise, accept and use stakeholder oriented policies (Wheeler and Sillanpää, 1998; Post *et al.*, 2002). Conscious that 'tools' for stakeholder analysis have their limitations, dialogue is recognised as key to stakeholder management (Wheeler and Sillanpää, 1998; Szwajkowski, 2000; Wiedermann-Goiran *et al.*, 2002). Good communication is acknowledged as an essential element for the promotion of CSR in organisations. Minkes *et al.* (1999: 331) proposed a six-step procedure to help top managers become more CSR focused and explained that 'such a program implies that business executives would need to understand how attitudes are developed and how an organisation and its employees are influenced'. Such comment suggests that no standard model of stakeholder management exists as each organisation is idiosyncratic, historically, culturally and structurally, as is each stakeholder constituency. Yet, stated specificities are also likely to evolve overtime if the organisation implements a 'collaborative communication strategy' which can 'change the perceptions and "rules of engagement" to create win-win outcomes' (Weiss, 2002: 33). Manager's tasks include monitoring and managing the organisation's relationships with each of the stakeholder groups, but also assessing and managing the relationships between the various stakeholder groups (Post *et al.*, 2002) with a view to creating synergies among stakeholders (Halal, 2000; Wiedermann-Goiran *et al.*, 2002).

Figure 1.3 summarises the main elements and factors of influence in stakeholder management. It is asserted that firms should engage in a constructive and open dialogue with various stakeholders. The synergies engendered can be either beneficial or detrimental to the corporation, depending on the nature of alliances between stakeholder groups. The dialogue, driven by leaders, aims to secure short-term performance and long-term organisational wealth, benefiting society (the sustainable perspective) as defined by the economic, social and political environment. The environment also influences stakeholders and firms through influencing members of society's expectations, values or priorities which affect dialogue which, in turn, affect the parameters defining performance, wealth or society's wellbeing, thus emphasising that stakeholder interrelationships are dynamic and context dependent.

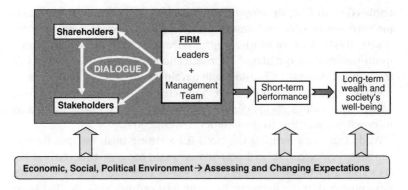

Figure 1.3 Stakeholder management.
Source: Adapted from Kakabadse *et al.* (2005).

Conclusion

Despite the potential lack of boundaries that can render CSR meaningless, a PricewaterhouseCoopers (2002) survey of the senior managers of 140 top US-based companies and their stance on sustainability showed that 75 per cent of the respondents have implemented some kind of sustainable business practice, essentially motivated by striving for enhanced reputation (90 per cent), competitive advantage (75 per cent) and cost savings (73 per cent). The 25 per cent who have not adopted sustainable practices justified their choice by the lack of clear business case (82 per cent), the lack of key stakeholder interest – including customers, suppliers and investors – (62 per cent) and the lack of senior management commitment (53 per cent) along with the difficulty to measure CSR/ sustainable performance and the lack of legal requirement to do so (PricewaterhouseCoopers, 2002). Thus, reputation emerged as a critical driver; 'the larger and more highly visible the company, the more likely it is to be developing sustainability programmes' (PricewaterhouseCoopers, 2002: 7).

Thus, what is underlined in this overview is that there is a real need to develop research on the business case for CSR and, in particular, to establish standards and quantifiable indicators to measure and monitor performance on economic, social and environmental practices. To date, CSR or sustainability are increasingly becoming the concern of large corporations. As the European Multi-stakeholder Forum on CSR concluded in its final report, there is a need to act at a global and collaborative level towards three main objectives, namely 'raising awareness and improving knowledge on CSR; developing the capacities and competences to help mainstreaming CSR and ensuring an enabling environment for CSR' (EMSF, 2004). Areas of further fruitful research would include adopting a multi-stakeholder, qualitative approach encompassing the impact of CSR on competitiveness and sustainable development; a social and environmental approach to public procurement, supply chain issues and partnership values compatability, technology transfer issues and CSR information available to stakeholders (EMSF, 2004).

Aside from emphasising the need for a strong business case for CSR supported by a committed and shared management, this chapter has also aimed to highlight some of the major characteristics of CSR that have emerged in the literature over the past century and the challenges facing future research and discussion on the relationships between business and the social world. Because the concepts of CSR and stakeholder are intertwined, the two approaches have been jointly examined in terms of both theory and practice.

In conclusion, Figure 1.4 identifies the major contributions to the concept of CSR. Distinction is drawn between the more academic contribution and that of business and civil society. On balance, academics tend to assess CSR more in terms of social contract than that of sustainability. Similarly, academics rather examine the influence of business through the lens of legitimacy whereas civil society refers to the power that business holds. Both academics and business and societal actors acknowledge a multi-stakeholder framework and the fact that CSR, in practice, is ultimately dependent on the influence of context (Carroll, 1989). Thus,

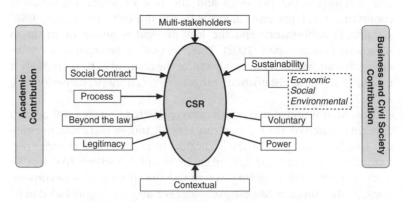

Figure 1.4   Corporate social responsibility – definitions and contributions.
Source: Adapted from Kakabadse *et al.* (2005).

when CSR is positioned as needing to go beyond the prescriptions of law, alternative thinking emerges which focuses more on the discretionary, or voluntary, aspects of CSR (Kakabadse and Morsing, 2006). Noted is that both academics and business and societal actors have identified similar themes for debate, but the terminology adopted distorts understanding the implementing and assessing of the effect of CSR (Ougaard and Nielsen, 2002).

Despite differences of view and language usage, particularly pertinent is that research demonstrates that leaders have a significant role to play in enhancing the social and environmental performance of their organisations. The increasing awareness people have of their leverage power can significantly change the responsibilities businesses have towards society. If organisations are to mature towards exercising greater responsibility, the proposition is that people should first reflect on their own position, behaviour, value system and expectations within their organisation. As can be seen throughout the remaining chapters of this book, the critical role leaders play in terms of CSR practice and promotion is given substantial attention.

References

Adidas Group. (2005), 'Corporate missions', available at http://www. adidasgroup. com/en/sustainability/mission_and_values/corporate_missions/default.asp (accessed: 14.12.05).

Amnesty International UK. (2003), 'Why do human rights matter to business?', available at http://www.amnesty.org.uk/business/why.shtml (accessed: 27.12.03).

Andrews, K.R. (1973), 'Can the best corporations be made moral?', *Harvard Business Review*, 51(3): 57–64.

Angelidis, J.P. and Ibrahim, N.A. (1993), 'Social demand and corporate supply: A corporate social responsibility model', *Review of Business*, 15(1): 7–10.

Argenti, J. (1993), *Your Organization: What Is It For?*, Berkshire: McGraw-Hill Publishing Co.

Arrow, K.J. (1973), 'Social responsibility and economic efficiency', *Public Policy*, 21: 303–317.

Athanasopoulou, A. (2005), 'Making corporate social responsibility research more useful: Thinking "outside the box" ', British Academy of Management Annual Conference, September. 13–15, Saïd Business School, University of Oxford.

Baker, M. (2003), 'Corporate social responsibility – What does it mean?', available at http://www.mallenbaker.net/csr/CSRfiles/definition.html (accessed: 27.12.03).

Barnard, C.I. (1938), *The Functions of the Executive*, Cambridge, MA: Harvard University Press.

Berenbeim, R. (2000), 'Global ethics', *Executive Excellence*, 17(5): 7.

Bloom, P.N. and Gundlach, G.T. (2000), *Handbook of Marketing and Society*, London: Sage Publications.

Bowen, H.R. (1953), *Social Responsibilities of the Businessman*, New York: Harper and Row.

Bowie, N.E. (2000), 'Business ethics, philosophy, and the next 25 years', *Business Ethics Quarterly*, 10(1): 7–20.

Carroll, A.B. (1979), 'A three-dimensional conceptual model of corporate performance', *Academy of Management. The Academy of Management Review*, 4(4): 497–505.

——. (1989), *Business and Society: Ethics and Stakeholder Management*, Cincinnati, OH: South-Western.

——. (1991), 'The pyramid of corporate social responsibility: Toward the moral management of organizational stakeholders', *Business Horizons*, 34(4): 39–48.

——. (1999), 'Corporate social responsibility', *Business and Society*, 38(3): 268–295.

Chen, R. (1975), 'Social and financial stewardship', *The Accounting Review*, July: 533–543.

Clarkson, M.B.E. (1995), 'A stakeholder framework for analyzing and evaluating corporate social performance', *The Academy of Management Review*, 20(1): 92–117.

CORE (The Corporate Responsibility Coalition). (2003), 'About the need for corporate responsibility', available at http://www.amnesty.org.uk/business/campaigns/core/need.shtml (accessed: 27.12.03).

Crowther, D. and Rayman-Bacchus, L. (2004), 'Introduction: Perspectives on corporate social responsibility', in D. Crowther and L. Rayman-Bacchus (Eds), *Perspectives on Corporate Social Responsibility*, Aldershot: Ashgate.

CSR Europe. (2003), 'FAQ, about CSR', available at http://www.csreurope.org/aboutus/FAQ/#csr (accessed: 27.12.03).

Danisco. (2005), 'Sustainability', available at http://www.danisco.com/cms/connect/corporate/about%20danisco/sustainability/sustainability_en.htm (accessed: 24.07.05).

Danone. (1974), 'Five priorities for a dual commitment to business success and social responsibility', available at http://www.danone.com/cmscache/MYSESSION~D7DE04B6CA1FED38C1256F0900563DAB/double_projetUS.pdf (accessed: 15.08.05).

Davis, K. (1960), 'Can business afford to ignore social responsibilities?', *California Management Review*, 2(3): 70–76.

——. (1973), 'The case for and against business assumption of social responsibilities', *Academy of Management Journal*, 16(2): 312–322.

——. (1975), 'Five propositions for social-responsibility', *Business Horizons*, 18(3): 19–24.

Davis, K. and Blomstrom, R.L. (1966), *Business and Its Environment*, Berkshire: McGraw-Hill Education.

Dobson, J. (1999), 'Is shareholder wealth maximization immoral?', *Financial Analysts Journal*, 55(5): 69–75.

Donaldson, T. and Preston, L. (1995), 'The stakeholder theory of the corporation: Concepts, evidence, and implications', *Academy of Management Review*, 20(1): 65–91.

Elkington, J. (1998), *Cannibals with Forks: The Triple Bottom Line of 21st Century Business*, Canada: New Society Publishers.

Emiliani, M.L. (2001), 'A mathematical logic approach to the shareholder vs stakeholder debate', *Management Decision*, 39(8): 618–622.

EMSF. (2004), 'European multi-stakeholder forum on CSR – final results and recommendations', 29 June, available at http://www.csreurope.org (accessed: 12.08.05).

Enterprise Europe. (2002), 'New economy, corporate social responsibility: stakeholder expectations', available at http://europa.eu.int/comm/enterprise/library/enterprise-europe/issue7/articles/en/enterprise07_en.htm (accessed: 20.05.04).

Epstein, M.J. and Roy, M-J. (2001), 'Sustainability in action: Identifying and measuring the key performance drivers', *Long Range Planning*, 34(5): 585.

Euroabstracts (The European Union). (2003), 'Responsible entrepreneurship: A collection of good practice cases among small and medium-sized enterprises across Europe', available at http://www.emc.be/library/doc0020.pdf (accessed: 20.10.05).

European Commission. (2004), 'European multi-stakeholder forum on CSR: Final results and recommendations', available at http://forum.europa.eu.int/irc/empl/csr_eu_multi_stakeholder_forum/info/data/en/csr%20ems%20forum.htm (accessed: 10.09.05).

Farmer, R.N. (1964), 'The ethical dilemma of American capitalism', *California Management Review*, 6(4): 47–58.

Ferraro, F., Pfeffer, J. and Sutton, R.I. (2005), 'Economics language and assumptions: How theories can become self-fulfilling', *Academy of Management. The Academy of Management Review*, 30(1): 8–24.

Follett, M.P. (1918), *The New State: Group Organization, the Solution of Popular Government*, New York: Longmans Green and Co.

Frederick, W.C. (1960), 'The growing concern over business responsibility', *California Management Review*, 2(4): 54–61.

———. (1978/1994), 'From CSR1 to CSR2: The maturing of business-and-society thought', *Business and Society*, 33(2): 150–164.

———. (1986), 'Toward CSR3: Why ethical analysis is indispensable and unavoidable in corporate affairs', *California Management Review*, 28(2): 126–141.

Frederick, W.C. (1987), 'Theories of corporate social performance', in S.P. Sethi and C.M. Falbe (Eds), *Business and Society: Dimensions of Conflict and Co-operation*, New York: Lexington Books, pp. 142–161.

———. (1998), 'Moving to CSR4: What to pack for the trip', *Business and Society*, 37(1): 40–59.

Freeman, R.E. (1983), *Strategic Management: A Stakeholder Approach*, London: Financial Times Prentice Hall.

———. (2004), 'A stakeholder theory of the Modern corporation', in L. Hartman (Ed.), *Perspectives in Business Ethics* (3rd Edition), Berkshire: McGraw Hill Higher Education.

Friedman, M. (1962), *Capitalism and Freedom*, Chicago, IL: University of Chicago Press.

———. (1970), 'The social responsibility of business is to increase its profits', 13 September, *The New York Times Magazine*, available at http://ca.geocities.com/busa2100/miltonfriedman.htm (accessed: 07.11.03).

Garriga, E. and Melé, D. (2004), 'Corporate social responsibility theories: Mapping the territory', *Journal of Business Ethics*, 53(1/2): 51–71.

Giddens, A. (1984), *The Constitution of Society: Outline of the Theory of Structuration*, Cambridge: Polity Press.

Goodpaster, K.E. (1991), 'Business ethics and stakeholder analysis', *Business Ethics Quarterly*, 1(1): 53–72.

Halal, W.E. (2000), 'Corporate community: A theory of the firm uniting profitability and responsibility', *Strategy and Leadership*, 28(2): 10–16.

Harrison, J.S. and Freeman, R.E. (1999), 'Stakeholders, social responsibility, and performance: Empirical evidence and theoretical perspectives', *Academy of Management Journal*, 42(5): 479–485.

Harrison, S. (1997), 'Corporate social responsibility: Linking behaviour with reputation', in P. Kitchen (Ed.), *Public Relations: Principles and Practice*, London: Thomson Learning.

Hess, D., Rogovsky, N. and Dunfee, T.W. (2002), 'The next wave of corporate community involvement: Corporate social initiatives', *California Management Review*, 44(2): 110–125.

Hillman, A.J., Keim, G.D. and Luce, R.A. (2001), 'Board composition and stakeholder performance: Do stakeholder directors make a difference?', *Business and Society*, 40(3): 295–313.

Hummels, H. (1998), 'Organizing ethics: A stakeholder debate', *Journal of Business Ethics*, 17(13): 1403–1419.

Johnson, G. and Scholes, K. (2001), *Exploring Corporate Strategy: Text and Cases* (6th Edition), Herts: FT Hall.

Jones, T.M. (1980), 'Corporate social responsibility revisited, redefined', *California Management Review*, 22(3): 59.

——. (1995), 'Instrumental stakeholder theory: A synthesis of ethics and economics', *Academy of Management. The Academy of Management Review*, 20(2): 404–437.

——. (1999), 'The institutional determinants of social responsibility', *Journal of Business Ethics*, 20(2): 163–179.

Jones, T.M. and Wicks, A.C. (1999), 'Convergent stakeholder theory', *Academy of Management. The Academy of Management Review*, 24(2): 206–221.

Jones, T.M., Wicks, A.C. and Freeman, R.E. (2002), 'Stakeholder theory: The state of the art', in N.E. Bowie (Ed.), *The Blackwell Guide to Business Ethics*, Oxford: Blackwell Publishers, pp. 19–37.

Juholin, E. (2004), 'For business or the good of all? A Finnish approach to corporate social responsibility', *Corporate Governance*, 4(3): 20–31.

Kakabadse, A. and Morsing, M. (2006), *Corporate Social Responsibility: Reconciling Aspiration with Application*, Hampshire: Palgrave Macmillan.

Kakabadse, N.K., Rozuel, C. and Lee-Davies, L. (2005), 'Corporate social responsibility and stakeholder approach: A conceptual review', *International Journal of Business Governance and Ethics*, 1(4): 277–302.

Kaptein, M. and Wempe, J. (2002), *The Balanced Company: A Theory of Corporate Integrity*, Oxford: Oxford University Press.

Kilcullen, M. and Kooistra, J.O. (1999), 'At least do no harm: Sources on the changing role of business ethics and corporate social responsibility', *Reference Services Review*, 27(2): 158–178.

Klonoski, R.J. (1991), 'Foundational considerations in the corporate social responsibility debate', *Business Horizons*, 34(4): 9–18.

L'Etang, J. (1995), 'Ethical corporate social responsibility: A framework for managers', *Journal of Business Ethics*, 14(2): 125–132.

Langlois, C.C. and Schlegelmilch, B.B. (1990), 'Do corporate codes of ethics reflect national character? Evidence from Europe and the United States', *Journal of International Business Studies*, 21(4): 519–539.

Lantos, G.P. (2001), 'The boundaries of strategic corporate social responsibility', *The Journal of Consumer Marketing*, 18(7): 595–649.

Maitland, I. (1997), 'Virtuous markets: The market as school of the virtues', *Business Ethics Quarterly*, 7(1): 17–31.

Margolis, J.D. and Walsh, J.P. (2003), 'Misery loves companies: Rethinking social initiatives by business', *Administrative Science Quarterly*, 48(2): 268–305.

Matten, D., Crane, A. and Chapple, W. (2003), 'Behind the mask: Revealing the true face of corporate citizenship', *Journal of Business Ethics*, 45(1): 109–120.

McAdam, R. and Leonard, D. (2003), 'Corporate social responsibility in a total quality management context: Opportunities for sustainable growth', *Corporate Governance*, 3(4): 36–45.

McWilliams, A. and Siegel, D. (2001), 'Corporate social responsibility: A theory of the firm perspective', *Academy of Management. The Academy of Management Review*, 26(1): 117–127.

Meznar, M., Chrisman, J.J. and Carroll, A.B. (1991), 'Social responsibility and strategic management: Toward an enterprise strategy classification', *Business and Professional Ethics Journal*, 10(1): 47–66.

Minkes, A.L., Small, M.W. and Chatterjee, S.R. (1999), 'Leadership and business ethics: Does it matter? Implications for management', *Journal of Business Ethics*, 20(4): 327–335.

Mitnick, B.M. (1995), 'Systematics and CSR: The theory and processes of normative referencing', *Business and Society*, 34(1): 5–33.

Moir, L. (2001), 'What do we mean by corporate social responsibility?', *Corporate Governance*, 1(2): 16–22.

Morris, S.A. (1997), 'Internal effects of stakeholder management devices', *Journal of Business Ethics*, 16(4): 413–424.

National Express Group. (2005), 'Corporate responsibility: Our approach', available at http://www.nationalexpressgroup.com/nx/cr/approach/ (accessed: 14.12.05).

Nisberg, J.N. (1988), *The Random House Handbook of Business Terms*, New York: Random House USA Inc.

Novethic. (2003), 'Glossaire – responsabilité sociale d'entreprise (RSE)', available at http://www.novethic.fr/novethic/site/guide/glossaire.jsp (accessed: 29.12.03).

Novo Nordisk. (2003), 'Social responsibility as a business principle', available at http://www.novonordisk.com/sustainability/soc_responsibility/default.asp (accessed: 29.12.03).

OECD (Organisation for Economic Co-operation and Development). (2003), 'Corporate responsibility, About', available at http://www.oecd.org/about/ 0,2337,en_2649_33765_1_1_1_1,00.html (accessed: 27.12.03).

Orlitzky, M., Schmidt, F.L. and Rynes, S.L. (2003), 'Corporate social and financial performance: A meta-analysis', *Organization Studies*, 24(3): 403–441.

Ougaard, M. and Nielsen, M.E. (2002), 'Beyond moralizing: Agendas and inquiries in corporate social responsibility', available at http://www.cbs.dk/centres/cvr/pdf/morten_ougaard_beyound_moralizing.pdf (accessed: 30.06.04).

Pesqueux, Y. and Biefnot, Y. (2002), *L'Ethique des affaires (Business Ethics)*, Paris: Ed. d'Organisation.

Pettigrew, A. (1987), 'Context and action in the transformation of the firm', *Journal of Management Studies*, 24: 649–670.

Pettigrew, A., Thomas, H. and Whittington, W. (2002), *Handbook of Strategy and Management*, London: Sage.

Phillips, R. (2001), 'Stakeholder legitimacy: A preliminary investigation', Georgetown University Business School Working Paper, Washington, D.C.

Post, J.E., Preston, L.E. and Sachs, S. (2002), 'Managing the extended enterprise: The new stakeholder view', *California Management Review*, 45(1): 6–28.

PricewaterhouseCoopers (2002), '2002 Sustainability Survey Report', available at: http://www.pwcglobal.com/fas/pdfs/sustainability%20survey%20report.pdf (accessed: 14.05.04)

Rhenman, E. (1968), *Industrial Democracy and Industrial Management. A Critical Essay on the Possible Meanings and Implications of Industrial Democracy* (N. Adler, Trans.), London: Tavistock Press.

Rhenman, E. and Stymne, B. (1965), *Företagsledning i en föränderlig värld (Corporate Management in a Changing World)*, Stockholm: Aldus/Bonnier.

Roman, R.M., Hayibor, S. and Agle, B.R. (1999), 'The relationship between social and financial performance', *Business and Society*, 38(1): 109–125.

Salls, M. (2004), 'An opposing view on corporate social responsibility', *Harvard Business School Working Knowledge*, available at http://hbswk.hbs.edu (accessed: 09.06.04).

Scholl, H.J. (2001), 'Applying stakeholder theory to e-government: Benefits and limits', available at http://www.ischool.washington.edu/jscholl/Papers/Scholl_IFIP_2001.pdf (accessed: 30.06.04).

Sethi, S.P. (1975), 'Dimensions of corporate social performance: An analytical framework', *California Management Review*, 17(3): 58–64.

Simmons, J. (2004), 'Managing in the post-managerialist era: Towards socially responsible corporate governance', *Management Decision*, 42(3/4): 601–611.

Singhapakdi, A., Vitell, S.J., Rallapalli, K.C. and Kraft, K.L. (1996), 'The perceived role of ethics and social responsibility: A scale development', *Journal of Business Ethics*, 15(11): 1131–1140.

Smith, A. (1991), *The Wealth of Nations*, London: Everyman's Library.

Smith, N.C. (2003), 'Corporate social responsibility: Whether or how?', *California Management Review*, 45(4): 52–76.

Sony Corporation of America. (2005), 'Corporate philanthropy – Sony in America: working together to make a difference', available at http://www.sony.com/SCA/philanthropy.shtml (accessed: 14.12.05).

Suchman, M.C. (1995), 'Managing legitimacy: Strategic and institutional approaches', *Academy of Management Review*, 20(3): 571–610.

Szwajkowski, E. (2000), 'Simplifying the principles of stakeholder management: The three most important principles', *Business and Society*, 39(4): 379–396.

Takala, T. (1999), 'Ownership, responsibility and leadership – A historical perspective', *International Journal of Social Economics*, 26(6): 742–751.

Tesco (2005), 'Corporate responsibility – Message from Sir Terry Leahy', available at http://www.tescocorporate.com/page.aspx?pointerid=32B0E699AB1A4CCC8D0 18E763CAF120D (accessed 14.12.05).

Thévenet, M. (2003), 'Global responsibility and individual exemplarity', *Corporate Governance*, 3(3): 114–125.

UK government's gateway to Corporate Social Responsibility. (2005), 'What is CSR?', available at http://www.societyandbusiness.gov.uk/whatiscsr.shtml (accessed: 28.08.05).

Unilever. (2003), 'CSR: Rebuilding trust in business – A perspective on corporate social responsibility in the 21st century', available at http://www.unilever.com/Images/A%20Perspective%20on%20Corporate%20Social%

20Responsibility%20in%20the%2021st%20Century_tcm13–5520.pdf (accessed: 29.12.03).

van Marrewijk, M. (2003), 'Concepts and definitions of CSR and corporate sustainability: Between agency and communion', *Journal of Business Ethics*, 44(2/3): 95–105.

van Marrewijk, M. and Werre M. (2003), 'Multiple levels of corporate sustainability', *Journal of Business Ethics*, 44(2/3): 107–119.

Vinten, G. (2000), 'The stakeholder manager', *Management Decision*, 38(6): 377–383.

Vogl, A.J. (2003), 'Does it pay to be good?', *Across the Board*, 40(1): 16–23.

WBCSD (World Business Council for Sustainable Development). (2003), 'Cross–cutting themes: The WBCSD's red thread', available at http://www.wbcsd.org/Plugins/DocSearch/details.asp?DocTypeId=251&ObjectId=MTU2NA&URLBack=%2Ftemplates%2FTemplateWBCSD2%2Flayout%2Easp%3Ftype%3Dp%26MenuId%3DMzk3%26doOpen%3D1%26ClickMenu%3DLeftMenu (accessed: 29.12.05).

Weiss, J.W. (2002), *Business Ethics: A Stakeholder and Issues Management Approach* (3rd Edition), London: Thomson Learning.

Wheeler, D. and Sillanpää, M. (1998), 'Including the stakeholders: The business case', *Long Range Planning*, 31(2): 201–210.

Wiedermann–Goiran, T., Perier, F. and Lépineux, F. (2002), *Développement durable et gouvernement d'entreprise: un dialogue prometteur*, France: éditions d'organisation.

Wilson, I. (2000), 'The new rules: Ethics, social responsibility and strategy', *Strategy and Leadership*, 28(3): 12–16.

Wood, D.J. (1991), 'Corporate social performance revisited', *The Academy of Management Review*, 16(4): 691–718.

2
CSR Penetrating the Supply Chain: Desire Lacking Reality

Nada K. Kakabadse, Andrew P. Kakabadse and
Richard Middleton

Introduction

Corporate social responsibility (CSR) has gained prominence both in the scholarly and popular media and is increasingly penetrating the agendas of corporate boards, NGOs and governments. The increased attention given to CSR has been partly fuelled by corporate excesses which have become manifest in various parts of the world, as well as the growing discomfort with the poverty divide between the 'haves' and 'have nots' epitomised by the increasing gap between developing and developed societies. Yet resistance still exists to the adoption of CSR principles, as the prevailing ideology of the 'invisible hand' of free markets dictates that economic wealth and its distribution require minimum intervention and regulation of market forces. Thus, Friedman's (1962: 133) argument that 'few trends would so thoroughly undermine the very foundation of our free society as the acceptance by corporate officials of a social responsibility other than to make as much money for their shareholders as they possibly can', although narrow minded by enlightened standards, is still favoured by those who hold that businesses are ultimately, if not uniquely, accountable to their owners and that the only reason for being in business is to make money for the business's investors (Margolis and Walsh, 2003). The focus on corporate financial performance (CFP) is justified by the dictum that 'the proper business of business is business. No apology required' (*The Economist*, 2005: 18). However, a growing body of evidence challenges such perspective as the prosperity of certain nations and interest groups results from other nations', groups' and individuals' misfortunes. The growing number of proponents of the 'stakeholder' or 'social responsibility' model of corporate governance hold that businesses are accountable to a broader populace who have a direct or indirect stake in the enterprise's activities (Halal, 2000). Although no clear agreement concerning the definition of CSR and stakeholders has emerged, the general implication is that enterprise management should be much more sensitive to environmental concerns and to the various actors who are likely to be impacted by the organisation's progress. The debate has advanced to considerations of corporate citizenship and the firm's role in society, thus giving rise to the expression 'from Friedman to Freeman', illustrating the shift in debate on the role of business in society (Kakabadse and Rozuel, 2004).

However, whether senior executives have genuinely become more accepting of the social consciousness statements of CSR or merely accepting of the debate as a public relations exercise, is not clear. Porter (2003), for example, argues that 'corporate leaders are now giving "lip service" to this but they do not ultimately understand it. No matter what they say in public, when you get behind the scenes with executives and directors, they will ask you: why should we invest in social initiatives?' (Porter, 2003: 4). At best, Porter (2003: 41) positions CSR as 'corporate philanthropy', or a noble ambition and considers it as a religion filled with priests (Porter, 2003). Yet, irrespective of what executives seemingly believe, the stakeholder debate towards promoting a more socially responsible market economy is paralleled by public and private enterprises experiencing pressure to transparently streamline their financial performance (Kakabadse and Rozuel, 2004). Such pressure has witnessed only certain enterprises having adopted CSR within their sphere of operations with the majority contemplating committing to CSR (Craig-Smith, 2003).

The growing public interest in CSR, and its variable penetration of the corporate agenda, inspired the study outlined in this chapter (Hess *et al.*, 2002). Discussed is a case study examining CSR application within the supply chain of an international company, surrogately termed the International Food Corporation (IFC). The study explores how stakeholders within IFC's supply chain variously interpreted and implemented CSR considerations. Preceding the analysis of the case study is a brief review of latest thinking of CSR emphasising the balance between CSR desire and organisational reality. Overall, it is concluded that prevailing market conditions dominate enterprise management application. Whatever top managements' aspirations, the study results highlight that once CSR 'leaves' the boardroom, the lack of disciplined and proceduralised follow through not only inhibits the effective application of CSR but also leaves senior management ignorant of lack of progress. Turning desire into reality emerges as a critical concern.

CSR interpretations

CSR is no new phenomena. From the earliest days of the industrial revolution, the movement towards enterprise's socially responsible behaviour has acted as a counter to the free hand given to the joint-stock company, later to be morphed as the multinational enterprise (MNE). Overtime, the corporation's social responsibilities have been captured in the acronym CSR which, in turn, has evolved into varying forms and meanings. Scandinavian countries have more championed concern with social wellbeing prompting the notion of a corporate responsibility towards social community. In contrast, Central European nations have shown greater concern for industrial farming, bioengineering and enterprise's effects upon biodiversity emerging with concerns for environmental sustainability, often in the form of a sustainable ecosphere. According to Central European interpretation, corporate responsibility attends to the needs of a silent stakeholder – the environment – consciously eco-efficient, delivering more value for less environmental burden. A third CSR position is that adopted by the Anglo-American economies. Their focus on economic and market development, giving rise to concerns of shareholders' trust of management, has advanced the notion of corporate ethics, namely, norms, laws, values and virtues that establish 'ethically' acceptable business practice. The good 'corporate citizen' is one who adopts a 'moral' orientation to their conduct of business and enterprise.

Thus, these three perspectives have sat side by side for over three decades (Shankman, 1999). However, over the last 15 years the perspective more adopted through Continental Europe has become that of sustainable development so as to 'meet the needs of today without compromising the ability of future generations to meet their own need' (Brundtland, 1987). Further, socially responsible behaviour has, overtime, become positioned as voluntary. The European Commission (EC, 2002: 5, 347) defines CSR as a 'concept whereby companies integrate social and environmental concerns in their business operations and in their interaction with their stakeholders on a voluntary basis'. The onus is placed on corporations to exercise their CSR commitments. By implication, assistance from governments and international institutions, such as the International Financial Reporting Standards (IFRS), and the International Accounting Standards Board (IASB) is assumed for the purpose of enabling socially responsible activities to be pursued. In contrast, the Anglo-American focus has been on regulation, notably the legal mandates from Sarbanes/Oxley, or voluntary codes policed by the stock exchanges of New York and London, both for the purpose of providing parameters for corporations to behave responsibly towards shareholders, suppliers and customers. Anglo-American practice adds credence to Porter's (2003) view of CSR as corporate philanthropy.

Supply chain sustainability

Irrespective of the three contrasting CSR interpretations or whether certain organisations seriously view CSR as a viable policy or not, an additional area of examination is the sustainability of CSR when entering into the 'bowels' of the organisation's configuration, namely the supply chain (Saunders, 1997).

Traditionally the supply side of the business equation, in effect the functions of purchasing and procurement, has been principally driven by cost effectiveness considerations over purchasing, supported by concerns of service and quality (Donaldson and Preston, 1995). Some argue that cost effectiveness has been achieved at the expense of sustainability as purchasing and procurement functions, in their drive for efficiency, are viewed as having paid little attention to social issues (Maignan *et al.*, 2002). In contrast, others argue that supply chain challenges have shifted to that of a value proposition as opposed to over-attention to cost (Saunders, 1997). However, most concur that the supply side of the organisation is well placed to demonstrate the extent of its social responsibility orientation, acting as the interface between internal needs and the external operating environment (Carter and Jennings, 2002). The significance of this interface, in terms of CSR, is illustrated by the phrase 'extended enterprise', adopted by the Chrysler Corporation when referring to its main supply management practices (Post *et al.*, 2002).

Maignan *et al.* (2002) propose that four principles of CSR need to be applied in any supply chain analysis, namely, respect for workers' rights, respect of local democratic institutions, protection of natural resources and the use of minority suppliers, all comparable with the categories identified by the UN Global Compact Initiative (UN, 2000). Definition of minority suppliers includes racial background, religion, gender and size of supplier enterprise (Maignan *et al.*, 2002). Although Maignan and Ralston (2002) found that supplier responsibilities are rarely mentioned by CSR sensitive stakeholders, Carter and Jennings (2002) suggest that supplier/CSR considerations can be understood by inquiring into how supplier commitment, trust and long-term relationships are forged. Long-term intentions which foster socially sustainable practice need to be examined against short-term, at times, opportunistic and noncommittal associations that challenge CSR application (Carter and Jennings, 2002). Such analysis highlights the quality of stakeholder linkages in the supply chain and the nature by which they were initiated, for example, transactional, individually exclusive, mutually beneficial (Post *et al.*, 2002). However, it is acknowledged that tension between the two standpoints of short-term financial gain for the shareholder and the longer-term sustainability and relationship development of stakeholders is likely to arise. The bridging of difference requires in-depth examination in order to ascertain the reality of sustainability (Margolis and Walsh, 2003; Mikkilä, 2003).

In particular, the purchasing function is faced with a substantial degree of tension stretch. If a material or service is cheaper overseas, one consideration focuses on cost to the organisation whilst another on the impact on local suppliers. The shareholder argument contends that pursuit of economies of scale should be undertaken irrespective of effects on local conditions. This view has provided fuel to the anti-globalisation argument. The opposing view challenges conventional thinking by putting suppliers first, thus challenging the accepted norms that markets exist for the benefit of consumers and shareholders (Mikkilä, 2003).

The study

Recognising the breadth of interpretation of CSR and its tensions in supply chain application, the aim of this inquiry is to investigate whether an organisation that publicly positions itself as socially responsible 'practises what it preaches', or if not, the nature of emerging practice 'on the ground'. The research site chosen was that of the International Food Corporation (IFC – company name changed to ensure confidentiality), a large European, multinational food products manufacturer. The IFC operates a divisional structure, totalling several thousand employees, spanning many countries with an annual turnover of US$ 4 billion. Of its several divisions, the study was pursued in the spices division (SD) which has evolved a reputation for social responsiveness. The IFC's approach to corporate sustainability reflects Brundtland's (1987) four pillars of: (i) safety, health, environment and quality (SHEQ); (ii) product safety (PS); (iii) environmental ethics (EE); and (iv) social issues and business integrity (SIBI). The fourth pillar, social issues and business integrity, includes employee rights, international society rights, security, compliance and business partner rights. The importance of sustainability is highlighted in the organisation's 2003–2004 annual report where as

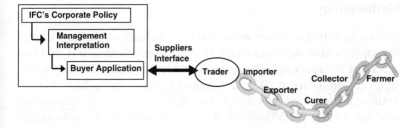

Figure 2.1 IFC's cascade of CSR.
Source: Adapted from IFC (2004).

much space is devoted to sustainability as to financial and commercial risk. Further, internal study results of IFC's social policy scorecard indicate that whilst 75 per cent of the production sites, covering 80 per cent of the employee base, live up to expectations in terms of social policy application, operations in the European Union and the United States emerged with higher scores in comparison to operations in other parts of the world (IFC, 2003). Further, a recently circulated internal sustainability report informs of the company's distinctly positive listing on the Dow Jones Sustainability Index, the FTSE4Good and other indexes (IFC, 2003). Towards the end of 2004, a relevant Continental European research group listed IFC as being one of the top five for social concern and sustainability out of 38 global food businesses. Figure 2.1 illustrates the CSR policy cascade process employed by IFC's spices division (SD).

In particular, the study focused on the SD's vanilla supply chain of the IFC, a particularly challenging part of the supply chain as the fragility of the vanilla plant and its pollination is paralleled by an equal sensitivity of relationship maintenance between the farmers at the source of the chain and the curing and preparation processes necessary for vanilla's ultimate manufacture and sale. At present, vanilla does not hold commodity status, but future initiatives to switch farming from Africa to India and the speeding up of the drying process are intended to realise economies of scale. African farmers, however, recognising threats to their livelihood have become suspicious of IFC, thus making a primarily trusting relationship even more fragile. Research access was secured by the research team through a former senior IFC manager who had evolved a wide network of contacts within the IFC supply chain, including IFC directors, buyers, traders, mid-level suppliers (i.e. curing houses) and farmers in a number of developing economies. In particular, three developing economies, two in Africa and one in India, hosted the study. These three sites provide for over 40 per cent of SD's supply chain.

Methodology

Interviews with and observation of key individuals within each unit in the supply chain was undertaken. The interview schedule was stratified according to functional role, seniority and levels of responsibility in the supply chain (Gerring, 2004; George and Bennett, 2005; Table 2.1). An outline of the interview schedule highlighting areas of discussion was sent out to IFC participants in advance of meeting. Semi-structured interviews then followed and, in the course of discussion, additional relevant contributors were identified for the purpose of further interviews. With external stakeholders (e.g. traders, curers, farmers), a less formal interview process was adopted often undertaken at the participant's place of work. At each research site a local facilitator acted as 'cultural interpreter' in order to provide for greater understanding of the nature of the views expressed (Yin, 1987). Once the interviews were complete and the notes transcribed, a manual coding of the interpretations of application of CSR policies within the vanilla supply chain was undertaken (Miles and Huberman, 1994). A total of 72 conversations were completed (Table 2.1).

Table 2.1 Study participants

Stakeholders	Participants	Method	CSR cascade
IFC top team	2 senior executives	Corporate CSR policies and documentation. Informal conversations.	Policy generation
Management	10 senior managers	Semi-structured interviews. Informal conversations. Observation.	Policy adoption Policy review
Buyers	12 buyers from IFC's spices division	Semi-structured interviews. Informal conversations. Observation.	Policy enactment
Traders	4 each from Madagascar, India and Uganda	Informal conversations. Observation.	Policy application (external)
Mid-supply stream	3 each from Madagascar, India and Uganda	Informal conversations. Observation.	Mid-supply stream application
Farmers	5 each from Madagascar, India and Uganda	Informal conversations. Observation.	Production application
Community leaders	4 each from Madagascar, India and Uganda	Informal conversations.	Effect of CSR policy application

Source: Compiled by authors.

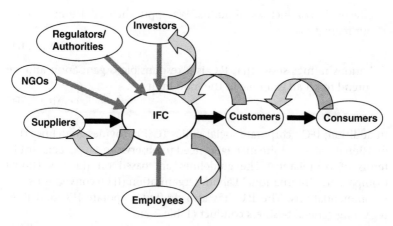

Figure 2.2 IFC's stakeholder and sustainable development policy.
Source: Adapted from IFC (2004).

Findings

Distinction is drawn between the responses of internal IFC employees and external stakeholders. Internal IFC employees are classified by role, location and level of responsibility, namely senior executives at corporate headquarters, divisional managers, buyers and auditors. External stakeholders are equally subdivided according to their responsibilities as traders, mid-term suppliers (i.e. importers, exporters, curers), farmers and members of the local community.

Corporate perspective: policy generation

Documents outlining IFC's policies towards stakeholders are illustrated in Figure 2.2. The commitment that the IFC has publicly made to promoting a sustainable development policy, taking account of internal and external stakeholder needs in order to redress concerns and constantly work towards improving critical relationships with suppliers, customers, consumers, employees and investors is captured in Figure 2.2. Executives of the company, in interview, declared with pride both horizontal attentiveness to social responsibility, namely, one supply chain from supplier to consumer, and also vertical attentiveness to employees and investors.

We are committed to CSR. In addition to our exemplary policies we employ respected consultants to advise us on how we should effectively conduct social audits. We apply their advice in training our managers!

Executive 1, IFC

Various ratings show that IFC is a responsible organisation and we intend to set an example in the food industry.

Executive 2, IFC

In addition, IFC's corporate social policy (CSP) provides guidelines that divisional, sales and site managers need to observe and report against in terms of compliance. The guidelines are based on the UN Global Compact and International Labour Organisation (ILO) conventions and recommendations. The IFC has also drafted corporate HR guidelines regarding general business conduct (Table 2.2).

In order to promote social responsibility practice in the supply chain, IFC corporate centre has issued a procurement policy framework, vendor evaluation guidelines and specific guidelines for suppliers, outlining what the organisation expects from its supply base, particularly attending to equal opportunity, freedom of association, abolition of forced labour and elimination of child labour. Senior executive management refer directly to the Brundtland (1987) report when discussing issues of sustainability and also highlight that IFC has signed the UN Global Compact Initiative (Maignan *et al.*, 2002).

The two corporate centre executives interviewed emphasised the proactive position adopted by IFC at the 2002 Round Table discussion on corporate sustainability hosted by the OECD. However, when requested to interpret the performance and contribution of particular divisions, such as the spices division (SD), to social responsibility, discussion centred more on economic drivers and the challenge of

Table 2.2   IFC's HR business conduct guidelines

Business Conduct Guidelines
General principles
Refrain from anti-competitive agreements
Communication outside IFC
Refrain from receiving bribery
Ensure fair marketing practices
Relations between employees and IFC
Employees should behave as worthy ambassadors for IFC

Source: Adapted from IFC's social issues.

integrating commodity arguments concerning price with social responsibility obligations.

Divisional senior manager perspective: policy adoption

Divisional senior managers acknowledged consistent receipt of corporate CSR policy and corporate core values communication. Further, they expressed distinct awareness that all employees were requested to undertake an online training programme concerned with issues of sustainability and social responsibility. The online programme was staff and management's first exposure to CSR and sustainable development training. The divisional managers interviewed displayed a knowledgeable understanding of IFC's CSR policies. However, the application of CSR policy taking into account daily practice and accommodation of local concerns, induced a broad and inconsistent range of responses.

> Policies are amended, clarified, modified or even opposed! ... Of course, by agreement with the executive!
>
> Senior Manager 1, Spices Division

> We have a checklist for policies because there are so many.
>
> Senior Manager 3, Spices Division

> The depth document, Raw Material Product Specification (RMPS), expected to cover every perceivable query that may arise from food or health, safety and product quality, doesn't cover sustainability or social policies, but only products.
>
> Senior Manager 4, Spices Division

> Sustainability is clearly mentioned in the 25 pages of the Raw Material Product Specification (RMPS), but there are over 1200 core suppliers covering a total of 8660 raw materials in the spices division alone. The task of administering these is enormous.
>
> Senior Manager 7, Spices Division

Overall, interviewees at divisional senior manager level displayed variance of view concerning the details of both product and social responsibility application, due to the volume of raw materials, core suppliers and covering IFC documentation. As captured in the comments of senior managers 4 and 7, quoting the very same document (RMPS), both held different recollections of its content due to the extent of detail.

Buyer perspective: policy enactment

In contrast to senior IFC management (corporate centre and divisional), buyers exhibited limited understanding of CSR and its sustainability as well as a low awareness of the online training course and existence of the documentation mentioned above. Their responses ranged from appreciation of CSR compliance to total ignorance (even rejection), some not even aware that IFC's suppliers could be delisted as a result of their social responsibility inattention.

> I've found CSR really interesting. It adds a whole new dimension to what I do and something for me to think about!
>
> Buyer 1, Purchasing Manager, Spices Division

> I feel that as a buyer it is not for me to accept any responsibility or concern for sustainability or social issues in our supply chain. That is not part of my job.
>
> Buyer 3, Purchasing Manager, Spices Division

> We need to know who we are dealing with in order to answer our own issues of traceability, so we ask where they obtain their materials. If they are unwilling to divulge the information, then it rings alarm bells. If they invest in marketing brochures and the like, it shows to us that they are serious.
>
> Buyer 4, Purchasing Manager, Spices Division

A number of buyers suggested that compliance with IFC's corporate CSR policy is a veneer and that reality is a focus on the 'hard' business concerns, such as price, quality and service (delivery, information, reliability). This view was also echoed in each developing country suppliers' buying departments, who expressed their primary goal as being cost saving, and devoting considerable time to meeting this goal. Yet, most interviewees concurred with Carter's (2000) suggestion that buyers represent the organisation to the outside world and lack of attention to CSR would eventually become evident.

> Spices traders are no different to any other in most respects. We deal with traders on a year to year, or crop cycle basis, whereas with manufacturers we tend to look for longer-term relationships.
>
> Buyer 5, Purchasing Manager, Spices Division

> My preference is not to use traders at all but to go straight to manufacturers, but there are cases such as with spices where this is difficult

to do. The primary guide as to which trader to use is price. If they are too cheap, it leads you to ask more questions. If they are too expensive, we look elsewhere. It means we have to read the markets as well. The traders are selling to us on their expertise and knowledge of the market, not on CSR issues.

Buyer 7, Purchasing Manager, Spices Division

Most of the time we look for the best price to the right specification. On occasion, decisions may include the potential for the supplier to provide a repeatable or sustainable supply in the future, but that is not to say that if a single trade opportunity does materialise it would not be taken.

Buyer 8, Purchasing Manager, Spices Division

What is the point of checking the sustainability stuff if they aren't getting the price or quality right or they can't deliver on time?

Buyer 9, Purchasing Manager, Spices Division

Buyers, similar to divisional senior managers, acknowledged that although sustainability and social responsibility policies have been an established part of IFC's culture for a number of years, only very recently have such policies been determinedly enacted by the corporate centre. Even with such push, still certain buyers expressed ignorance of the detailed content of CSR policy. Others simply indicated that they did not believe in the business viability of CSR when they were, as managers, equally being tasked to be attentive to costs. Unable to reconcile the paradoxical dichotomy between costs and social responsibility responsiveness, a reaction by many was to position CSR as 'someone else's responsibility'.

SHE quality audit perspective: policy review

Between February and September 2004, a number of processes were introduced by the corporate centre to ensure that the CSR message was consistently promulgated throughout the organisation in order for a common foundation of understanding to be established. In addition, a reputable international consultancy organisation (not named) who were awarded the responsibility for auditing the effectiveness of CSR and sustainability application advised on how to conduct social audits especially focusing on the safety, health and environment (SHE) function. SHE also held the direct responsibility of 'training the trainers' in an effort to involve employees. However, at a presentation to divisional managers outlining the responsibilities of the SHE function, no mention was made of CSR or IFC's position on social policy. At the meeting, SHE audits were positioned as that of risk assessment, pursued regularly or in the event of failure. Although the SHE function was considered by the corporate centre as responsible for examining the quality of CSR application and its sustainability, functional myopia was seen to lead to a lack of cross-functional interaction.

> In reality, auditing within the spices division is practically nonexistent in any region. So there is no possibility of buyers participating in the process.
>
> Senior Manager 1, Spices Division

> Audits are a major omission. They are not being done locally and there is no buying involvement as far as I know.
>
> Senior Manager 3, Spices Division

> Even if training was given to both the management and the buyers, where would they find resources and time to conduct audits? Therefore it is not a priority.
>
> Senior Regional Buyer 1, Spices Division

> There always seems to be more going on in Europe and we're always being told they do training better over there. Where do they get the time? And then why don't they do audits?
>
> Senior Regional Buyer 2, Spices Division

> By their nature, traders' risk assessment is likely to be lower than a manufacturer. A manufacturer has a factory and more direct responsibility for the product. The visit I made to Madagascar was driven by determining the security of our money rather than social or product risk.
>
> Senior Regional Buyer 3, Spices Division

Although buyers indicated a lack of awareness of the corporate centre-sponsored online training initiative, reflecting the newness of the project, they did express eagerness to participate in the training process in order to update their knowledge and their capacity to apply CSR concepts. Online training was not viewed as burdensome as the interviewees indicated that the greater proportion of CSR policy communication was conducted electronically. However, little emerged from interview with SHE personnel concerning the degree of follow-up by corporate centre management for them to appreciate the level and quality of CSR application, down the organisation. However, management did admit that weakness existed in communicating CSR policy updates or amendments.

> There is definitely a breakdown in communications, particularly with regards to updates and this must be tackled now that other projects are nearing completion.
>
> Senior Manager 3, Spices Division

> The role of the division is to ensure that policy is communicated to, and applied by, the end users. In this instance, at the interface with external stakeholders, the suppliers.
>
> Senior Manager 1, Spices Division

Although it was claimed by corporate centre management that 'all suppliers are treated in the same way regardless of where they are based or where they source from, and each is also subject to a risk assessment', interviewees confirmed audit assessment as being focused on product risk, product quality and quality systems in order to determine risk levels, rather than quality or CSR sustainability. Unusually, it was reported that price was not included in risk assessment. In fact, a full risk audit was only pursued if the response of suppliers to a pre-audit questionnaire indicated that a particular supplier merited full-scale auditing. It emerged that the senior management of SD were reliant on traders taking the responsibility to conduct their own audits. Further, buyers in interview indicated that not only was reliance on supplier honesty in terms of form filling extensive but that supplier ability to complete pre-audit forms was itself variable.

Traders' perspective: external CSR policy application

In contrast to other interviewees who highlight inconsistency of application of CSR and sustainability policies according to location and level within the organisation, traders emphasised their focus on price. The interviewees indicated that down the vanilla supply chain any, even inconsistent, concern for social policy and sustainability is substituted at the interface with the curers and farmers with attention to especially cost and product quality. It was stated that as 'an after thought' buyers may include CSR and sustainable supply chain concerns with curers and farmers. Such a finding is supported by Maignan and Ralston (2002) who indicate that suppliers rarely mention CSR, except in circumstances of needing to differentiate between two otherwise equal suppliers.

> Our job is to cut costs and keep costs low and buy locally.
>
> Commodity Trader, India

> Sustainability means having finances arranged in our country with our own bank account in a local bank. We used these finances to invest in a small factory for local processing of other materials, not only vanilla, and to have our own local person on the ground.
>
> Vanilla Trader, Madagascar

In terms of supplier compliance with CSR, at the time of interview, no formal supplier agreement was in operation. The only documentation available was the 'Sustainability Guidelines for Suppliers', distributed electronically, or manually direct from the key contact supplier, to those on the vendor list of certain select sites. The suppliers who indicated that they were informed and influenced by the 'Sustainability Guidelines for Suppliers' resided in the developed Western world and even then a difference was drawn between European and US buyers.

> Europeans are a big way into sustainability. It never really comes up with the US buyers ... but again it always comes to price.
>
> Vanilla Trader, India

> Sustainability is more important in Europe than in the US ... for us it is easer to sell to US buyers ... it is not that suitability is not important for us locally it is just that it means different things – here it means basic survival.
>
> Vanilla Trader, Uganda

Additional observation in countries of vanilla origination highlighted no 'real' concern towards social responsibility adoption. Other stakeholders, such as buyers and importers, supported these observations.

> I have seen no evidence that traders invest themselves. As a rule they 'dress up' the local facilities in order to give the impression of having 'their own' place but really it is a partnership with farmers and this can change from year to year, season to season.
>
> Senior Manager, Spices Division

Yet, a minority of traders considered themselves as socially responsible, actively attempting to direct second-hand computers into local schools and funding the temporary migration of workers from outlying areas to the curing house for the purpose of providing employment. Certainly, some local peer pressure was reported acting as a stimulus to improve local standards of life.

On investment in curing houses one buyer reports:

> Investments in us are unrelated to global market conditions, but are the result of prevailing standards in the local market and peer pressure. It was not so much Western buyers leading us in a direction, more us coming to terms with their direction.
>
> Senior Buyer, Uganda

> I am new to vanilla trading but my relationship with spice farmers and the local farming association has been established over a prolonged period of time and is a true partnership and trust. I knew how the local environment functions and where and how I can help.
>
> Commodity Trader, Madagascar

Curers' perspective: mid-supply stream application

Overall, interviewees highlighted that the smaller suppliers within the developing world are seldom aware of IFC's sustainability policies. In Madagascar, for example, curing houses for vanilla tend to have an established relationship with exporters/importers and traders. In the new growth markets where the vanilla industry is less well established, such as Uganda and India, these relationships are not as strong, which reflects in the level of CSR application. In Uganda and India, mid-level suppliers reported their refusal to accept IFC's CSR initiative or even guidance on how to adapt to global vanilla fluctuations. As a result, Uganda and India curers felt that IFC was not being honest with them.

> Many smaller curers like myself are not used to dealing with Western standards or expectations.
>
> Vanilla Curer 1, India

> Natural products are difficult to predict in terms of final quality and, for vanilla in particular, with the additional processing such as curing, it is easy to impair the final quality. Buyers do not understand our risks.
>
> Vanilla Curer 3, India

> If I cannot deliver the expected quantity of the final product, traders won't buy from me and I have to feed my family.
>
> Vanilla Curer 2, Uganda

> We work with the farmer and often invest with them in planting schemes ... our business is affected by the farming crop.
>
> Vanilla Curer 1, Madagascar

The theme to emerge from the curers is of low levels of trust between them and the IFC on issues of world market developments in vanilla and their effect on local conditions. It was the curers' view that little opportunity exists to seriously examine CSR and sustainability application within developing country localities.

Farmers' perspective: production application

Farmers strongly emphasised their lack of control over pricing, production and product quality of vanilla. They also expressed the view that all others in the supply chain were making money out of them. At a trade conference held in Cannes in the Autumn of 2004, one of the authors witnessed a polarisation of response from delegates, representing every facet of the vanilla industry – farmers, curers, exporters, traders, processors and food manufacturers from various countries – concerning the establishment of a 'vanilla association'. Farmers and curers supported the formation of a 'vanilla association' whilst traders and upstream buyers described it as a 'cartel', or an association that would control price.

> The problem this year is that traders and major companies have formed a cartel and are determined to hammer down price. That is the major reason why there are no takers.
>
> Planter

> Everybody above us is making money on our labour. High prices in the market do not benefit us as others are keeping the money that is rightfully ours.
>
> Spice Farmer

> If I am to achieve my yields, I need to be sure that my workers are trained properly in how to pollinate vanilla. That costs! Where am I supposed to get the money for that?
>
> Vanilla Grower

These last comments refer to the fact that vanilla, by nature, is a crop that requires support and protection from its surroundings. It was reported in an interview that vanilla is seldom grown in isolation from banana or coffee. Further, ecological sustainability is not threatened by the expansion of vanilla, thus placing vanilla as a supplementary, fiscal crop. Vanilla is usually grown as a complementary crop to coffee, banana or rice, foods needed by the farming family. Hence, harvesting is not the concern but more curing. Although farmers are responsible for growing green beans (vanilla), market demand has led many farmers in areas such as Madagascar to attempt the curing process themselves under the belief that they can realise a greater proportion of the finished product and thus attract increased revenue. Unfortunately, as stated in the interviews, the quality of the final product suffered as a result of early picking, partly to prevent theft during the high value years and partly due to poor processing techniques which involved blanching under semi-controlled conditions. However, current market conditions of short supply has allowed for a lower quality final product to become acceptable. The interviewees strongly emphasised that little investment has been made by the multinational food companies to train for better standards when currently such cost can be absorbed in the final market price.

Local perspective: effect of CSR policy application

One of the authors had the opportunity to discuss the plight of the vanilla industry with the leaders of the Ugandan government, who emphasised their willingness to co-operate with the buyers:

> What you want, we can do.
>
> President Museveni, Uganda

> We can provide whatever you require and in the quantity and quality required. Your demand needs to be clear in order for the farmers to commit to the production demanded.
>
> Mr Ruhemba Kweronda, Minister of State for Presidential Affairs, Uganda

> We have a significant natural resource that has been untapped for two decades. New demands for our products provides us with an economic driver and an opportunity to catch up.
>
> Dr Maggie Kigozi, Executive Director, Investment Authority, Uganda

> We are putting in place an initiative to increase the area under vanilla to 15000 hectares by 2007, the terminal year of the Tenth Five Year

Plan (2002–07). About one third of this area will receive support from the Board.

Chairman, Spices Board, India

It also emerged from conversation that new entrants to the vanilla market, such as Uganda and India, have adopted a more 'commercial' approach than established countries as Madagascar, where vanilla is grown by 'thousands' of subsistence farmers. Madagascar, for example, hosts over 80,000 vanilla farmers of which only a few are large landowners. The vast majority of farmers run un-profitable holdings dependent on subsidy. Although not a native plant of India, the vanilla price spike has encouraged farmers from compatible regions to consider diversification into this new cash crop from their traditional tea, banana and other spices portfolio. Currently, few vanilla bean plantations exist amongst the new entrants. Yet the potential for these plantations to become established producers is high. The effect of switch of supply on the established vanilla growing local communities is likely to be substantial, particularly as certain IFC corporate centre managers have already expressed an interest to switch allegiance to India and Uganda. The view is that the Indians are more likely to be commercially aware (the emergent Indian vanilla farms are larger than their counterparts in Madagascar and more scale efficient) and hence, more comfortably interrelate with IFC. Overall, it was suggested in interview that the Indians are viewed as likely to place fewer CSR sustainability demands on IFC, adding to their attraction.

Discussion

The emerging view from this study is that the greater the number of interfaces and linkages in the CSR/sustainability policy design and application chain, the less likely CSR is to be effectively applied (Table 2.3). Not only external but internal stakeholders within IFC professed ignorance of the company's sustainability and CSR practices.

Additionally, a culture of resistance to working collaboratively had developed in Madagascar partly due to the number of smallholdings and their survival orientation. In contrast, in India and Uganda farming co-operatives were reported as formed for marketing the finished product. In Madagascar the curing houses hold the responsibility for providing an outlet for their local farmers from a given area, whereas in the other two countries, farmers have a more involved and collaborative relationship with the curers.

Table 2.3 Research findings

Viewpoint	Role	CSR and sustainability
Internal		
Corporate center	Establish policies, guidelines and sustainability report.	High level of commitment from executive. Detailed CSR policies in place. Regular CSR reporting. Highly influenced by local stakeholders.
Division	Interprets corporate policies and guidelines.	Reliance on exchanges of paperwork between suppliers and the division. Lack of integrative mechanisms. Rarely follow up on CSR policy. Focus on financial targets.
Operations (buyers)	Apply relevant/ interpreted guidelines.	CSR not generally covered during procurement discussions. Focus on price, quality and service.
Audit management; SHE quality	Apply relevant guidelines; conduct audits.	Insubstantial audits conducted.
External		
Traders (direct interface)	Commercial supply of material.	CSR rarely mentioned.
Mid-supply stream, importers, exporters, curers	Conversion and shipping of materials from the farmers to saleable goods.	CSR rarely mentioned. Focus on fiscal return.
Farmers producers)	Growers of the material.	CSR not mentioned. Concern with fiscal return.
Local community	Politicians and organisations able to influence local social issues.	Aware of issues, but focus on establishing a market for their produce in order to attract revenue.

Source: Compiled by the authors.

However, despite other developments, the critical finding to emerge is the basic mistrust between the links in a supply chain predominated by concern for economies of scale and financial gain. The farmers indicated that they do not receive a fair price. The curing houses expressed that they do not realise appropriate margin and the traders also claimed that their margins are small.

Figure 2.3 illustrates the relationship of each link in the supply chain from corporate centre through to division, buyers and further down to

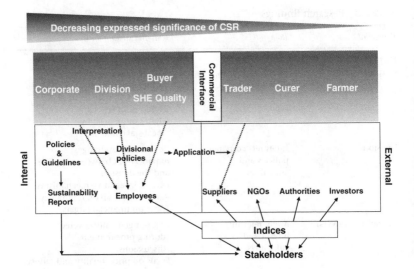

Figure 2.3   CSR and sustainability significance in the vanilla supply chain.
Source: Compiled by the authors.

farmers. What emerges is that IFC's internal stakeholders on whom the corporation relies to influence external stakeholders within the supply chain, namely traders, curers and farmers with regard to CSR policies, do not display a similar degree of enthusiasm for CSR as the corporate centre. In fact, outside the corporate centre, concentration is on fiscal return.

The corporate centre emerges as active in issuing policies and guidelines supportive of the Sustainability Report. The Sustainability Report provides the sustainability indices which identify an organisation's ranking and supposed competence in terms of sustainability and CSR within the formally defined supply chain. Yet, the research reveals that the expressed significance of sustainability and CSR dilutes further down the supply chain to the point where sustainability and CSR are of little relevance in a context where the prime concern is survival. No evidence emerged highlighting genuine stakeholder dialogue as an integrative mechanism for promoting CSR sustainability policies. Managers and buyers considered that they are afforded little discretion for such policy application, 'we do not have latitude in our decision making to take into account stakeholder impact, as our award system is target and not CSR oriented.' The target focus at the bottom of IFC's vanilla supply chain is concerned with developing new growing areas for the vanilla crop. The three to five year average in beginning to realise return from the planting of new vines is instrumental in determining viability for new entrants. The time and efficiency of the curing process is already viewed by IFC's management as taking too long and improved 'engineering' in different parts of the world as likely to induce a better return on investment.

Additional to the conflict between fiscal focus and social responsibility, and outside of IFC's control, is the current structure of vanilla farming communities. In Madagascar, one of the authors witnessed virtually every family member contributing to the farming of vanilla, particularly through the use of child labour, emerging with the conclusion that such practice was not 'forced' but more enforced by social expectation. Further, the quality of local educational facilities varied. Where 'reasonable' educational facilities were available, families genuinely attempted to ensure that their children attended educational programmes. In more remote areas, where education and healthcare was lacking, the income from vanilla sales was more likely to be spent on healthcare provision than education. Hence, the prevalence of a survival, short-term oriented mind-set.

> Developed, industrialised nations and organisations within them (e.g. industry, academic or NGO) have the 'luxury' of time and resource to consider the issues of sustainability and social responsibility as they don't have the fundamental concerns of day-to-day existence that subsistence farmers have.
>
> Local Politician, Madagascar

Further, and unwittingly, CSR pursuit can become an imposition on local communities.

> The right thing to do', 'onto people and societies' that have a different focus on establishing their own level of fiscal income.
>
> Local Trader, India

> The developed world, having established their own income base and resultant strengths, want to impose considerations that could possibly slow down the rate of progress in developing countries.
>
> Community Leader, Uganda

Similar to Margolis and Walsh (2003), the inquiry into the IFC supply chain confirms that firms are faced with reconciling contrasting financial and social responsibility demands. The supposed 'no man's land' between corporate financial performance (CFP) and corporate social performance (CSP) emerges as favouring the meeting of financial targets. Within the enterprise, differences arise. IFC's spices division' orientation is contractarian whilst the corporate centre's public position is that of social responsibility but nevertheless still holding line management to account for meeting their targets.

The emerging lack of mutual interrelation between profitability, legality, ethics and philanthropy combined with regulation, codes of practice, voluntary initiatives and stakeholder engagement, contrasts with McIntosh *et al.*'s (2003) conclusion of greater business and social responsibility integration. Within IFC, reward for CSR application was not afforded to management and employees. In order to enhance CSR policy application effectiveness, Husted (2003) proposes that CSR needs to be budgeted for, similar to any other project, in order to counteract both inconsistency and incoherence between CSR policy design and application.

Noting Clarkson's (1995) reality check that differences of response arise between level of organisation and individuals, still no evidence emerged from the IFC inquiry supporting Kitchin's (2003) concept of determined intent, typified by open dialogue and participation in CSR debate. The study confirms observations by Saunders (1997) and Maignan *et al.* (2002) that the purchasing and procurement functions enable corporate efficiency and control, but are not concerned with broader social issues.

Being aligned with the corporate centre's immediate external stakeholders, namely the media, press and professional associations within Continental Europe, does not address the need for CSR policy application as suggested by Craig-Smith (2003). IFC principally defends its reputation in Continental Europe and therefore the risk to reputation lies within that region and less so further afield (Crowther, 2004). Responding to perceived critical and influential stakeholders, such as European politicians, explains the centre's CSR promotion but operational lack of follow through, undermining the potential for a 'licence to operate' (Dahl, 1972; Kakabadse and Rozuel, 2004). To redress the situation, Joyner and Payne (2002) strongly argue for target setting so that tangible evidence of return in investment verifies CSR application. A conclusion to emerge from this study is that, particularly for large organisations, a 'one size fits all' approach is not appropriate (Piacentini *et al.*, 2000).

The findings emerging from this study focus on a specific, limited commodity, where price determines the functioning of the supply chain (Ortiz-Martinez, 2004). More niche and higher value proposition product supply chains may better integrate price demands with the nurture of global and local networks pursuing CSR application (Post *et al.*, 2002). Certainly, Carter (2000) and Carter and Jennings's (2002) suggestion that the purchasing and procurement functions determine the practice of CSR, is borne out. Further inquiry into CSR application requires greater examination of the interface between the organisation and its local communities than attending to the finesse displayed by the corporate centre in policy design.

References

Brundtland, G.H. (1987), *Our Common Future: The World Commission on Environment and Development*, Oxford: Oxford University Press.

Carroll, A.B. (2000), 'Ethical challenges for business in the new millennium: Corporate social responsibility and models of management morality', *Business Ethics Quarterly*, 10(1): 33–42.

Carter, C.R. (2000), 'Ethical issues in international buyer–supplier relationships: A dyadic examination', *Journal of Operations Management*, 18(2): 191–208.

Carter, C.R. and Jennings, M.M. (2002), 'Social responsibility and supply chain relationships', *Transportation Research. Part E, Logistics and Transportation Review*, 38E(1): 37–52.

Clarkson, M.B.E. (1995), 'A stakeholder framework for analyzing and evaluating corporate social performance', *Academy of Management. The Academy of Management Review*, 20(1): 92–117.

Craig-Smith, N. (2003), 'Corporate social responsibility: Whether or how?', *California Management Review*, 45(4): 52–76.

Crowther, D. (2004), 'Corporate social reporting: Genuine action or window dressing?', in D. Crowther and L. Rayman–Bacchus (Eds), *Perspectives on Corporate Social Responsibility*, Aldershot: Ashgate; pp. 140–160.

Dahl, R. (1972), 'A prelude to corporate reform', *Business and Society Review*, 1(1): 17–23.

Donaldson, T. and Preston, L.E. (1995), 'The stakeholder theory of the corporation: Concepts, evidence and implications', *Academy of Management. The Academy of Management Review*, 20(1): 65–91.

European Commission (EC). (2002), *Communication from the Commission Concerning Corporate Social Responsibility: A Business Contribution to Sustainable Development*, Brussels: EU Commission.

Friedman, M. (1962), *Capitalism and Freedom*, Chicago, IL: University of Chicago Press.

George, A.L. and Bennett, A. (2005), *Case Study and Theory Development in the Social Sciences*, Cambridge, MA: MIT Press.

Gerring, J. (2004), 'What is a case study and what is it good for?', *American Polecat Science Review*, 98(2): 341–354.

Halal, W.E. (2000), 'Corporate community: A theory of the firm uniting profitability and responsibility', *Strategy and Leadership*, 28(2): 10–16.

Hess, D., Rogovsky, N. and Dunfee, T.W. (2002), 'The next wave of corporate community involvement: Corporate social initiatives', *California Management Review*, 44(2): 110–125.

Husted, B.W. (2003), 'Governance choices for corporate social responsibility: To contribute, collaborate or internalize?', *Long Range Planning*, 36(5): 481–498.

IFC (International Food Corporation). (2003), *Knowledge for Sustainability, IFC Sustainability Report 2002/2003*, IFC, World.

——. (2004), *CSR Training Manual*, IFC, World.

Joyner, B.E. and Payne, D. (2002), 'Evolution and implementation: A study of values, business ethics and corporate social responsibility', *Journal of Business Ethics*, 41(4): 297–311.

Kakabadse, N. and Rozuel, C. (2004), 'The meaning of corporate social responsibility in a local french hospital: A case study', Seminar on the 'Stakeholders and Corporate Social Responsibility European Perspectives', C.N.A.M. (Conservatoire National des Arts et Métiers) and L.I.P.S.O.R.(Laboratoire d'Investigation en Prospective, Stratégie et Organisation), Paris, June 4.

Kitchin, T. (2003), 'Corporate social responsibility: A brand explanation', *Journal of Brand Management*, 10(4/5): 312–326.

Maignan, I., Hillebrand, B. and McAlister, D. (2002), 'Managing socially-responsible buying: How to integrate non-economic criteria into the purchasing process', *European Management Journal*, 20(6): 641–648.

Maignan, I. and Ralston, D.A. (2002), 'Corporate social responsibility in Europe and the U.S.: Insights from businesses' self-presentations', *Journal of International Business Studies*, 33(3): 497–514.

Margolis, J.D. and Walsh, J.P. (2003), 'Misery loves companies: Rethinking social initiatives by business', *Administrative Science Quarterly*, 48(2): 268–305.

McIntosh, M., Thomas, R., Leipziger, D. and Coleman, G. (2003), *Living Corporate Citizenship*, London: FT Prentice Hall.

Mikkilä, M. (2003), 'Acceptability of operations as an indicator of corporate social performance', *Business Ethics: A European Review*, 12(1): 78–87.

Miles, M.B. and Huberman, A.M. (1994), *Qualitative Data Analysis: An Expanded Sourcebook*, Beverly Hills, CA: Sage Publications.

OECD. (2002), 'The round table discussion on Corporate Sustainability', Directorate for Financial, Fiscal and Enterprise Affairs, OECD, Paris.

Ortiz–Martinez, E. (2004), 'Disclosure and stakeholder needs', in D. Crowther and K.T. Caliyurt (Eds), *Stakeholders and Social Responsibility*; Penang: Ansted University Press, pp. 163–183.

Piacentini, M., MacFadyen, L. and Eadie, D. (2000), 'Corporate social responsibility in food retailing', *International Journal of Retail & Distribution Management*, 28(11): 459–469.

Porter, M. (2003), 'CSR – a religion with too many priests? – Dialogue with Mette Morsing', *European Business Forum*, 15: 41–42.

Post, J.E., Preston, L.E. and Sachs, S. (2002), 'Managing the extended enterprise: The new stakeholder view', *California Management Review*, 45(1): 6–28.

Saunders, M. (1997), *Strategic Purchasing and Supply Chain Management* (2nd Edition), Harlow, Pearson Education Limited.

Shankman, N.A. (1999), 'Reframing the debate between agency and stakeholder theories of the firm', *Journal of Business Ethics*, 19(4): 319–334.

The Economist. (2005), 'The good company: A survey of corporate social responsibility', 22 January, 374(8410): 1–18.

UN (United Nations). (2000), Global Compact Initiative – Corporate Social Responsibility, June, UN, available at http://www.un.org/Depts/ptd/global.htm (accessed: 20.11.04).

Yin, R.K. (1987), *Case Study Research: Design and Methods*, California: Sage Publications.

3
Corporate Social Responsibility (CSR) in Healthcare: Case Study of a Local French Hospital*

Andrew P. Kakabadse, Nada K. Kakabadse and Cécile Rozuel

Introduction

Hospitals, despite corporate social responsibility's (CSR's) business identity, hence the term 'corporate', are not spared CSR considerations especially as they are exposed to budgetary restrictions and greater pressure for compliance from health authorities. As Johnson (2004: 288) explains: 'managers must know how to recognise, understand and resolve ethical problems that arise in both the managerial context and clinical setting. Yet healthcare managers and clinicians often have been at odds over how to solve ethical problems, sometimes even disagreeing over whether a moral dilemma exists at all'. On the basis that fiduciary disciplines and concern for community are likely to be ever greater demands, this chapter investigates how CSR is perceived by the stakeholders of one French hospital and how social responsibility concerns are addressed within the hospital.

After having introduced the context in which CSR, in general and in France is debated today, current research into healthcare, particularly from the perspective of developments in business and society, will be briefly reviewed. A study of CSR in a local French hospital will be presented in this chapter, starting with an explanation of the research methodology adopted, followed by an outline and discussion of the key findings. In conclusion, suggestions will be provided concerning possible future research into CSR and its integration with real life challenges (Blair *et al.*, 1989).

The corporate social responsibility debate

The relations between society and business are viewed as a prodigal area of research (Moir, 2001). A variety of reviews of conceptual and empirical studies that explore and analyse the nature of business's duties, rights and responsibilities towards society are now regularly published (Jones, 1980; Carroll, 1999; Garriga and Melé, 2004). Each provides new insights on the complexity and richness of the debate. Discussion on the role of business in society has all too often been summed up as a tension of the 'shareholder vs. stakeholder debate' whereby the 'shareholder' or 'profit centred' model of corporate governance assumes that businesses are ultimately accountable to their owners (Berle and Means, 1932/1968; Friedman, 1970), whilst proponents of the 'stakeholder' model argue that accountability should apply to, all the groups affected by a firm's activity, either positively or negatively (Halal, 2000; Freeman, 2004). Even, as shown in Chapter 1, no clear agreement on the definition of stakeholders exists; the concept implies that the firm's management teams need to be sensitive to the overall environment and its various actors whose decisions and actions are likely to affect the organisation's development. The concept not only refers to purely profit-making organisations but also to any model of enterprise and suggests that the organisation needs to set up an adequate framework for a more open decision process.

Partly for reasons of decision transparency but also through examination of concepts of social equity and human rights, CSR-oriented research has expanded tremendously over the past 50 years. Studies on business and society interrelations now range from philosophical enquiries on the nature of ethics and the ontology of business activity, to the 'business case' for CSR and 'hands-on' studies designed to help implement a CSR strategy. Recent research has challenged the widely acknowledged 'economic paradigm' as reductive, inappropriate, unproductive and even a harmful view of our world, implying that there is more to humanity than self-interested rational individuals seeking to enhance their short-term material wealth (Frederick, 1998; Korhonen, 2002; Fryer, 2005). Through the CSR debate, the very place of business as a core institution in society is questioned in parallel with the need for it to more deeply respect the fragile but indispensable connection and interdependence it has with the natural environment. Indeed, although trade as an activity is probably as old as mankind, only since the industrial revolution and the creation of incorporated enterprises has business gained such power and importance in society (Bakan, 2004). Because corporations possess such influence, a strongly held view is that they ought to be accountable to all those they affect. However, as the private enterprise is not structurally bound to do so, various writers have put forward the view that we, as citizens, need to seriously ponder on the social world we want for the future and thus design a new basis for a more integrative and balanced society (Smée, 2003a; 2003b).

The case for societal design has been heightened by the globalisation debate, whereby multinational corporations whose interests are held to be more economically inclined than social; their impact has prompted a variety of responses to the perceived exploitation of human, social and natural resources. Globalisation, or rather the integration of economies across the world, is condemned by some for having deepened the gap between rich and poor societies and indeed, the wealth gap within societies themselves (Korhonen, 2002). Alternatively, others stress that the market economy nature of globalisation has stimulated growth in terms of productivity and wealth (Tavis, 2000). Yet few challenge that the created wealth is unevenly distributed within and across the nation states which has given rise to 'greed' and self-seeking behaviour at the expense of other relevant stakeholders (Kakabadse and Kakabadse, 2001).

The contrast to what many see as the Anglo-American shareholder value platform, from which corporate philanthropy arises, is that of CSR from a stakeholder perspective. In Continental Europe where corporate governance adopts more of a stakeholder philosophy, an ever greater number of corporations are becoming CSR responsive (EABiS, 2003). One noticeable difference between corporate philanthropy and that of a stakeholder orientation is the pursuit of social as well as business partnerships (Scholl, 2001). The emergence of partnerships between corporations and nongovernmental organisations (NGOs) has been a one-stakeholder-oriented mechanism to overcome distrust between the two and to help authenticate responsible corporate citizens from fakes. Independent audits, discussion forums and employees' volunteering are examples of the new relationships formed between social entities previously held to be irreconcilable (Novethic, 2002).

CSR in France

Turning to France in particular, a survey by KPMG of French-listed corporations pointed out that the critical driver for the establishment of ethical committees within the organisation were institutional shareholders and consumers (Pinel, 2001). Similarly, responsibility towards customers was rated the most important element of the social responsibilities of a corporation in a study on consumer's perceptions of CSR (Maignan and Ferrell, 2003). CSR pursuit within France, as in other stakeholder societies not only focuses on the firm but also on the public agency. The Organisation for Economic Co-operation and Development (OECD), for instance, has set up a department working on public governance and management issues, as well as a global governance forum and other programmes and work groups to reflect on determined areas of public policy making and governance models. Through such effort, OECD released its Principles of Corporate Governance in 1999 insisting that 'good, effective public governance helps to strengthen democracy and human rights, promote economic prosperity and social cohesion, reduce poverty, enhance environmental protection and the sustainable use of natural resources and deepen confidence in government and public administration' (OECD, 2004). Yet, within France as in other socially minded stakeholder economies, public sector organisations are experiencing pressure to improve their rate of return on public investments and to enhance their financial performance. Thus market expectations for public and private enterprises have become similar. Providing a public good for the benefit of society no longer (if ever) exempts public enterprises from being profitable, reducing costs and competing for market share. Countries with a long tradition of national enterprises and welfare state, especially in Continental Europe, have been most affected by the discipline of fiduciary scrutiny. Despite such tension and the recent waves of privatisation, Continental European governments have not been sufficiently pressured to enter into a U-turn from the societal creep of marketisation. Thus, within stakeholder societies, the emergence of public organisations becoming more 'corporate' in their behaviour and practice has prompted the drive to greater consideration of CSR as a distinct element of corporate strategy.

With ever greater financial scrutiny and stakeholders' demand to be informed, the public organisations are being required to comply with demands of transparency, access to information and public participation as well as competitiveness and investment profitability in a sustainable way. Indeed, the 'new' French, as other Continental European public organisations, is being positioned as increasingly citizen and business-centred, whose performance is transparent and measurable. Improving public organisations' governance has, in turn, given greater impetus toward the creation of sustainable partnerships and public accountability toward stakeholders. Towards this end, the French government has created the national council on sustainable development (CNDD), composed of various civil society representatives from business to

nongovernmental organisations (NGOs) whose aim is to help government deliver a sustainable development strategy (Smée, 2003a; 2003b).
In fact, the development of CSR in France illustrates the 'Continental
Europe' view of CSR. France, like most of its European counterparts, is
often depicted as possessing a 'communitarian ideology' which asserts
'the needs of the community and the benefits of consensus', as opposed
to an individualist approach to society (Maignan and Ferrell, 2003).
Consequently, the French are more likely to expect private sector enterprises to conform to social norms of acceptable behaviour and be fully
involved in the community (Maignan and Ferrell, 2003). The long tradition of 'Etat-Providence', namely the State taking extensive charge of
social distress and providing basic support and protection to everyone,
paralleled by the inheritance of business and society relationships punc-
tuated by negotiations between employers and powerful unions and
arbitrated by the State, have contributed to a particular understanding of
the place of the corporation in society (Capron and Gray, 2000). As early
as 1977, France is the only country to have obliged firms beyond 300
employees to produce an annual social report ('*bilan social*') (Capron and
Gray, 2000; Maignan and Ferrell, 2003). Since then, France has established several measures such as taking into account environmental and
social concerns when allocating procurement contracts or more significantly, the 2001 law on new economic regulations ('*loi NRE*') which makes
it compulsory for companies listed on the Stock Exchange to publish
information on how they manage their impact on the environment and
society (*Ministère des Affaires étrangères*, 2004). Similarly, directives and
initiatives are being developed by, or in conjunction with, the State in
order to integrate CSR and sustainable development indicators, criteria
and concerns within corporate strategic management including the promotion of socially responsible investment (notably through pension
funds), NGO corporation partnerships and the creation of an observatory
on CSR (*Observatoire sur la Responsabilité Sociétale des Entreprises*) whose
aim includes the spread of 'best CSR practice' (*Ministère des Affaires
étrangères*, 2004; ORSE, 2005). A project gathering scholars and managers
developed through the '*Centre des Jeunes Dirigeants de l'Economie Sociale*'
(i.e. 'a voluntary grouping of young managers with converging interests
on issues of "social enterprise" or "social economy firms" '), recently
aimed to identify indicators to evaluate the motivation of socially
responsible corporations (Capron and Gray, 2000).

    CSR deliberation and initiatives have been an integral part of the
French agenda in terms of effectively operationalising social responsibility
practice as well as monitoring and assessing CSR performance

(*Medical News Today*, 2004). Future developments, however, will most likely be pursued in line with the European Union's (EU) efforts on CSR. In fact, the EU is thought of by some as a positive example of the step-wise establishment of an international regulatory framework for CSR as captured by its country members' experiences (Gendron *et al.*, 2004).

CSR and the healthcare sector

A particular area that has attracted CSR study has been that of the healthcare sector. Numerous commentators acknowledge that healthcare organisations operate in a 'hyperturbulent' environment characterised by fast-paced change, the result of which has been to turn healthcare into an economic good like any other sector (Kakabadse, 2004). As a result, healthcare managers are required to balance the contrasting demands of stakeholders and the disciplines of economic efficiency (Fottler *et al.*, 1989; Stevens, 1991; Kumar and Subramanian, 1998; Palank, 2000; Rotarius and Liberman, 2000; Olden, 2003; Ford *et al.*, 2004; Wells *et al.*, 2004). Today, healthcare organisations 'provide high clinical quality, high levels of functional quality (i.e. patient satisfaction) and cost effective patient care' with the scarce resources they are allocated (Fottler and Blair, 2002). Therefore with a view to reducing uncertainty (a direct consequence of the fast changing healthcare environment), healthcare organisations have begun to seek new partnerships with stakeholders, thus placing these organisation managers in the position of needing to develop collaborative relationships (Rotarius and Liberman, 2000).

In order to induce greater collaborative relationships, numerous healthcare studies have examined the process of stakeholder management from the perspective of balancing the powerful and contrasting expectations of stakeholders. In their 1989 study, Fottler *et al.* identified three broad categories of stakeholders:

Internal stakeholders, 'those who operate entirely within the bounds of the organisation and typically include management, professional and nonprofessional staff';

Interface stakeholders, 'those who function both internally and externally to the organisation' and include amongst others the medical staff, stockholders, taxpayers or other contributors; and

External stakeholders, split into three sub categories; those who provide inputs into the organisation (e.g. suppliers, patients or funds providers); those who compete with it (e.g. other hospitals or related health organisations) and those who have 'a special interest in how the organisation functions' (e.g. government regulatory agencies, professional associations, labour unions, the media or the local community).

Each stakeholder group described has a characteristic relationship with the organisation. Indeed, 'whereas the internal and interface stakeholders are at least partly supportive of the hospital, many of the external stakeholders are neutral, non-supportive or hostile', especially those who have a special interest in the organisation's management (Fottler *et al.*, 1989: 527). To some extent, the attitude of external stakeholders towards the healthcare organisation depends on various factors which include demographic characteristics, economic dynamism and communication of (and knowledge of) the organisation's services and strategy (Olden *et al.*, 2004; Wells *et al.*, 2004).

One conclusion to emerge from examination of the hospital-stakeholder relationship is that 'the number and diversity of stakeholder groups and their power *vis-à-vis* the healthcare organisations have increased' (Fottler *et al.*, 1989: 530). This suggests that effective stakeholder management is becoming ever more critical. However, the nature of effective stakeholder management is open to dispute. Some consider that what is required is improved functionality, namely the development of various proactive tool kits (or models) aimed at helping managers map the key stakeholders, link them to critical issues and clearly delineate managerial responsibilities for stakeholder management (Fottler *et al.*, 1989: 536). In contrast, Olden (2003) explains that stakeholder management application may not be sufficient for realising desired healthcare provision and that hospital managers should focus more on collaborating with stakeholders in order to deliver 'community health goods'. Whilst stakeholder management implies being aware of stakeholder claims, stakeholder collaboration purports the full understanding of these claims and their fitting into the broader conception of a hospital's mission (Olden, 2003).

The study

The study reported in this chapter examines CSR adoption within a small to medium-sized French hospital with an annual budget of around €25.5 million. The hospital, a primary employer in its town with 400 employees, cares for some 7,500 inpatients and provides consultation services to 45,000 outpatients annually. For reasons of confidentiality, the site shall be referred to as Bonne Santé Hospital. The catchment area of the Bonne Santé Hospital has in its charge small, rural traditional villages gathered around a larger town providing major services. There exist a wide diversity of incomes within the hospital's catchment area and even though the inhabitants' profile has changed with younger couples and an increased number of immigrants entering the region, the population is mainly elderly with deeply embedded roots in that locality.

The public healthcare sector in France is undergoing restructuring with a view to reducing the State's overall responsibility for healthcare (Griffith and White, 2005). Two recent 'health crises' have also revived the polemic on the functioning of the public health service and the collaboration, or rather lack of collaboration, between public establishments and local general practitioners (GPs) (Le Monde, 2003d).

In France, there exist some 1000 public hospitals and 470 not-for-profit private healthcare organisations that overall operate with 750,000 employees and a total budget of €50 billion (Le Monde, 2003a). The Ministry of Health provides general guidelines and policies but the ARH (Regional Agency for Hospitalisation) implements national policies, allocates funds according to the Ministry's guidelines and monitors the medical and financial management of hospitals in their region.

Public hospitals in France currently face several critical issues, although other European countries present the same structural problems. Physical deterioration due to poor levels of investment, an insufficient number of staff, ill conceived and inadequately implemented work regulations, a general and deep uneasiness amongst staff concerning the future of the public hospital, particularly in realising the mission of 'equal access to healthcare for all' and a highly bureaucratic, even paralysing, management model are just some of the challenges identified (Le Monde, 2003b).

A plan entitled 'Hospital 2007', highlights measures aimed at renovating deteriorated establishments and replacing the traditional 'national budget' allocation by a system of 'tariff per activity' (DHOS, 2003). Such development is accompanied by a decentralisation of authority, encouraging competition for fund allocation between 'centres of activity' and between healthcare practitioners (DHOS, 2003; Le Monde, 2003a; 2003c).

Study design

Aiming to appreciate the subjective reality of each research participant, the study has adopted an interpretivist perspective supported by inductive reasoning (Mason, 1996; Gillham, 2000; Saunders et al., 2002). The aim of interpretivist studies is to understand the meanings, interpretations, motives and intentions people use in their everyday lives which, in turn, directs their behaviour (Blaikie, 1993). Adopted is a constructivist ontology whereby social reality is the product of processes through which social actors negotiate the meanings of actions and situations, namely a concern with how individuals interpret the conditions in which they find themselves. Such epistemology is derived from everyday concepts and meanings, requiring the researcher to enter the everyday social world of his/her respondents in order to grasp the socially constructed meanings and then reconstruct them into a socially scientific language (Blaikie, 1993). In this study, we attempt to build a model representing the meaning of CSR for stakeholders in the Bonne Santé Hospital. The research design follows a qualitative case approach (Scholz and Tietje, 2001: 10) whose focus is on the dynamic relationship between the organisation and its stakeholders, as perceived by the study participants in relation to CSR. Case study appeared to be the most appropriate choice for exploring understandings of CSR due to its capacity to penetrate contextually contemporary phenomenon (Yin, 2003: 6). The choice to adopt a single case study was justified by the assumed typicality of the case within the region (Leavy, 1994). Indeed, Bonne Santé Hospital was considered by both the researchers and respondents to be representative of many other local hospitals in France. The findings from this single case study were, therefore, assumed to be 'informative' about the experiences of other similar establishments (Robson, 2002: 59; Saunders et al., 2002: 96; Yin, 2003: 41).

As opposed to other studies which provide respondents with an established CSR framework (Maignan and Ferrell, 2003), the research project introduced here was designed to allow the participants to provide their definition of CSR, thus offering unique insight into the 'real' understanding of social responsibilities. Data was collected using semi-structured interviews. At the time of data collection, the hospital had already, for a few months, been involved in a compulsory assessment and accreditation process examining the quality and safety of the medical establishment which, even at that stage, had identified the need for social dialogue.

The respondents were categorised into three main groups, namely executives and top managers; medical/paramedical professionals and support staff and external stakeholders comprising patients, primary healthcare providers (e.g. local GPs) and secondary healthcare providers (e.g. local chemists, first aid workers, and other healthcare representatives). The coding of data reflects the distinction made between three groups; 'executives' which includes the hospital's executives and top managers; 'employees' which includes medical/paramedical professionals and support staff and 'external stakeholders' which includes all the categories mentioned as above. Unfortunately, certain stakeholders were difficult to access and as a result, key policy makers (i.e. executives and top managers) did not participate in this study.

Forty-seven interviews were conducted in French by bilingual French-English speaking researchers. Data from each of the interviews was coded and then contrasted with other interview data in order to elicit main themes and categories. These categories were used for coding the interview transcripts and the contents of various documents referred to in discussion (Miles and Huberman, 1994). The codes were used to identify respondents' descriptions of their expectations and understanding of the responsibilities of the Bonne Santé Hospital and to build a tentative model representing the meanings held of CSR within this site as well as understanding how respondents constructed this meaning.

Research results

Four overarching themes emerged in terms of the study respondents' understanding of CSR within the Bonne Santé Hospital, namely notions of extended care involving medical care and community care, leadership, the importance of externalities and dialogue. However, each stakeholder group emphasised different elements within each theme.

Each of the themes are examined in depth. Drawing on the themes identified in interview and the interdependence between the themes, a model illustrating the meaning of CSR in Bonne Santé Hospital is constructed (see Figure 3.6) followed by a summary of the CSR expectations of Bonne Santé Hospital's stakeholders and the implications for social responsibility practice.

Extended care

Extended care is perceived as an outcome of dialogue between actors involved directly or indirectly in both medical care and community care (Figure 3.1).

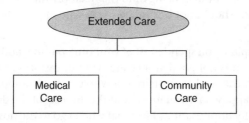

Figure 3.1 Extended care.
Source: Adapted from interviews.

The notion of 'care' emerged as being at the core of the hospital's mission. Yet, what participants meant by 'care' was not unanimous. Two sub-themes emerged, namely the medical care provided by the hospital and the role the hospital plays, or ought to play, in the local community, with the first sub-theme being named 'medical care' and the second referred to as 'community care'. The term 'extended care' was portrayed to encompass both sub-themes of care in an integrated manner. For instance:

> The hospital has to preserve health and take care of the patients as best as it can.
>
> Executive 8: 1

> The hospital's duty is to provide care, but it also acts as a local employer and a partner for local economic and social development.
>
> External Stakeholder 11: 1

The respondents referred to the medical treatment of patients as the primary role of the hospital and thus, medical care is introduced first.

Medical care

The respondents considered that the prime mission of Bonne Santé Hospital was to provide high quality medical treatment and to ensure the best possible medical care. However, patients as well as primary healthcare providers and medical professionals highlighted the importance of social interaction occurring in parallel to the provision of medical care (Table 3.1 and Figure 3.2), involving dedicating time to talk to patients and their families, explaining what is being done and making patients feel as comfortable as possible whilst in hospital.

In brief, the social process considered critical to the effective provision of medical care, was described as entailing the recognition that patients are, above all else, human beings and that relationships between the doctor and patient should not be limited to the care of only the sick organ.

> At the hospital, you spend most of your time waiting, and when you're feeling sick it is not good, it increases your uneasiness ... I think it has to do with the medical system as a whole ... but you don't go to the hospital happily, so if you must be at the disposal of the doctors and so on, it's really unpleasant ... I feel that when I go to the hospital, I waste a lot of time but they don't have much time to care about me.
>
> External Stakeholder 10: 5

Table 3.1 Medical care: emergent themes

Sub-themes	Sub-themes	Meaning
Treatment		The mission of a public hospital to provide good quality medical treatment.
Process	Medical Social	Enhancing the 'human' side of care, especially towards patients and their families.
Structure		The impact of the physical and organisational structure of the hospital, for instance in terms of communication flows.
Training		The provision of high quality, regular and adequate training.
Culture	Communication Behaviour Recognition and motivation Management system	Influence of management style and level of communication on the staff's behaviour, morale and motivation.

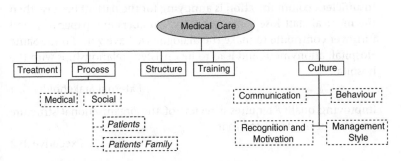

Figure 3.2 Medical care.

Source: Adapted from interviews.

There is a need for more time to enhance the human contact aspect of care to patients. Relationships with patients do affect the reputation, and it has consequences on the patients' choice to go to the hospital or to the private clinic.

Employee 1: 2

Doctors don't say much to patients. ... We are nothing when we're at the hospital, there is an issue of communication and a 'caste effect', especially when doctors use medical jargon, so you have to make your presence felt to obtain information; this is slightly easier when you're related to someone who works at the hospital, but that is not fair because everyone should have equal access to information.

External Stakeholder 9: 1 and 3

However, in contrast to the positive socially oriented perspective, internal stakeholders identified Bonne Santé Hospital's structure as 'compartmentalised'; first, between the administrative staff and the medical/paramedical staff and second, between the medical wards themselves. This reported inadequacy was seen to impede broader social interaction and even affect medical application in the sense that insufficient communication between wards could lead to incomplete medical records and patients being submitted to undergo the same examination twice. It was emphasised that co-operation should replace competition between wards.

Each ward is like a small fortified castle with its chief, its lord and its employees, and so on even though the employees' boss is ultimately the hospital director; and everyone defends its small village.

Executive 9: 2

Insufficient communication is annoying for the patient because then the medical staff lose some reactivity. Cumbersome paperwork and turnover contribute to make the dialogue we have with Bonne Santé Hospital, anonymous and lead to inconsistent relationships with the hospital.

External Stakeholder 6: 4

Improving quality requires a review of the organisational structure and the means dedicated to it.

Executive 3: 2

Everyone is important, from the top management to the support staff. It is a matter of collective performance, not an individual competence.

Executive 13: 2

Concerns over training and the culture of the hospital were also highlighted by the medical/paramedical professionals. The interviewees recognised the need for developing training programmes on specific topics concerned with quality, responsibility, accountability and confidentiality since they considered themselves as inadequately prepared to address these non-medical points.

The staff does not receive training on hygiene, although it has been requested in the past. No initiative has been launched for that purpose. Yet, there is a need for regular updates on hygiene-related issues.

Employee 13: 2

Responsibilities are assumed to be known. There are some training sessions on professional and medical confidentiality, but it's the responsibility of each individual to ensure he or she knows whatever he/she ought to know.

Executive 7: 3

The issue of culture was alluded to in terms of communication, recognition and motivation, management style and behaviour. Communication in Bonne Santé Hospital was seen as a concern, partly due to the resentment felt by the medical/paramedical professionals towards the top managers who were rarely present in the wards and were not seen as acknowledging the work of the medical staff. This created unease amongst staff who subsequently refrained from getting involved in the hospital's development.

Communication between wards is poor, there is no dialogue and no willingness to engage in dialogue. ... We are informed [on national standard guidelines] through memos, but there is neither follow-up nor support of these initiatives.

Employee 18: 2

The management style is 'to divide and rule'. Top managers think administrative, but an administrative viewpoint is different from a medical viewpoint, and the medical service is very varied.

Employee 14: 2

The lack of a clear organisational project affects the degree of staff's investment in Bonne Santé, and alters the global motivation and the atmosphere at work.

Employee 21: 2

Top managers lack leadership. Yet, it is up to them to give the impulse to the whole organisation, so that it can diffuse to all levels. There is a need to make employees be actors instead of mere performers, and to give people a sense of responsibility.

Employee 5: 1

Community care

Community care was viewed as the mission of the hospital in terms of provision of service to the local community beyond that of medical duties

Table 3.2 Community care: emergent themes

Sub-themes	Meaning
Information provision	Improvement of information flows to the community and enhancing the hospital's openness.
Partnerships	Endorsement of a more active role in the community along with local actors.
Education/prevention	Use of the hospital's skills and capabilities to better serve the needs of the community.

Figure 3.3 Community care.
Source: Adapted from interviews.

(Table 3.2 and Figure 3.3). This aspect of care was viewed as important more by external stakeholders and by some medical/ paramedical professionals but by few executives/senior managers.

Internal stakeholders perceived healthcare education and prevention as important to realising the mission of the hospital towards the community. In contrast, patients identified a need for the better provision of information concerning the hospital's technical (medical) and social practice. Also primary and secondary healthcare providers expressed a wish to develop partnerships between the hospital and the community. This was a contentious point as tension was reported to exist between the public and private health sector in France. Recent reforms in France have been aimed at controlling medical expenditure by curbing the number of people attending the casualty department for minor injuries whilst making GPs more available after hours.

> The hospital should be the place for medical information, training and prevention to the public. All three come together: it is about (1) teaching on how to save somebody's life, (2) informing on healthy lifestyles to avoid problems, and (3) ensuring psychological and technical follow-up in case of serious diseases. ... The hospital should be a platform for discussion and action.
>
> Employee 23: 1 and 5

We don't really know what's going on in the hospital. We lack information on its management, on its development. Bonne Santé is not open enough to external stakeholders, even though we work along with it. ... When the patient is out, it's over, there is no follow-up. This comes from a lack of dialogue from the very start.

External Stakeholder 6: 5

Up to this date, there hasn't been enough co-operation. Yet, it is necessary to work together to survive. Co-operation should be developed.

External Stakeholder 4: 3

In terms of providing better healthcare and social community service, one point was stressed by the interviewees, namely, the lead top managers should provide initiative in improving the overall work atmosphere, work ethic and work dedication of employees in the hospital. The view expressed was that until morale improves, the desire to forge ever better community relations will remain muted.

Leadership

All internal stakeholders, to varying degrees, acknowledged the critical importance of leadership in promoting and supporting more responsible behaviour and a greater dedication to healthcare provision and to Bonne Santé as the employing organisation. Both medical/paramedical professionals and support staff expected top managers to initiate change that enhanced medical and community care practice, or at least to support such initiatives when proposed by the staff. Four main factors were identified as influencing the quality of leadership; managers' personalities, power games and politics, managers' behaviour and quality of training (Table 3.3 and Figure 3.4).

Most internal stakeholders, including managers, considered that the way an organisation is managed is significantly dependent on the personality/style of senior management. External stakeholders, medical/

Table 3.3 Leadership: emergent themes

Themes	Meaning
Leadership	Influence of top managers (namely managers' personalities and behaviour, quality and adequacy of their training and effect of power games) on the hospital's culture, its overall functioning and dialogue with stakeholders.

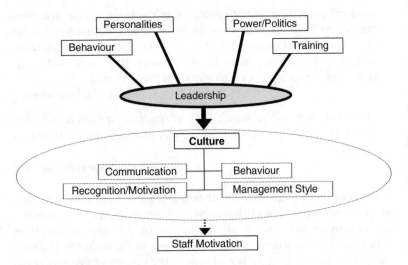

Figure 3.4   Leadership.
Source: Adapted from interviews.

paramedical professionals and support staff concurred, indicating that the personality of the clinical director strongly determines the functioning and atmosphere of his/her ward.

> The quality of dialogue within the ward is dependent on the clinical director's personality and on whether he/she pays attention to other people or not.
>
> Employee 16: 3

> The doctors and clinical directors make the reputation of the wards.
>
> External Stakeholder 2: 3

To the detriment of Bonne Santé, the respondents considered that the hospital's management had been inflicted for years by power games and political strategies between clinical directors and top managers, which substantially contributed to the unease and loss of motivation felt by most of the staff as well as being an obstacle to the development of a constructive dialogue with the local community. Indeed, personal interests were seen to prevail over Bonne Santé Hospital's interests.

> Bonne Santé is the scene of games of influence, of rivalries and 'clans', which create tensions within the organisation. ... These

games of influence and power for instance affect the priority order given to problems which need to be addressed.

Employee 21: 2

Staff feel weary and consider Bonne Santé Hospital as a workplace to which you have an obligation to go. This creates stress and aggressiveness which are both fostered by top managers' games of power. All this has a consequence on overall performance.

Employee 18: 4

The majority of staff interviewed expected top managers to be models of motivation and exemplary behaviour, particularly in promoting Bonne Santé Hospital's development. However, they concluded that the power games and the personalities of top managers restrained the development of appropriate leadership.

How the structure progresses and improves depends on top management.

Executive 3: 4

The dynamic must come from the top and diffuse all over the organisation.

Executive 12: 2

Bonne Santé Hospital needs more executives and this is an organisational problem. It needs executives who have been trained as executives because the job comes with responsibilities, including communication within the ward and with other wards.

Employee 18: 5

The quality of management also related to the training managers received. For example, clinical directors are required to accept both medical and administrative responsibilities and yet, many confessed to having only medical capabilities and not necessarily the skills to manage a ward and the people who work in it.

The person who is a candidate [to become a clinical director] should have compulsory training, for instance a one-week training programme on how to manage a ward, how to communicate in a ward, how a hospital is managed because, up to now, clinical directors have been chosen on the sole basis of their medical qualities, than on their age and their qualifications but these have nothing to do with it.

> Managing a ward has nothing to do with medical qualities. You can be an excellent surgeon and a very bad clinical director.
>
> Executive 9: 2

> The hospital does not have enough executives with an appropriate training, which is essential because the position comes with greater responsibilities.
>
> Employee 18: 4

The respondents considered that overall Bonne Santé's performance is relatively good given its constraints and problems, essentially because their staff are sufficiently dedicated to providing good quality care. However, it was mentioned that performance would increase if the staff's individual sense of responsibility was channelled into a global project headed by the hospital's management team.

> Everyone has his own medical responsibility, but there is insufficient administrative monitoring which is a necessary drive for organisational dynamic and cohesion. Staff work very differently [in each ward].
>
> Executive 12: 3

> Employees are responsible for what they do, but a global project would provide support for making little supplementary efforts (financial or other).
>
> Executive 4: 5

The deeply held view to emerge in interview was that the quality of leadership perceived in Bonne Santé Hospital was poor and not responsive to the needs of the staff which, in turn, damaged the culture of the organisation. Relationships were perceived as negative. Poor leadership was reflected through insufficient and in-appropriate communication (internal and external), in the lack of recognition of the value of the staff and in the non-collaborative management style which discouraged effort above the minimum and, in turn, led to the de-motivation of staff. The central role of leaders and the need for effective leadership in order to promote CSR initiatives was clearly emphasised by many internal and external stakeholders.

Externalities

Interviewees identified two main sub-groups of externalities (Table 3.4 Figure 3.5) which Bonne Santé Hospital could not control or easily influence. The first group was labelled 'supervisory authorities', which promotes national policy issues or legislation with which a public hospital must comply including quality standards and flexibility of working hours.

Table 3.4 Externalities: emergent themes

Themes	Sub-themes	Meaning
Supervisory authorities	Funding Regulations	Influence of regulatory bodies affecting the resources allocated to the hospital and the norms to pursue.
Demographics	Ageing population Minorities diversity Resource poverty Values	Influence of social changes on the hospital's activity.

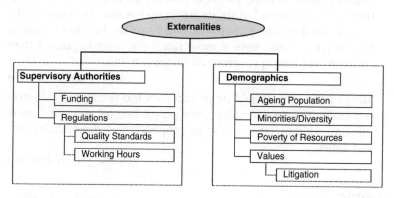

Figure 3.5 Externalities.
Source: Adapted from interviews.

The second group was labelled 'demographics' and referred to social changes that are likely to affect any public hospital's functioning and role.

The 'demographic' factors included an ageing population, the presence of minorities which could cause tension within wards and the increased number of patients who have to contend with insufficient resources for treatment and hospitalisation. Certain respondents also expressed concern regarding the increasing tendency to litigate. Justified or not, litigation is expensive and damaging to organisation reputation and the general work morale. Generally, these externalities were felt to increase pressure and stress on the hospital's staff, forcing un-welcome developments.

GPs sometimes have relational problems with the hospital, for instance when there are not enough beds to hospitalise patients. But this lack of beds is chronic, and the conflict is inevitable, it is part of the healthcare system.

External Stakeholder 1: 4

The 'minimum policy' mind-set affects both staff and patients, because it affects the overall performance of the hospital, but this state of facts is not specific to Bonne Santé.

Employee 23: 2

I am afraid that the new laws and the problem of insufficient staff turn the hospital into a social actor only, taking charge essentially for the elderly or the people in financial difficulty. Public sector organisations ending up being for some people only [...] with a ghettoization between private healthcare sector on the one hand and public hospital on the other [...] epitomising a two-tier healthcare system. The hospital should have a social role, even more important than currently, but with appropriate buildings and staff.

Executive 9: 4

More information should be provided on individual and collective responsibilities. In particular, since people become more and more litigious, it is important to develop people's knowledge of their rights and duties.

External Stakeholder 9: 3

Dialogue

Irrespective of the issue under examination, the need for improved dialogue was clearly emphasised as critical to the performance improvement of Bonne Santé Hospital (Table 3.5 and Figure 3.6). Patients, patients' families (social process and information provision) and local healthcare providers (partners) stated that better quality dialogue between them and Bonne Santé Hospital was fundamental in order to develop more progressive schemes for health education and prevention. Such initiatives involve open dialogue between the hospital managers and staff on the one hand, patients, local healthcare providers and local authorities on the other.

Effective extended care was seen as only possible if open dialogue became established between management, medical practitioners and community representatives. With a few exceptions, dialogue within the hospital as well as between the hospital and the community was not supported by substantial initiatives or projects of collaboration, and many participants were unaware of the existing structures purported to provide a platform for dialogue. The following statements

Table 3.5   Dialogue: emergent themes

Themes	Meaning
Dialogue	Fair and open dialogue between the various stakeholders involved in the hospital's development in terms of defining needs and priorities for action.

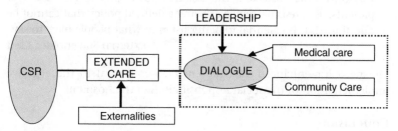

Figure 3.6   Dialogue and CSR.
Source: Adapted from interviews.

clearly called for multi-stakeholder dialogue, principally initiated by the hospital:

> Patients can contact the conciliation committee which acts as a mediator in case of dissatisfaction. This initiative works well and allows for a better apprehension of how the hospital works by the public, besides showing managers' interest for Bonne Santé's image.
>
> Employee 14: 2

> The patients' evaluation when leaving the hospital is like a permanent enquiry into the image of the hospital. Yet, the results are not disclosed, this information is not exploited enough.
>
> Employee 12: 4

> The dialogue within the hospital and with the community barely exists. It is never assessed and re-defined, we operate in the continuity of what we already have set up, but that is not necessarily enough.
>
> Employee 3: 3

> There should be information and training meetings on the care the hospital provides. In some activities, like obstetrics, the hospital could come and present their work techniques to local healthcare actors.
>
> External Stakeholder 1: 3

The hospital, because it has a huge economic and social role, especially financial, is already open to the town, that is to the town council. But the dialogue should include other actors.

Executive 6: 2

All stakeholders should be represented in the dialogue. The dialogue hospital-community currently exists but is limited and works one-way only. One obstacle is the assumed power physicians have over patients, as care is perceived as being a defined policy that cannot be questioned. It is essential to better listen to what people have to say.

External Stakeholder 11: 3

The need for enhanced dialogue emerged as central to the effective implementation of the social responsibilities of the hospital.

Conclusion

A tentative model is proposed to represent the social responsibilities of the hospital as perceived by its stakeholders (Figure 3.7). In particular, the notion of dialogue has proved to be the key element that brings together all the emerging themes. Indeed, developing appropriate social processes in medical care is essentially about establishing dialogue with patients and patients' families and listening to their needs and demands. Interviewees stressed that they see interaction and communication with patients as integral and, for some, an essential part of care.

Improving the structure of the hospital, providing adequate training programmes and enhancing organisational culture was additionally viewed as requiring dialogue between top managers and the medical/paramedical and support staff. Similarly, developing effective and adequate community care was viewed as calling for an open dialogue with the stakeholders involved, including external healthcare providers (GPs, private healthcare establishments, local chemists, local specialised practitioners, etc.), the town council and, notably, the whole local community in order to determine priorities in terms of education and prevention. Studies carried out in small hospitals suggest that the local community's perceptions, experience and attitude towards the hospital seriously affect the relationships they develop and even the functioning and survival of the hospital itself (Olden *et al.*, 2004; Wells *et al.*, 2004). In France, provision of services in response to local needs, such as effective and free family planning services in regions where families are young and resources limited, are financially subsidised in relation to activity and occupancy rates. The more patients register at

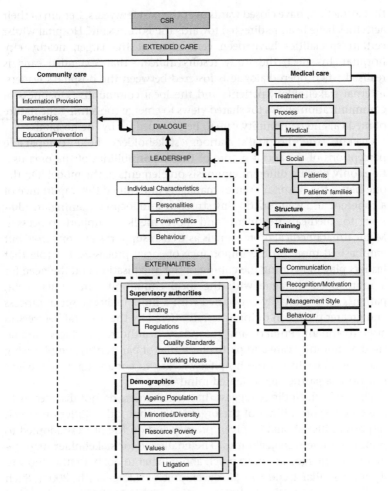

Figure 3.7 The CSR model of Bonne Santé Hospital.
Source: Compiled from interviews.

the hospital, the more resources will be granted. Unfortunately, local hospitals which do not have the opportunity to attract a high intake of recipients are awarded fewer resources limiting their capacity to purchase specialised equipment or to offer a wider range of services which, in turn, reduces their attraction for patients. Thus, working closely with, and gaining the support of, the local community appears to be particularly critical for small and medium-sized French hospitals. Indeed, the two other local hospitals in the region of Bonne Santé, unable to induce that attraction, have closed wards over the past few years. Certain of their activities have been re-directed towards the Bonne Santé Hospital whilst certain specialities have been centralised at the larger, nearby city hospital. In effect, the study results indicate that 'extended care' is realised when open dialogue is fostered between the hospital's leaders, internal stakeholders, patients and the local community. Openness of communication allows for shared views to emerge concerning the nature of medical and community care to be provided for by the hospital.

Overall, the hospital's various stakeholders hold comparable perceptions of the social nature of the responsibilities of the organisation, only placing different emphasis on elements of the model. On the one hand, the hospital's senior managers underlined the importance of a coherent and well-functioning structure and focused training, in addition to medical treatment and post medical support processes. Medical/paramedical professionals as well as support staff concurred but emphasised more on the importance of social processes, the role that leaders play in defining the culture of the organisation and the need for a more open dialogue with the local community. In similar vein, patients were primarily concerned with a more inclusive social process and greater provision of information offered by the hospital before and after treatment. Primary and secondary healthcare providers emphasised community care and particularly that of partnership, emphasising that the leadership of the hospital was key to enhancing dialogue and nurturing a partnership oriented mind-set.

The research findings suggest that stakeholders do not disagree as to the core responsibilities of the organisation but rather differ on which responsibilities should be given priority and on the process adopted to prioritise these responsibilities. The challenge for stakeholder management has emerged as not so much about 'what to do' but rather 'how to do it', a similar trend to CSR development (Craig-Smith, 2003). Such findings contrast Wood (1991) or Hummels' (1998) suggestion that various stakeholders of an organisation hold different expectations on both the what and the how. In fact, Bonne Santé Hospital's stakeholders indicate that they share a common understanding of CSR and what they overall expect from the organisation. The critical difference lies between the views of top managers who focused more on the minimum role the hospital can play in society and on the provision of essential medical care, whilst the other stakeholders held greater expectations of the hospital in terms of community care (Hitt, 1990).

The findings from this study parallel certain of the key conclusions to emerge in the stakeholder literature. First, that dialogue is at the heart of stakeholder management. Although Burchell and Cook (2006) point out that 'dialogue on CSR' is a hazy concept, they insist that multi-stakeholder dialogues, either direct or intermediated and more or less formal, are perceived as an important element for progress and development on these issues by most of the participants. Whilst stressing the need to really listen to one another, they emphasise the way true dialogue creates an inspiring 'learning environment' (Burchell and Cook, 2006: 155). Second, that managers are indeed the critical leaders most able to promote socially responsible principles throughout the organisation. Indeed, as suggested by Szwajkowski (2000), good communication is an essential element of stakeholder management and is fundamental to the development of CSR (Ford *et al.*, 2004). Exposure to meaningful dialogue ultimately 'moulds' the perceptions of stakeholders and leads to shared understanding (Weiss, 2002). The idea that enhanced communication would eventually modify people's perception of the hospital in terms of quality of service and its overall reputation was identified so by the internal stakeholders at Bonne Santé Hospital. The participant's view that communication is a management priority, supports Szwajkowski's (2000) argument that it is top management's responsibility to foster good communication for effective CSR application. The emerging model of CSR practice at the Bonne Santé Hospital places leadership at the heart of establishing sound dialogue. This conclusion supports Thomas and Simerly's (1995) proposition of the determinant role of top managers in defining the nature of the firm's corporate social performance (CSP).

Corporate social responsibility has emerged as a continuous process of negotiation between stakeholders and not the pursuit of a fixed set of objectives. Societal values and cultural characteristics influence the expectations of stakeholders (Maignan and Ferrell, 2003). The adoption of national and international standards and codes of conduct provide a basic platform of shared principles for organisations to adopt. However, providing for that additional level of social care is the result of the negotiation and interactions between stakeholders. For Bonne Santé, providing medical care acted as their *raison d'être*. Community care provision acted as an additional service in exchange for funding and a 'licence to operate'.

Additional to dialogue and leadership as determinants of medical, community and extended care, the notion of legitimacy was also referred to in some interviews. Certain stakeholders, in particular external stakeholders, pointed out the impact that the Bonne Santé Hospital has on the local community. Bonne Santé Hospital was recognised as not only a healthcare provider but also the main employer in the town and the principal local hospital in the region competing with the neighbouring city's medical infrastructure. Bonne Santé was positioned as a strong and powerful actor in the community, economically, socially and politically. If Bonne Santé was seen as not fulfilling its responsibilities or not responding to the community's expectations, then the community considered itself as free to remove the legitimacy it granted the hospital. In fact, a number of Bonne Santé managers expressed concern that local people preferred to go to a local private clinic, a direct competitor, rather than the hospital for certain simple operations. Unfortunately for Bonne Santé, the hospital could not amortise the cost of its expensive surgical equipment with low cost operations. The management felt they needed to maintain up-to-date equipment to perform challenging and often expensive operations the private clinic could not offer. Although, the provision of such service was detrimental to Bonne Santé Hospital's financial position, on the positive side Bonne Santé was viewed by community stakeholders as fulfilling its social responsibilities.

Replication of this case study, but in another context, would be particularly interesting validating or challenging the CSR model presented. The study of Bonne Santé Hospital brought to light the significant influence of externalities on CSR application. Although some previous research has examined the role institutional and non-institutional actors play as drivers for CSR development (Jones, 1999), it would be of value to explore the extent to which society's legitimate expectations of an organisation ultimately affect its ability to respond to pertinent stakeholders' expectations. Another key theme requiring enquiry is the link between organisational reputation and stakeholder expectation and trust of the institution. In particular, examining the nature of effective dialogue and its link to relationship improvement between the organisation and stakeholders (and between stakeholders themselves) would be valuable. Finally, we suggest that more qualitative research be pursued in order to appreciate what social actors believe to be the responsibilities of organisations in various economic and social contexts, including the examination of the reasons behind such beliefs.

As market-driven philosophy is increasingly becoming 'the global rule', both public and not-for-profit organisations are becoming exposed to similar criteria for performance assessment. Although ethical considerations are nothing new to the healthcare sector, the marketisation of society throws up ethical challenges to the management of healthcare organisations. Today, members of healthcare organisations need to learn how to deal with increasing pressure from investors concerned with the most efficient use of funds as well as from an ever demanding society. Thus, hospital staff are caught between requirements to be more efficient, more available, more cost-effective, more in touch with the public needs and more involved but, all too often, with too limited resources, little support and ignorance of how such contrasting demands are becoming increasingly challenging.

It is paradoxical that, on the one hand, CSR is gaining recognition from high-level public institutions (UN Special Representative on Business and Human Rights, the European Union's Green Paper on CSR), but, on the other, short-termism and profitability are distinctly disseminating into public sector activities and public organisations in countries with a strong tradition of welfare state. France is confronted with such a phenomenon as are its European neighbours, particularly Belgium and Germany. Yet despite serious concern, the study has shown that various stakeholders' expectations are not too dissimilar to each other and that in promoting open dialogue, leaders in conjunction with other internal and external stakeholders are enabled to drive through change.

References

* The original version of this article entitled 'Meaning of corporate social responsibility in a local French hospital: a case study' by Nada K. Kakabadse and Cécile Rozuel and published in Society and Business Review (2006), 1: 7–96 has been considerably adapted. We thank Emerald Publishing for their permission to include this work in this book.

Bakan, J. (2004), *The Corporation: The Pathological Pursuit of Profit and Power*, London: Constable and Robinson.

Berle, A.A. and Means, G.C. (1932/1968), *The Modern Corporation and Private Property* (Revised Edition), New Brunswick, USA: Transaction Publishers.

Blaikie, N. (1993), *Approaches to Social Enquiry*, Cambridge: Polity Press.

Blair, J.D., Savage, G.T. and Whitehead, C.J. (1989), 'A strategic approach for negotiating with hospital stakeholders', *Health Care Management Review*, 14(1): 13–23.

Burchell, J. and Cook, J. (2006), 'It's good to talk? Examining attitudes towards corporate social responsibility dialogue and engagement processes', *Business Ethics: A European Review*, 15(2): 154–170.

Capron, M. and Gray, R. (2000), 'Accounting in Europe – experimenting with assessing corporate social responsibility in France: an exploratory note on an initiative by social economy firms', *The European Accounting Review*, 9(1): 99–109.

Carroll, A.B. (1999), 'Corporate social responsibility', *Business and Society*, 38(3): 268–295.

Craig–Smith, N. (2003), 'Corporate social responsibility: Whether or how?', *California Management Review*, 45(4): 52–76.

DHOS. (2003), 'Hôpital 2007', n°2, available at http://www.sante.gouv.fr/htm/dossiers/hopital2007/h2007_1.pdf

EABiS. (The European Academy for Business in Society) (2003), 'EABiS' 2nd Colloquium in Copenhagen', available at http://www.copenhagencentre. org/sw1459.asp Copenhagen: Copenhagen Business School, September 19–20.

Ford, R., Boss, R.W., Angermeier, I., Townson, C.D. and Jennings, T.A. (2004), 'Adapting to change in healthcare: aligning strategic intent and operational capacity', *Hospital Topics: Research and Perspectives on Healthcare*, 82(4): 20–29.

Fottler, M.D. and Blair, J.D. (2002), 'Introduction: New concepts in healthcare stakeholder management theory and practice', *Healthcare Management Review*, 27(2): 50–52.

Fottler, M.D., Blair, J.D., Whitehead, C.J., Laus, M.D. and Savage, G.T. (1989), 'Assessing key stakeholders: Who matters to hospitals and why', *Hospital and Health Services Administration*, 34(4): 525–546.

Frederick, W.C. (1998), 'Moving to CSR4: What to pack for the trip', *Business and Society*, 37(1): 40–59.

Freeman, R.E. (2004), 'A stakeholder theory of the modern corporation', in L.P. Hartman (Ed.), *Perspectives in Business Ethics* (3rd Edition), New York: McGraw–Hill/Irwin.

Friedman, M. (1970), 'The social responsibility of business is to increase its profits', *The New York Times Magazine*, available at http://ca.geocities.com/ busa2100/miltonfriedman.htm (accessed: 07.11.03).

Fryer, M. (2005), 'Exploration of the ethical rationales advanced in support of the shareholder theory and the paradigmatic assumptions that underpin them', *a paper presented at a Joint Conference: 9th Annual Conference of the European Business Ethics Network–UK Association (EBEN–UK) and 7th Ethics and Human Resource Management Conference*, Surrey: Royal Holloway, University of London.

Garriga, E. and Melé, D. (2004), 'Corporate social responsibility theories: Mapping the territory', *Journal of Business Ethics*, 53(1–2): 51–71.

Gendron, C., Lapointe, A. and Turcotte, M.-F. (2004), 'Responsabilité sociale et régulation de l'entreprise mondialisée', *Relations Industrielles/Industrial Relations*, 59 (1).

Gillham, B. (2000), *Case Study Research Methods*, London: Continuum International Publishing Group Ltd.

Griffith, J.R. and White, K.R. (2005), 'The revolution in hospital management', *Journal of Healthcare Management*, 50(3): 170–189.

Halal, W.E. (2000), 'Corporate community: A theory of the firm uniting profitability and responsibility', *Strategy and Leadership*, 28(2): 10.

Hitt, W.D. (1990), *Ethics and Leadership: Putting Theory into Practice*, Columbus, OH: Battelle Press.

Hummels, H. (1998), 'Organizing ethics: A stakeholder debate', *Journal of Business Ethics*, 17(13): 1403–1419.

Johnson, R.B. (2004), 'Hospital ethics review committees and business ethics: What managers can learn', *International Journal of Management*, 21(3): 286–291.

Jones, M.T. (1999), 'The institutional determinants of social responsibility', *Journal of Business Ethics*, 20(2): 163–179.

Jones, T.M. (1980), 'Corporate social responsibility revisited, redefined', *California Management Review (pre-1986)*, 22(3): 59–67.

Kakabadse, A. and Kakabadse, N. (2001), *The Geopolitics of Governance: The Impact of Contrasting Philosophies*, Hants: Palgrave Macmillan.

Kakabadse, N.K. (2004), 'The modern architects of Enlightenment: Moulding corporate citizens', *Corporate Governance: International Journal for Enhancing Board Performance*, 4(4): 5–10.

Korhonen, J. (2002), 'The dominant economics paradigm and corporate social responsibility', *Corporate Social Responsibility and Environmental Management*, 9(1): 66–80.

Kumar, K. and Subramanian, R. (1998), 'Meeting the expectations of key stakeholders: Stakeholder management in the healthcare industry', *S.A.M. Advanced Management Journal*, 63(2): 31–40.

Le Monde. (2003a), 'L'hôpital public menacé par la pénurie d'argent et de personnel', available at http://www.lemonde.fr (accessed: 27.11.03).

——. (2003b), 'L'hôpital en danger', available at http://www.lemonde.fr (accessed: 27.11.03).

——. (2003c), 'M. Mattei propose de renforcer le pouvoir des directeurs', available at http://www.lemonde.fr (accessed: 27.11.03).

——. (2003d), 'Jean–François Mattei accuse les médecins de ville de participer à l'engorgement des hôpitaux', available at http://www.lemonde.fr (accessed: 01.12.03).

Leavy, B. (1994), 'The craft of case–based qualitative research', *Irish Business and Administrative Research*, 15: 105–118.

Maignan, I. and Ferrell, O.C. (2003), 'Nature of corporate responsibilities: Perspectives from American, French, and German consumers', *Journal of Business Research*, 56(1): 55.

Mason, J. (1996), *Qualitative Researching*, London: Sage Publications Ltd.

Medical News Today. (2004), 'French report says its health system needs big changes', available at http://www.medicalnewstoday.com/medicalnews.php?newsid=5499 (accessed: 20.12.04).

Miles, M.B. and Huberman, A.M. (1994), *Qualitative Data Analysis: An Expanded Sourcebook* (2nd Edition), Thousand Oaks, CA: Sage Publications (USA).

Ministère des Affaires étrangères. (2004), 'Responsabilité sociale des entreprises', available at http://www.diplomatie.gouv.fr/fr/thematiques_830/droits-homme-democratie_1048/droits-economiques-sociaux-culturels_4720/responsabilite-sociale–entreprises_17059.html (accessed: 11.08.05).

Moir, L. (2001), 'What do we mean by corporate social responsibility?', *Corporate Governance*, 1(2): 16–22.

Novethic. (2002), 'De la contestation au partenariat, panorama des relations ONG–Entreprises', available at http://www.novethic.fr/novethic/site/article/index.jsp?id=19542 (accessed: 07.08.05).

OECD (Organisation for Economic Co-operation and Development). (1999), *OECD Principles of Corporate Governance*, Paris: OECD Publication Service.

——. (2004), 'Public governance and management', available at http://www.oecd.org/topic/0,2686,en_2649_37405_1_1_1_1_37405,00.html (accessed: 14.05.04).

Olden, P.C. (2003), 'Hospital and community health: Going from stakeholder management to stakeholder collaboration', *Journal of Health and Human Services Administration*, 26(1/2): 35–57.

Olden, P.C., Szydlowski, S.J. and Armstong, N.G. (2004), 'Health promotion and disease prevention by small rural hospitals: Reasons, obstacles, and enablers', *Journal of Healthcare Management*, 49(2): 89–102.

ORSE. (2005), 'Objectifs et missions', available at http://www.orse.org/fr/home/index.html (accessed: 11.08.05).

Palank, E.A. (2000), 'Healthcare survival: The new rules of the game', *Physician Executive*, 26(5): 40–43.

Pinel, J.-M. (2001), 'L'application des règles de la corporate governance dans les entreprises françaises' (Application of corporate regulations in French enterprises). In P. D'Humières and A. Chauveau (Eds), *Les pionniers de l'entreprise responsable (Pioneers of Responsible Enterprise)*, Paris: Editions d'Organisation.

Robson, C. (2002), *Real World Research* (2nd Edition), Oxford: Blackwell Publishing.

Rotarius, T. and Liberman, A. (2000), 'Stakeholder management in a hyperturbulent healthcare environment', *The Healthcare Manager*, 19(2): 1–7.

Saunders, M.N.K., Lewis, P. and Thornhill, A. (2002), *Research Methods for Business Students* (3rd Edition), Herts: FT Prentice Hall.

Scholl, H.J. (2001), 'Applying stakeholder theory to e-government: Benefits and limits', available at http://www.ischool.washington.edu/jscholl/ Papers/Scholl_IFIP_2001.pdf (accessed: 30.06.04).

Scholz, R.W. and Tietje, O. (2001), *Embedded Case Study Methods: Integrating Quantitative and Qualitative Knowledge*, London: Sage Publications Ltd.

Smée, V. (2003a), 'Le gouvernement lance la stratégie nationale du développement durable', *Novethic*, available at http://www.novethic.fr/novethic/site/dossier/index.jsp?id=35843&dos=35887 (accessed: 14.05.04).

——. (2003b), 'Une très forte attente de la société civile', *Novethic*, available at http://www.novethic.fr/novethic/site/dossier/index.jsp?id=35888&dos=35887 (accessed: 14.05.04).

Stevens, R.A. (1991), 'The hospital as a social institution, new-fashioned for the 1990s', *Hospital and Health Services Administration*, 36(2): 163–173.

Szwajkowski, E. (2000), 'Simplifying the principles of stakeholder management: The three most important principles', *Business and Society*, 39(4): 379–396.

Tavis, L.A. (2000), 'The globalization phenomenon and multinational corporate developmental responsibility', in O.F. Williams (Ed.), *Global Codes of Conduct: An Idea Whose Time Has Come*, Notre Dame, IA: University of Notre Dame Press.

Thomas, A.S. and Simerly, R.L. (1995), 'Internal determinants of corporate social performance: The role of top managers', *Academy of Management Journal*: 411–415.

Weiss, J.W. (2002), *Business Ethics: A Stakeholder and Issues Management Approach* (3rd Edition), London: Thomson Learning.

Wells, R., Lee, S.-Y.D., McClure, J., Baronner, L. and Davis, L. (2004), 'Strategy development in small Hospitals: Stakeholder management in constrained circumstances', *Healthcare Management Review*, 29(3): 218–228.

Wood, D.J. (1991), 'Corporate social performance revisited', *Academy of Management The Academy of Management Review*, 16(4): 691–718.

Yin, R.K. (2003), *Case Study Research: Design and Methods* (3rd Edition), London: Sage Publications Ltd.

4
Investment Brokers' Orientation towards CSR

Andrew P. Kakabadse, Nada K. Kakabadse and Reeves Knyght

Introduction

The grand narratives of community and nationhood, that for a century, acted as a social glue and kept the many fragments of society cohesive, appears to have been replaced by the narrative of economics which 'forces' everything and everyone into the perspective of the market, where profit has emerged as the primary standard of excellence. Consequently, market economics have almost assumed the *de facto* role of a secular religion. As a consequence, corporations are increasingly penetrating all spheres of civil society.

In response, repeated calls have been made for corporations to reconsider their role within society. Such civic society demands have pressurised corporations to re-align their value systems, but with little effect. Their mission, vision, policy deployment, decision making and reporting of corporate affairs have promoted the current worldview of shareholder dominance (van Marrewijk and Werre, 2003). Yet despite resistance, the increasing convergence of ecological and social issues have facilitated the merging of the concepts of sustainability and responsibility positioning them as a pressing issue for corporate consideration in addition to the traditional focus on the interests of financiers and owners (Keijzers, 2000). Whether this all-embracing form of emerging economy can deliver social justice outcomes is examined in this chapter through exploration of corporate social responsibility (CSR) interpretation and application within financial institutions.

Examination of CSR pursuit in the 'niche' banking arena delves into the image and reality of the private-equity industry, controlling the really 'smart' money that wields lasting influence, but behind a veil of secrecy. Until the late 1970s, the main activities of the private elites, carried out mostly by the investment arms of a few wealthy families (e.g. Rockefellers, Whitneys) was that of buying shares in private companies in the hope of selling them at a higher price later (*The Economist*, 2004). By the 1980s, the industry progressed to that of a main street identity. Fundamental changes in the type of deals executed brought in new challenges, particularly those of better governance and greater transparency.

However, 'breaking into' the investment industry in order to investigate any phenomena is not easy. Through 'behind the scenes' influence and endeavour, access was gained allowing for exploration of CSR meaning and application with reference to the investment broker's role in boutique investment banking. Using role theory to underpin the research, this study examines the investment banking dealer's role in relation to CSR. The aim of the inquiry is to shed light on the 'secretive' nature of investment banking and brokers in order to increase our understanding of how investment brokers perceive CSR, and how and whether they enact it or not!

Investment dealers: boutique bank

Although the concept of an investment dealer differs widely across geographies, to be recognised as an investment dealer by the Investment Dealers Association (IDA), registered firms must display a minimum prescribed level of capital and have all employees legally licensed in accordance with local regulations and the Securities Exchange Commission. Further, in certain markets, investment dealers are divided into discount firms and full-service firms. Discount firms offer lower commission rates and do not provide administrative support (back-office services) to their clients, whereas full-service dealers provide full back-office support for clients (IDA, 2002). These types of firms also differ to the extent that they diversify their activities in capital markets. A full-service firm will handle everything from researching companies to financing new issues and trading them on the stock market. Non full-service investment dealers focus on one or more single lines of business such as retail sales, institutional sales or investment banking (Department of Finance Canada, 2002). Additionally, investment dealers often change roles acting as a principal or an agent, depending on the contract they have accepted (CSI, 2003).

Boutique banks are investment dealers that incorporate a specialisation strategy by focusing on a niche market where competition is scarcer (Thornton, 2002). Thus, smaller investment dealers can break into an industry and potentially capitalise on large profits without, initially, directly competing with established and entrenched chartered banks and larger investment dealers. The dot.com industry is a prime example of a successful boutique bank strategy. However, in tough economic times, increased competition from boutique banks is even evident to the media. In a recent article from *The Wall Street Journal*, Craig and Putka (2002) argue that in a recession, the larger banks will avert their attention to smaller niche-market type deals seeing as there are fewer large deals available. Despite such pressure, boutique banks provide the same structure as a full-service investment dealer but have shown themselves to be more agile and able to counteract such competition.

Investment dealer's role

The investment dealer's role is complex and for reasons of sound governance, principally the protection of investor's capital, the industry has its own standards promoted by bodies as the Investment Dealer's Association (IDA), Private Equity Industry Guidelines (PEIG), Security and Exchange Commissions, Securities Institutes and various states'/countries' disclosure rules. In turn, the industry requires investment dealers to have a 'high degree of specialised knowledge about securities issuers, investors and the constantly changing securities markets. An entrepreneurial spirit of innovation and calculated risk-taking are among its hallmarks', whilst 'change and volatility are frequently the norm' (CSI, 2003: 1–26). In support, Anonymous (1998) describes investment dealers as highly competitive, operating in an industry that measures the value of employees by the amount of money generated daily. Outside North America, the private equity industry is less developed although a variety of standards exist. In the United States, the PEIG group, a collection of large investors and private-equity funds work on providing guidelines for the industry's systems of valuation. The European Union (EU), on the other hand, has had valuation guidelines for some time, whilst the United Kingdom is still working on its own guidelines (*The Economist*, 2003). In Swaziland, for example, Partners Group and other innovative firms have advised on bonds backed by private-equity and hedge-fund investment, traded on exchanges which can be purchased by retail investors for a few thousand dollars (*The Economist*, 2003). Thus, irrespective of controls and guidelines, various studies have suggested that, during the 1990s, European-based private equity funds that were mostly focused on buy-outs, delivered higher returns than their US counterparts (*The Economist*, 2004).

Various boutique banks' policy and procedure manuals (CIB, 2003; UKIB, 2003; USIB, 2004) use the terminology 'frontline employees/ department' to refer to employees that are directly involved in making investment-related decisions that commit the firm, or have direct contact with the firms' clients, to provide advice and/or the support of investment decisions. Frontline departments include corporate finance, research analysis and institutional and retail sales and trading.

Investment banking/corporate finance refers to the range of financial tools that can be adopted to finance a company, such as the finance of mergers and acquisitions and initial public offerings (IPOs) (CIB, 2003; UKIB, 2003; USIB, 2004). Employees are paid according to a commission-based system determined by their capacity to assist companies and governments to raise capital by issuing different types of securities such as equity, debt, private placements, commercial paper and medium-term notes (CIB, 2003; UKIB, 2003; USIB, 2004).

Retail and institutional sales and trading, or brokers, are those groups of employees often referred to as investment advisors, brokers, account representatives and investment sales representatives (CIB, 2003; UKIB, 2003; USIB, 2004). Retail and institutional sales people and traders decide what securities to advise to their clients (CIB, 2003; UKIB, 2003; USIB, 2004). In so doing, it has become common practice for each broker to develop their own list of clients, in turn being required to make advisory decisions that are aligned with the clients' investment objectives (CIB, 2003; UKIB, 2003; USIB, 2004). Specifically, a trader will perform the actual function of making the trade, ensuring payment is directly debited from the proper accounts and that valid notification of trade completion is submitted back to clients (CIB, 2003; UKIB, 2003; USIB, 2004).

CSR and the financial sector

Two centuries after Malthus's (1798) *An Essay on the Principle of Population*, the issue of limitations to growth and its consequences for the world was re-visited in 1972 by the Club of Rome, not in relation to the accelerating growth of the population but in assessing the devastating effect human activities have on the ecological environment (van Marrewijk, 2003). The Club of Rome's findings also represented a global appeal for all members of society to take responsibility for the ecological environment. Building on such a platform, the World Commission on Environment and Development (1987) produced a report entitled *Our Common Future* (the Brundtland report), defining sustainable development (SD) as development that meets the needs of the present without compromising the ability of future generations to meet their own needs. In effect, the Brundtland report positioned sustainable development as requiring responsible behaviour from both the individual and the corporation. Therefore what of the financial sector?

Financial institutions exert considerable political and social power not least by the way in which economic, instrumental rationality has contributed to the privatisation of the public sphere. However, their CSR concerns and adoption, particularly by boutique banks and other specialist financial institutions, have been a neglected area of inquiry. Van Marrewijk and Werre (2003) have argued from a developmental evolutionary perspective that each individual and organisation responds to outside challenges in accordance to their own awareness and abilities, especially in the field of investment banking. Thus, whether each bank chooses to be 'compliance-driven' (i.e. CSR is a duty and obligation or correct behaviour), 'profit-driven' (i.e. CSR is a tool for risk reduction and profit maximisation), 'care-driven' (i.e. CSR consists of balancing economic, social and ecological concerns), 'systemic-driven' (i.e. CSR is a way of progress and suitability), 'holistically-driven' (i.e. CSR is the DNA of each person and/or organisation) or to opt out of pursuing CSR concerns, is open to choice (van Marrewijk and Werre, 2003).

Others (Korten, 2001, Zadek, 2001), from the behaviourist perspective, argue that the more intensely an entity preserves its own individuality and wholeness, the less it serves its communities or its partners in the broader community and vice versa. Such a view is particularly pertinent to investment banking, as the securities industry is identified as dynamic, engendering a competitive working environment, whereby employees are positioned as responsible for maintaining their own business, motivated by their own self-determined compensation (Willman *et al.*, 2001; Hebb and Fraser, 2002). On this basis, tensions have been reported to arise between rights and responsibilities, individuality and membership and autonomy and heteronomy. Korten (2001: 13) suggested that globalisation accentuates these tensions, with most multinationals over-emphasising their self-preservation and thus ignoring their participatory role within the community at large therefore creating a 'threefold global crisis of deepening poverty, social disintegration and environmental degradation'.

Thus, whether due to the stage of human and organisational development (van Marrewijk and Werre, 2003), or in response to growing consumer and citizen dissatisfaction, changing demographics such as more sophisticated, well-educated and better-informed members of society (i.e. consumers, suppliers, investors and employees) and/or pressure from nongovernmental organisations that drives the tightening of regulation and greater transparency (Vogl, 2003), an increasing number of corporations are now embracing, at least, the 'rhetoric' of CSR through a variety of activities such as codes of ethics, codes of conduct, audit principles and standards and the evident implementing of CSR initiatives. Especially within the EU community, certain stakeholders, when making investment decisions consider how socially responsible, or otherwise, are certain outcomes, emphasising the need for businesses to take into account the social, economic and environmental impacts of their actions (*Enterprise Europe*, 2002).

Even in the financial sector, stock exchanges and other financial institutions around the world are increasingly compelling listed companies to provide information on their CSR activities. In France, all companies listed in 2000 on the Paris Bourse (now EURONEXT consisting of the merged Amsterdam, Brussels and Paris stock exchanges) are required to include, in their financial statements, information about their social and environmental performance. In South Africa, the Johannesburg Stock Exchange (JSE) requires that all listed companies comply with a CSR-based code of conduct. In addition, in the United Kingdom, the Association of British Insurers (ABI) has issued guidelines which set out information on social, environmental and ethical matters which institutional investors now expect to see disclosed in the annual reports of listed companies.

The study

Despite playing a fundamental role in the development and sustenance of a nation's economy, there have been few published studies on the profile and nature of investment banks and investment advisors. Being exploratory in nature, the research presented in this chapter is framed within an intepretativist philosophy that holds that knowledge of reality is gained through social construction in terms of use of language, consciousness, shared meaning, documents, tools, and other artefacts; phenomena which assist understanding through the meanings that people assign to them (Klein and Myers, 1999). In particular, brokers from three boutique firms (i.e. specialised investment dealer banks) based in Canada, the United Kingdom and the United States participated in this study. Ensuring the participants and their institutions' anonymity, only the participants' department and their institutional code name (e.g. CIB, UKIB, USIB) is used. A total of 124 interviews were conducted (Table 4.1).

Table 4.1 Sample

Site	Number of participants
Canada (C)IB Toronto	41
United Kingdom (UK)IB, London	40
United States (US)IB, New York	43
Total	124

The interviews were conduced from 2003 through to end 2005 and typically lasted 60 minutes. While their general protocol was determined in advance, questions were supplemented during interview in order to probe emergent themes and to expand upon explanations (Harris and Sutton, 1986). The flexible, semi-structured interview sought to explore investment brokers' perceptions of their role and role enactment as well as their capabilities.

Underlying the interviews, a framework of role theory was adopted. Katz and Kahn's (1966) study of roles explained how each focal unit, whether individual or group, is presented with a set of role expectations that influence behaviour within the organisation. Role theory explains that a role is shaped according to a threefold process, the role holder's expectations, the expectations of significant others and the extent to which the role holder perceives and accepts those expectations and behaves accordingly (Rodham, 2000). The key to effective role behaviour is the process of 'learning the expectations of others, accepting them and fulfilling them' (Katz and Kahn, 1966: 188), although 'what matters is not if [*sic*] the impression is correct but the impact it can have on the other recipient' (Jones, 1993: 85). Considering that, for an investment advisor, role demands are dynamic and often contradictory, including the requirement to be simultaneously strategic, flexible, efficient, cost-effective and client-oriented, the focus of this study was on the incumbent role holder's subjective perception of context and role expectation.

The population total was determined by adopting the approach of Seidman (1998) and Glaser and Strauss (1967). Seidman (1998) argued that interviewers should know when they have conducted a sufficient number of interviews, in line with Glaser and Strauss's (1967) saturation argument. After 124 interviews at the three sites, similar themes were repeatedly reported (Table 4.1). Information saturation appeared to have been reached and hence no further interviews were deemed necessary.

To improve reliability, participants were asked to check their interview transcripts for accuracy. Being an exploratory and interpretative study, data was analysed adopting categorisation and sub-categorisation techniques (Stutton and Callahan, 1987). Each interview transcript was coded thematically and reviewed (Insch *et al.*, 1997). Reviewed codes were iteratively sorted according to emergent themes. The initial categories were identified from the literature (e.g. compensation, extra role-behaviour) and further confirmed through primary data (Glaser and Strauss, 1967). The findings were provided to the participants, contributing to the ecological validity of the study in order to enable further learning.

Study findings

The interviewees identified four main factors that impact investment dealers' ways of working and application of CSR: industry culture/work context, compensation systems, role enactment and skills. The study's aim was to describe and understand investment dealers' manner of working and its effect on CSR application. Figure 4.1 below depicts the themes identified and the logic that the chapter follows.

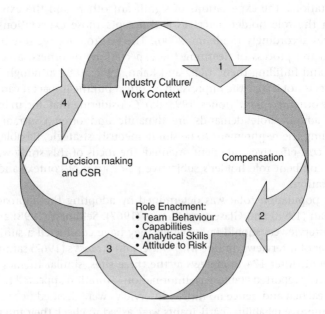

Figure 4.1 Investment brokers' CSR application.

Source: Compiled by the authors.

Industry culture/work context

The literature of the past 20 years illustrates how the culture of both the organisation and that of the broader sector(s) within which the organisation operates impact on a range of interdisciplinary topics such as leadership (Chatman and Cha, 2003) and productivity (Kirkman and Shapiro, 2001). In financial services companies, where the core assets are a firm's human capital, macro (Keltner, 1995) studies indicate that industry culture profoundly influences investment decision making. The current comparative analysis between brokers of three distinctive organisational settings indicates that certain overarching similarities in brokers' attitudes toward CSR are influenced by industry culture.

> This business is about money. So I work not only in a competitive industry but also in competitive organisations. In a way, it is a culture of paradox. It is cut throat on the one hand but a great camaraderie on the other. You can say that we work hard but we also play hard. It is the only way to effectively deal with the build up of stress.
>
> Retail Sales and Trading, UKIB

> Some call this an entrepreneurial culture, which it often is. I call it highly underhanded culture with many opportunities. But one has to have imagination and be able to take the pressure to work in this industry that has a money cult. Some cannot take it and they leave, some make mistakes that you read in the paper but the majority of people in the industry just love doing what they do best; putting deals together and making money.
>
> Institutional Sales and Trading, USIB

> The industry is generally clubby, which to outsiders appears opaque and, to some, even sinister. There are considerable differences between firms. For example we are a tightly run private bank whilst private equity firms such as [Carlyle] are staffed with powerful former politicians who have global access. But one has to accept that wherever there is money, there is an aura of secrecy and suspicion. That is the context you operate in and that is why our clients come to us.
>
> Institutional Sales and Trading, CIB

The participants suggest that the 'survival of the fittest' corporate culture promotes a 'tournament model' orientation, a point supported by previous research (Bebchuk *et al.*, 2002).

Compensation

Compensation emerged as a strong influencing factor on role perception and behaviour, particularly in terms of the propensity to take risk as well as on the application of CSR. In the participating boutique firms, compensation varied according to the kind of investment deal with which each became involved or stayed fixed depending on the type of transaction (sales). The study participants described brokers who worked in boutique investment banking as, in their terms, lavishly paid (*The Economist*, 2004), often receiving an annual management fee of 1.5–2.5 per cent of the fund's assets and share of any profit made from the fund's investment after the initial capital had been repaid to limited partners, a payment known as 'carried interests' (20 per cent of the net profit but can be up to 30 per cent; *The Economist*, 2004). On such a basis, the interviewees stated that most compensation plans tended to be focused on profitability and profit-related accomplishment held little or no incentive for corporate social responsibility application.

> I am responsible for my revenue, and nobody else is. We are paid based on a percentage allocation of the commission earned off every deal … find a deal, that's a commission … structure the deal … that's a commission … organise the financing … that's another commission.
>
> Corporate Finance, CIB

> I make my money and I make as much as I can. I make fixed commission on trades. If I participate in financings I can earn a finder's fee.
>
> Retail Sales and Trading, CIB

> My job is to structure the deal and satisfy my client. That forms the basis for my compensation. CSR is a top management issue, not mine. I follow organisational guidelines set up by the compliance department and as long as I am within guidelines, I think that I am socially responsible.
>
> Retail Sales and Trading, USIB

The findings also indicate that the compensation system influences the way knowledge and information are exchanged (or not). Reward is oriented to the individual rather than the group which can negatively impact on the creation of an *ésprit de corps*. Emphasising the importance of individual contribution through individual bonus assigned on the basis of criteria decided by the group, rather than on a collective bonus that is related to the profitability of the company, reward reinforces the importance of individuality and minimises concern for CSR application. Overall, the findings support previous research that investment banks' employees view themselves as 'running their own business' as a result of the self-determined nature of compensation (Fenton-O'Creevy *et al.*, 2004).

Role enactment

Individually determined compensation induced a perception of being self-employed and that experience emerged as deeply influencing the way employees enacted their role, particularly in terms of how they worked with one another. Furthermore, the compensation system was identified as determining how individuals dealt with knowledge and information sharing.

> I am primarily a salesman ... and will always be and only second, I manage the other brokers.
>
> Retail Sales and Trading Branch Manager, CIB

> My role is what I make it to be. I set my own goals and targets and it is up to me to achieve them. ... It is all about making money and chasing the next deal. If you involve too many people, then your commission is whittled down to almost nothing.
>
> Institutional Sales and Trading, UKIB

> In a way I am self-employed. As long as I keep making deals that make money, my job is secure and no questions are asked. So I see my role as a deal and money maker. A long way behind are my other responsibilities.
>
> Institutional Sales and Trading Branch Manager, USIB

Employees concurred that they wished to make 'as much money as possible'. As a result, the flow of investment information was reported by the study participants as impeded because individuals attached ownership to information and exchange based on the perceived value it would provide them.

Team behaviour

Again compensation is identified as influential on dealers' relationships with colleagues, their motivation and ultimately their manner toward information exchange, attitude to risk, decision making and CSR. As has clearly emerged, employees reported avoiding working with each other in a 'team like manner' as to do so, affected the proportion of commission they earned. Such behaviour resulted in employees, often brokers, shouldering tasks that fell outside their remit as investment advisors. In fact, the majority of brokers indicated that they often undertook several corporate finance roles.

> I do whatever it takes to generate revenues. That includes sourcing deals, creating deals, structuring deals and trading stock.
>
> Institutional Sales and Trading, CIB

> It really depends on the nature of the deal. However, that being said, more often than not I will trade, sell and finance deals. I am not just a salesman.
>
> Institutional Sales and Trading, CIB

> We made some mistakes and the press was not kind to us and now we have to be very careful. Perhaps we are now too careful and too risk averse. However, when I can, I ensure that I do as much as I can myself in order to keep up the commission levels.
>
> Institutional Sales and Trading, USIB

All respondents indicated that they were willing to extend their job roles, as they perceived a positive correlation between the tasks they undertook and potential revenue.

> If the client shows real concern with an ethical, environmental and social issue, then I will go out of my way to ensure that the deal satisfies all those concerns. It is good business sense.
>
> Institutional Sales and Trading, UKIB

Capabilities

Being personally capable (reported as self-awareness or the ability to read one's own emotions and self-management, in effect, the ability to control emotions and act with honesty and integrity in a reliable and effective manner), being socially capable (reported as social awareness, or the ability to understand others' perspectives and feelings, appreciate their strengths and weaknesses, communicate clearly and convincingly, disarm conflicts, and build strong personal bonds) and a positive attitude to risk, were raised in interview as being of primary importance to the continued effective performance of investment brokers.

> You have to know yourself in this business. You have to know how much you can take and what effect you have on others.
>
> Institutional Sales and Trading, UKIB

I know there are a lot of numbers in this business but in reality it is all about understanding others, how they will react, what they feel, all of which are important in completing a deal, which really is all about influencing them.

Institutional Sales and Trading, USIB

Thus, relationship building and networking skills were seen as prerequisite for effective performance as a broker. Indeed, being personally and socially capable were considered so vital that some argued these should be developed prior to assuming the brokers role.

Relationships in this business are key, that's where you get the information. It's all that matters. If you want to be successful, you must be able to form and maintain relationships.

Retail Sales and Trading, CIB

Maintaining and growing relationships. This is a very personal business. You must have good network but also know how to maintain it.

Corporate Finance, USIB

A trusted network is mandatory. People have to trust you and you have to trust them. Personal trust and integrity are very important as well as ability to work under pressure.

Corporate Finance, UKIB

In contrast to previous comments concerning the individualistic nature of investment banking, the interviewees reported valuing trust, networking and the forming and maintaining of collegiate bonds. However, balancing individuality with collegiality was considered challenging. Such capability was reported as developed 'on the job' and sustained through individual attention and nurture.

Analytical skills

Besides being people friendly, the study's participants also emphasised that a key capability of being an investment broker was that of being able to demonstrate and apply analytical skills and good judgement.

Analytical skills are mandatory. You need to analyse information and you need to analyse how all the rules and standards and regulations that come along will impact your deal and sometimes it may be financial regulation, air traffic controller regulation or environmental regulation. It all depends on the deal.

Institutional Sales and Trading, UKIB

If you have analytical skills, you do not need to depend on analysts, you can structure the whole deal yourself and that means securing a large piece of the pie as well as a speedier deal.

Corporate Finance, USIB

Attitude to risk

Compensation was again reported as a significant determinant of each individual's attitude to risk. Moreover, each investment dealers' propensity to risk was reported as an important consideration to the way investment information is exchanged. In turn, each broker's orientation to risk was further reported as affecting his/her attitude to CSR, inter-role conflicts, sense of responsibility to the organisation, their personal survival and how each viewed oneself as a member of the broking community (Green, 1993).

How do I justify to myself morally? I think that I am actually helping the economy and creating jobs for other people ... that's the rationalisation.

Corporate Finance, USIB

I am very analytical. I only take calculated risks. Investment decisions must be calculated as value-adding opportunities. If CSR is part of that equation then it will be duly considered.

Institutional Sales and Trading, USIB

I only invest if it's a sure thing. I analyse, I calculate ... I do it all. Trusting gut instincts are not enough for me: my pay cheque is on the line ... I have a mortgage to pay. That takes over any CSR considerations.

Corporate Finance, CIB

Some guys go after low risk/low profit deals as opposed to the more valuable high risk/high profit deals or what we call 'vanilla deals'. Others prefer a difficult investment project that makes it hard for outsiders to monitor. I personally like complex deals that require new thinking – ground breaking stuff, even if I have to hedge risks.

Retail Sales and Trading, UKIB

Decision making and CSR

In contrast to decision theory which suggests that individuals are intendedly and boundedly rational (Simon, 1957), brokers reported that they faced internal (personal) conflicts and conflicts of interest in pursuing CSR. The findings of this study capture Cyert and March's

(1964: 118) observation that due to environmental uncertainty, individuals resort to quasi-resolutions of conflict since perfect resolutions are impossible. The respondents identified themselves as not systematic in their approach to CSR, sometimes driven by their own moral standing and, at other times, according to client demand.

> The basic decision process should start with asking yourself; why am I in investment banking in the first place and what is my benefit to the industry and myself? For example, the guiding principle I use is to always focus on growing revenues and profits. If I can also create a few jobs in the companies in my portfolio then I am doing some social good but the main focus is making money.
>
> Institutional Sales and Trading, UKIB

> I also think that CSR is social hypocrisy, as I know that there is an inverse relationship between the anti-social nature of the company's business and money spent on CSR. I know that our clients in tobacco, oil and armaments spend more money on CSR than our clients in manufacturing, food or infrastructure businesses. People are morally driven but the spectra of morality is very wide. My decisions are based on risk factors and service to clients. If I don't provide a professional service, my client will walk away and that is not good business nor is it responsible.
>
> Corporate Finance, UKIB

> The investment decision-making process is dynamic and multi-dimensional. Each deal is different and requires an inner imagination or vision of the deal as well as concrete strategies on how to make it a reality. CSR is not part of that process but our compliance department may have a considerable impact on a deal's original idea, whether for legal or CSR reasons, but that is business.
>
> Institutional Sales and Trading, USIB

> It is a dilemma, whether we should finance the Sakhalin pipeline, which to various degrees will disturb the feeding ground of a near-extinct breed of grey whales, whose population consists of only 120 members. The first phase of the Sakhalin oil and gas pipeline project, off the east coast of Russia, is worth $12 billion whilst the Sakhalin-2 project will generate $45 billion worth of oil and liquefied natural gas and is vital for the future of the embattled client's firm. I keep postponing making the decision and asking for more environmental impact studies. I need more information to make the decision.
>
> Corporate Finance, USIB

Sometimes it takes months of analysis to do a deal and sometimes it takes a few days or even a few minutes. A guy came in the other day and made a presentation, within 20 minutes he walked out with a $2 million cheque. ... CSR is not a separate issue of concern but rather the overall soundness of a deal ... return on investment, potential risk, legality.

Retail Sales and Trading, CIB

Conclusion

The emergent findings from the interviews suggest that the social context within which brokers work, the structure of reward and compensation and the nature of the work are instrumental in understanding brokers' perceptions and attitudes to CSR. Investment banks reward profit making, thus positioning CSR as a more minor and additional concern or a form of compliance driven by the industry or the employing bank. Towards this end, CSR is interpreted by some as responding to minimum legal requirements. Others view CSR as an element of the economic, social and environmental aspect of their operations, determined by client demands and generally what makes 'good business sense'. Some evidence has emerged that investment advisors are under increasing pressure to consider CSR under the banner of responsible investment. On this basis, brokers' concern for generating revenue may have, in the future, to be re-focused to take account of long-term benefits for a broader array of stakeholders. However, the study respondents emphasised that the move for taking into account sustainable stakeholder benefit will be the initiative of the organisation or the industry sector, but not the individual broker (banker).

To examine, in greater depth, some of the conclusions arising from this study, further empirical research is required, covering how brokers perceive CSR in relation to its impact on corporate image, how they prioritise their stakeholders' interests, how do brokers' attitudes to CSR change overtime and how brokers compare their CSR performance with that of their peers. Additionally, the attitude of banks' top managers to CSR requires investigation. As one broker confessed:

I make money. All this other stuff (CSR, governance, codes of conduct) is for them upstairs. If they say do it, will I do. Until they say that I don't.

Corporate Finance, UKIB

References

Anonymous (1998), 'Investment dealer dynamics: Reflections of a Bay Street cowboy', available at http://www.rapport.ca/pdf/cowboy/19_cowboy.pdf (accessed: 12.02.06).

Bebchuk, L.A., Fried, J.M. and Walker, D.I. (2002), 'Managerial power and rent extraction in the design of executive compensation', *University of Chicago Law Review*, 69: 751–846.

Chatman, J.A. and Cha, S.E. (2003), 'Leading by leveraging culture', *California Management Review*, 45(4): 20.

CIB. (Canadian Investment Bank) (2003), *Company Policy and Procedures Manual*, Toronto: CIB.

Craig, S. and Putka, G. (2002), 'Deals and deal makers: Robertson Stephens: No deals for a deal maker – Once-hot investment boutique rode the dot-com IPO wave, now struggles to find a buyer', *Wall Street Journal (Eastern edition)*, p. C.1.

CSI (Canadian Securities Institute). (2003), *The Canadian Securities Course*, Toronto: The National Education of the Organization of the Canadian Securities Industry.

Cyert, R.M. and March, J.G. (1964), *Behavioral Theory of the Firm*, New Jersey: Prentice Hall.

Department of Finance Canada. (2002), 'Canada's securities industry overview', available at http://www.fin.gc.ca/toce/2002/cansec_e.html (accessed: 03.06.03).

Enterprise Europe. (2002), 'Corporate social responsibility: stakeholder expectations', 7: 2.

Fenton-O'Creevy, M., Nicholson, N., Soane, E. and Willman, P. (2004), *Traders: Risks, Decisions, and Management in Financial Markets*, Oxford: Oxford University Press.

Glaser, B.G. and Strauss, A.L. (1967), *The Discovery of Grounded Theory: Strategies for Qualitative Research*, Chicago, IL: Aldine.

Green, R.M. (1993), *The Ethical Manager*, London: Macmillan.

Harris, S.G. and Sutton, R.I. (1986), 'Functions of parting ceremonies in dying organizations', *Academy of Management Journal*, 29(1): 5–30.

Hebb, G.M. and Fraser, D.R. (2002), 'Conflict of interest in commercial bank security underwritings: Canadian evidence', *Journal of Banking and Finance*, 26(10): 1935.

IDA (Investment Dealers Association of Canada). (2002), *Annual Report 2001–2002*, Toronto: Investment Dealer Association.

Insch, G.S., Moore, J.E. and Murphy, L.D. (1997), 'Content analysis in leadership research: Examples, procedures, and suggestions for future use', *The Leadership Quarterly*, 8(1): 1–25.

Jones, P. (1993), *Studying Society: Sociological Theories and Research Practices*, London: Collins Educational.

Katz, D. and Kahn, R.L. (1966), *The Social Psychology of Organizations*, New York: Wiley.

Keijzers, G. (2000), 'The evolution of Dutch environmental policy: The changing ecological arena from 1970–2000 and beyond', *Journal of Cleaner Production*, 8(3): 179–200.

Keltner, B. (1995), 'Relationship banking and competitive advantage: Evidence from the U.S. and Germany', *California Management Review*, 37(4): 45–72.

Kirkman, B.L. and Shapiro, D.L. (2001), 'The impact of cultural values on job satisfaction and organizational commitment in self-managing work teams: The mediating role of employee resistance', *Academy of Management Journal*, 44(3): 557–569.

Klein, H.K. and Myers, M.D. (1999), 'A set of principles for conducting and evaluating interpretive field studies in information systems', *MIS Quarterly*, 23(1): 67–88.

Korten, D.C. (2001), *When Corporations Rule the World* (2nd Edition), Bloomfield, CT: Kumarian Press.

Malthus, T. (1798), 'An essay on the principle of population, as it affects the future improvement of society with remarks on the speculations of Mr. Godwin, M. Condorcet, and other writers', available at http://www.ac.wwu.edu/~stephan/malthus/malthus.0.html (accessed: 20.10.06).

Rodham, K. (2000), 'Role theory and the analysis of managerial work: The case of occupational health professionals', *Journal of Applied Management Studies*, 9(1): 71–81.

Seidman, I. (1998), *Interviewing as Qualitative Research: A Guide for Researchers in Education and the Social Sciences*, New York: Teachers' College Press.

Simon, H.A. (1957), *Models of Man*, New York: Wiley.

Stutton, R.I. and Callahan, A.L. (1987), 'The stigma of bankruptcy: Spoiled organizational image and its management', *Academy of Management Journal*, 30(3): 405–436.

The Economist. (2003), 'Private equity: Parting the veil', available at http://www.economist.com/finance/displayStory.cfm?story_id = 2304358 December 18 (accessed: 05.04.06).

——. (2004), 'Survey: Private equity: The new kings of capitalism', available at http://www.economist.com/surveys/displayStory.cfm?story_id = 3398496 November 25 (accessed: 05.04.06).

Thornton, E. (2002), 'Revenge of the Boutique Banks', *BusinessWeek*, October 28.

UKIB (United Kingdom Investment Bank) (2003), *Investment Dealers Guide*, London: UKIB.

USIB (United States Investment Bank). (2004), *Corporate Procedures Manual*, New York: USIB.

van Marrewijk, M. (2003), 'Concepts and definitions of CSR and corporate sustainability: Between agency and communion', *Journal of Business Ethics*, 44(2/3): 95–105.

van Marrewijk, M. and Werre, M. (2003), 'Multiple levels of corporate sustainability', *Journal of Business Ethics*, 44(2/3): 107–119.

Vogl, A.J. (2003), 'Does it pay to be good?', *Across the Board*, available at http://www.conference-board.org/articles/atb_article.cfm?id=73 (accessed: 25.03.06)

Willman, P., Fenton O'Creevy, M.P., Nicholson, N. and Soane, E. (2001), 'Traders, managers and loss aversion in investment banking: A field study, *Accounting, Organizations and Society*, 27(1, 2): 85.

World Commission on Environment and Development (1987), *Our Common Future*, Oxford: Oxford Paperbacks.

Zadek, S. (2001), *The Civil Corporation: The New Economy of Corporate Citizenship*, London: Earthscan Publications Ltd.

5
Ethical Considerations in Decision Making: Case Study of the United Kingdom's Acute Private Healthcare Industry

Andrew P. Kakabadse, Nada K. Kakabadse,
Cécile Rozuel and Kerry Elliott

Introduction

Increasingly, the healthcare sector, worldwide, is exposed to a large and diverse array of pressures, agendas and perspectives which makes any choice hard to make and equally difficult to defend. Indeed, the orientation chosen for any national healthcare system is the result of compromise which is sustainable as long as the various relevant stakeholders are willing to concede part(s) of their expectations. At the same time, the quality of healthcare is a particularly sensitive concern for the public which, in turn, makes it a critical topic for political leaders, particularly as the care of the patient is provided for increasingly through private corporations which generally operate on the basis of 'classical' profit or rent-seeking behaviour (Kakabadse and Rozuel, 2006).

The private healthcare sector, as of year 2000, represented 25.3 per cent of the UK healthcare market (HMR, 2000: 1). Today, private healthcare consists of a number of different sub-sectors such as primary care services, acute care, psychiatric care, long-term care and private medical insurance. It is private acute care which, to date, only accounts for a small proportion of services offered that has been earmarked for growth as a result of the current political climate focused on reducing the barriers between public and private healthcare services and encouraging partnership between the two (DOH, 2006).

Parallel to the injection of private capital into healthcare, patients and other stakeholders are increasingly demanding that health delivery organisations be held accountable for their decisions and actions. In effect, as firms are being scrutinised for the strategies they pursue and the healthcare products and services they offer, the industry is becoming largely a consumer-driven business (Medrise, 2004). Indeed, more and more patients are willing to travel to obtain the treatment they feel is best rather than settle for moderately adequate care (Watson Wyatt Worldwide, 2001). Such agility is facilitated through information on alternative treatments being now readily and easily accessible via the Internet, despite the fact that the Web is also a medium used by marketers for 'attracting, capturing and retaining healthcare consumers' (Medrise, 2004). In effect, consumers (patients) today are better informed. The ease in finding information about a disease, operation or alternative treatment amounts to being just a few clicks away. A question, though, remains concerning whether the medical profession today feel threatened and intimidated by patients easily accessing information or whether they welcome the chance to discuss with their clients their illness in greater depth.

As a result of having a better educated and more aware populous, as well as private investment in health provision, the boundary between information and promotion is often blurred. Further, since health is such a critical issue, healthcare professionals, as well as consumers, are becoming increasingly aware that establishing clear ethical standards are particularly important in helping determine what is right and appropriate. Ethics in healthcare covers a wide range of issues, from the personal motive behind dedication to care to the relevance and quality of medical training and ultimately to the notion of objective, unprejudiced and fair diagnosis. Certainly, particular intractable moral problems associated with healthcare have been with us since Hippocrates, whilst others have emerged through scientific and technological advancement. What, however, is clear in today's world is that health is a matter of public concern. As such, the State is integrally involved, through public funding and/or through public organisations, in the maintenance of a sound and fair healthcare system. Unfortunately, practice does not always match intent. The National Institute of Clinical Excellence has, since its foundation, sought to evaluate new types of treatment available and to approve of their use, or not, in order to prevent 'postcode lottery' (i.e. service quality that depends on the location of one's domicile). Indeed, apart from a short period of GP (General Physician) fund-holding in the 1990s, the levels and types of treatments available in any particular area have been the responsibility of individual health authorities which, in reality, for the last 55 years have been driven by cost-based decisions (Department of Health, 2000). This has had a devastating effect on various patient groups, especially for those requiring drugs for multiple sclerosis and cancer, on the basis of their being available in some areas but not in others.

Thus, due to its very public and politically sensitive nature, the ethics of the healthcare industry have undergone scrutiny. Reputation, transparency, timely and accurate financial reporting, especially in an industry where long-term competitiveness depends on extensive research and development expenditure, has required disciplined governance. Certain efforts in this direction have attracted scepticism and have been labelled as 'covering our backs' to prevent litigation rather than more positive reasoning rooted in a sincere belief of providing high quality healthcare for the public. In fact, the situation in the United Kingdom through the formation of PPPs (public private partnerships) has even more muddied the waters, as private organisations are adopting methods to market their services according to their own ethical inclination.

As a result of fundamental structural changes in healthcare which are assumed to have 'stretched' the ethical challenges facing healthcare managers, a study of an acute care private provider in the United Kingdom, referred to here for privacy reasons as CHUK, was considered as pertinent to pursue. The study explores the ethical standards adopted in the marketing of acute care and how key stakeholder groups, namely consultants, patients and marketing and business managers, arrived at decisions and the 'quality' of ethical standard behind such decisions. Examined will be the ethical standards considered important when evaluating acute care issues. The ethical challenges include: profit making and its relationship to patient safety and well-being; the nature of 'informed consent'; the depth of each individual's understanding of the implications and possible outcome of proposed interventions or alternatives; the conditions under which patients would not be resuscitated; confidentiality of patients records – paper or electronic, and the considerations concerning decisions regarding their medical treatment such as the patient's clinical condition, the ability to pay and the moral or religious judgement of the doctor concerned. The first part of this chapter briefly reviews the major moral philosophies and introduces key concepts of business ethics. The current place and state of ethics in the UK healthcare sector will also be examined. The second part of this chapter focuses on the research study pursued. Elements of moral theory are adopted in order to highlight differences and similarities in stakeholders' decision-making processes. Finally, the conclusions emerging are discussed in conjunction with providing recommendations concerning best-practice in healthcare as well as providing guidelines for the 'ethical' marketing of private acute care.

Ethics and organisations

An increasing number of studies outline that no negative relationship exists between a corporation's financial performance and its social or 'good citizen' performance (Aupperle *et al.*, 1985; Meznar *et al.*, 1991; Waddock and Graves, 1997; Orlitzky *et al.*, 2003). Questions remain, however, as to whether sound financial performance allows for improved corporate social responsibility (CSR) performance and whether elevated CSR standards nurture greater return on investment. In order to prove the point, but from the other end of the spectrum, certain writers argue that irresponsible and unethical behaviour is damaging, both, financially and in terms of image and reputation (Orlitzky *et al.*, 2003). However, the nature of ethical behaviour and acting in a 'good and right' manner has been open to dispute. On the one hand, environmentalists would view the altering of dimensions of context, or as Skinner (1971) proposes, intentional control of peoples behaviour, is acceptable and even needed in order to increase overall moral performance. On the other hand, conscience and concluding for oneself the nature of right and wrong, irrespective of the dynamics of context, is an ethical position with a long history. The point being made is that the spread of moral philosophy is extensive. In this chapter, attention is given to four critical platforms of ethical foundation, namely, duty-based (deontological), consequentialist, justice and virtue-based ethics concepts (Figure 5.1).

Duty-based ethics

Deontological, or duty-based ethics stress that acting morally amounts to each doing their duty whatever the consequences. Christian ethics are exemplars of duty-based ethics. Christian ethics, based on the Ten Commandments have heavily influenced Western understanding of morality (Warburton, 1995), providing people with absolute commands decreed by an external authority (i.e. God) whose rightness is unquestionable. The absolutism and complete reliance on God's command is at the heart of the challenge of practising Christian ethics, essentially because 'real meaning' is subjected to personal (self-interested) interpretation.

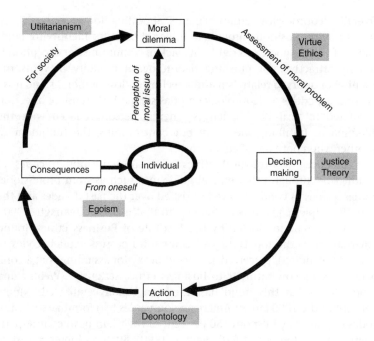

Figure 5.1 Social system.
Source: Compiled by authors.

The argument of a 'just war' illustrates the dilemma of defending oneself under attack or even arguing that a killing is justified under the rule of God. For that matter, every single religion which attracts extremism or fanaticism faces the same criticism on the basis that intra and inter-religious conflicts are the result of several leaders asserting their own interpretation of sacred texts.

In contrast, the moral philosophy of Immanuel Kant (1990) avoids the trap of dogmatism by relying on pure reason to define moral commands. The rationale of Kantian ethics is its reliance on duty as the most fundamental moral motivation, which means that an action is judged on the basis of its motive (what one aims to do) rather than on its outcome (what eventually happens). According to Kantian ethics, certain universal unconditional and obligatory rules exist which are defined by the moral authority of reason, referred to as 'Categorical Imperatives', namely,

1. act according to the maxim of universal law which impacts on all;
2. act so that a human being is not treated as a means to an end.

Overall, deontological ethics remains appealing for several reasons. Deontological positions provide a universal basis for identifying landmarks of what is good and right. The lack of compromise or exception is equally attractive, for pursuing deontological morality prevents the opening of doors to relativism and a feeling of 'loss of moral standards'. In contrast, critics of deontology emphasise that little sense of direction is offered to 'real-life' challenges when a person is faced with the dilemma of fulfilling ones duty but contravening the fulfilment of another when both are of equal worth.

In practice, deontological ethics are endorsed through codes of conduct or through other ethical guidelines such as from professional bodies. Codes of conduct have flourished over the past decades and the Caux Principles constitute a reference to that matter (Cavanagh, 2000). Recent research, conducted by the Institute of Business Ethics, found out that 80 of the top 100 listed companies possess explicit codes of ethics (or conduct), perceived as 'a valid proxy for assuming that a company took its commitment to business ethics seriously' (Webley and More, 2003). Yet this trend has not been equally embraced. Ninety per cent of the 2000 largest American companies had formulated ethical codes of practice whilst only 50 per cent of their European counterparts seem to have done so (*The Economist*, 1990). Such a difference can be partly explained by cultural and social traditions associated with doing business on both sides of the Atlantic. The other is that enforcing principles or guidelines is precisely the concern of deontology since the principles are either too general or 'absolutely' interpreted and applied when a more complex 'moral' scenario requires attention.

Thus, situational ethics are attractive to many because the moral agent can become 'enmeshed' in daily life and not stand above it to consider universal principles (Polanyi, 1966). Yet despite its drawbacks, most professional bodies, including those in healthcare, now possess codes of conduct that their members are required to adopt, such as from the General Medical Council and the Nursing and Midwifery Council (GMC, 2001; NMC, 2004). The codes stress the 'duty of care' healthcare professionals owe to patients but various elements regarding employees, customers, providers and other stakeholders vary in their emphasis according to each code.

Consequentialist ethics

In contrast to rule-based morality, consequentialist ethics focus on the consequences of each person's action and assess the morality of that action according to its outcome. Consequentialism allows for relativism and exceptions to rules in so far as doing what is right, may require adopting 'not so right' means or at least means that are not strictly morally praise-worthy. Two major consequence-based philosophies, namely Utilitar-ianism and Egoism, are briefly examined.

Utilitarianism assesses the ethical quality of a judgement by its conse-quences. The individual 'calculates' the costs and benefits of the various possible scenarios and makes a choice based on the optimal utility of his/her action. Two principle versions of utilitarianism exist, such as act-utilitarianism which states that from the 'utility calculus method' are derived rules of behaviour, and rule-utilitarianism which, on the contrary, considers that general rules come first and define what actions are right or not (Vardy and Grosch, 1999).

Two well-known philosophers Jeremy Bentham (1789/1970) and John Stuart Mill (1998) are acknowledged as the proponents of act-utilitarianism, portraying that the ultimate intent of life is attaining the greatest happiness for the greatest number of people. Morality is assessed by the consequences of a certain action assumed to be taken purpose-fully by the agent. When a set of actions bring a maximised utility, then some rule may be tentatively derived.

On the other hand, rule-utilitarianism 'determines what is morally right by the consequences of following a particular rule' (Vardy and Grosch, 1999: 71). As such, the rule takes precedence over the action even if the consequence of the action is of greater utility than that provided for by following the rule. Actually, rule-utilitarianism combines the universal appeal of deontology with the pragmatic approach of consequentialist theories in order to create an option that enforces strict compliance to rules (hence avoiding relativism) along with a sense of shared beneficial outcome (hence promoting justice to the greatest possible extent).

However utilitarianism has attracted criticism. Principally, it is difficult to define and ultimately measure happiness. The notion of hap-piness is important as the essence of utilitarianism is the greatest good for the greatest number. Bentham (1789/1970) attempted to overcome that obstacle by substituting happiness for pleasure and the absence of pain, a concept easier to measure in terms of intensity or duration. In that sense, pleasure is not purely physical but can refer to a blissful men-tal state. However, even that notion remains unsatisfactory for the per-ception of mental (and even physical) fulfilment is similarly subjective (i.e. some people are more sensitive to pleasure than others and, at sim-ilar level of pleasure, one person may be ecstatic whilst another may be just satisfied). The challenge of finding a common notion on which to anchor the decision-making process, remains.

Thus, Utilitarianism has been denounced for its 'instrumental' approach but praised for its 'practicality'. To a certain extent, the vocabulary adopted for business, such as 'win/lose', is a reflection of a rational calculus which provides the best winning outcome. This 'Cartesian' way of reaching decisions on moral issues does have merit, especially when resources are scarce and pressure to perform increases. Such thinking drove Gould (1975: 634) to declare that 'in the name of justice as well as efficiency, we have got to adopt new methods of medical accounting'. One example of such method is assessing the relative importance of threats to health in terms of the loss of life according to the number of years of life expectancy. Calculations are based upon the assumption that all who survive their first perilous year ought then to live onto the age of 70, with any extra year on top being a bonus. In Denmark, for example, there are 50,000 deaths a year but only 20,000 among citizens in the 1–70 year range (WHO, 2004). The annual number of life/years lost in this group is 264,000 (total). Of these, 80,000 occur because of accidents and suicides, 40,000 because of coronary heart disease and 20,000 are due to lung disease (WHO, 2004). On the basis of these figures, and adopting a utilitarian perspective, a large proportion of the 'health' budget ought to be spent on preventing accidents and suicides and a lesser, but still substantial, amount on attempting to prevent and cure lung and heart disease. Further, much less would be spent on cancer which is predominantly a disease of the later part of life and therefore contributes relatively little to the total sum of life/years lost. Little would go towards providing kidney machines and even less towards treating haemophiliacs. Thus, according to this logic, no money would be available for trying to prolong the life of a sick old man/woman of 82. No doubt that if such a view were proposed today, it would create an outburst of indignation.

Yet, the health service that was established in the United Kingdom in 1948 by the Minister for Health (Bevan, 1948) little resembles the one we are struggling to manage today. Medical advancement and technological progress have outstripped the resources allocated and patients' knowledge and demands exceed capacity to meet expectations. Without adopting the extreme view of cutting off funds to cure rare diseases, the challenge exists of establishing a framework that accounts for ethical concerns whilst allocating scarce resources to meet an ever greater demand.

In contrast to utilitarianism, the consequentialist philosophy of egoism asserts that individuals act exclusively in their own self-interest. Acts on behalf of others or out of a sense of moral duty are, in fact, a disguise for self-motivation and self-centredness. Machiavelli, one of the best known advocates of ethical egoism, explains in *Il principe (The Prince)* (1532/1961) how political rulers need to show both 'moral' and 'immoral' characteristics to achieve and maintain power. In support, Bentham (1789/1970) believed that egoism was in the nature of every one but should not be seen as purposeless or vain. The reason is that moral egoism represents a duty of self-improvement. On this basis, actions should be taken to improve one's personal virtue, intelligence or happiness. The difference between utilitarianism and egoism is that the latter does not prescribe the objective of the happiness of others. It should be noted that not acting towards the happiness of others does not mean that the happiness of others is sacrificed or disregarded but only that self-happiness takes precedence.

Justice theory (norms/law)

The third moral position is that captured in John Rawls's *A Theory of Justice* (1971). Rawls (1971) formulates two principles of justice, namely that:

1. each person has an equal right to basic liberties. In effect, all can pursue the life they desire providing that does not directly or indirectly harm another person (Vardy and Grosch, 1999). The principle of liberty argues that people have inherent rights such as the freedom of speech, the right to vote and the right to due process of law, and that, in turn, they have the right to exercise these liberties; and
2. each person is likely to pursue different aims and the 'social contract' underpinning communities should allow for these differences. Rawls's (1971) principle of difference assumes that inequalities will occur but social and economic inequalities are to be arranged so that they are:
   • to the greatest benefit of the least advantaged, and
   • attached to offices and positions open to all under conditions of fair equality and opportunity.

Fundamental to Rawls's (1971) justice theory is the notion that social structures should be designed to provide a maximised minimum (or 'maximin') to the most deprived in society (Vardy and Grosch, 1999). In this sense, of all the moral platforms, justice theory has been identified as particularly relevant to the UK healthcare market as it is dominated by the NHS, known as one of the largest public healthcare systems in the world (HMR, 2000: 1). This tax-based public healthcare system illustrates justice theory in action, since the population pay taxes so that comprehensive healthcare services can be provided to all its citizens based upon individual need (HMR, 2000: 1).

To a large extent, justice theory adopts a pragmatic view of society and human self-interest in that not doing harm to others and providing the minimum necessary support to those deprived, provides the platform of how today's communities should function. Indeed, justice theory avoids the trap of defining 'goodness' or 'happiness' with which other moral theories struggle. However, justice theory is critiqued for its out-of-touch nature on the basis that people do not act on grounds other than their strict self-preservation. As the essence of Rawls (1971) is the creation of social safeguards available to all requiring social support now and at any point in the future, the question remains whether the will to invest and maintain such a social structure (e.g. continue to pay taxes) is uniformly sustainable across all sectors of society.

Virtue ethics

Largely inspired by Greek philosophers and particularly formulated by Aristotle, virtue ethics focuses on 'how man should be' rather than on 'what man should do' (Vardy and Grosch, 1999). The basic argument is that the source of the good life for man lies in his character, on the basis that virtue is embedded in one's personality. Virtues are not statements of what to do or not to do but rather qualities or inclinations which, if practiced in a balanced manner, help someone to become a virtuous agent. The agent has to practice to develop these virtues through adopting practical reason to understand which virtue(s) should be developed and why it is important to do so. Thus, the 'good' person is someone who has developed a 'good' character, namely one who understands the virtues they have adopted and who, through habit and/or education, has fostered a state of balance of his/her character which makes them act 'right', or apply the 'good' action 'naturally' (Solomon, 2002). Emotions are neither neglected nor rejected but are handled carefully and mastered through practical reason and the wisdom gained through experience.

By shifting the focus from action to individual character, virtue ethics are spared the critique of other moral philosophies including the arbitrage between consequences and motives. Virtue ethics place emphases on the responsibilities of each person concerning what constitutes morality and 'moral performance'. Yet attractive as they are, virtue ethics have not been extensively adopted in management thinking, largely due to their less predictable and more individualistic nature.

Ethical concerns in healthcare

In the highly competitive healthcare industry, ethically laden consider-ations have risen to the fore, particularly in areas such as marketing and sales promotion which have been given ever greater prominence (Solomon, 2002). The functions of marketing and sales focus on main-taining existing customers' loyalty and interest whilst increasing rev-enue and gaining further market share. A classical moral dilemma facing marketing is that of choosing a profitable decision over a morally responsible one (Abratt and Sacks, 1988). The balance between achieving enterprise profitability and acting in accordance with basic human rights is delicate to define and maintain. For instance, launching an intensive campaign for plastic surgery is a questionable exercise given that its effects may include people becoming more dissatisfied with their body (when compared against an idealised ideal), increasing debt levels due to patients borrowing money for surgery which, in turn, causes further anxiety and stress. In turn, the promotion of a 'quick' and superficial fix may well ignore the real problems which are more deeply rooted in the individual's psyche. Should the quest for the 'body beautiful' and the supportive advocacy for a stereotyped image, which is likely to change with fashion, be part of the acute care sector's agenda? Whilst safety and improvement are matters of concern for acute care hospitals, the question that arises is; what are the boundaries of communication and promotion that private healthcare providers should respect, particularly concerning the health of the community rather than of the betterment of the organisations' bottom-line?

The importance of understanding ethical issues and establishing ethical standards for practicing healthcare is distinctly recognised, par-ticularly when healthcare is determined by the 'rules of the market' (Evans, 1991). Within the United Kingdom, the NHS's poor perform-ance in relation to endemic infections such as MRSA, staff shortages, old fashioned and dilapidated buildings and long waiting lists afford the pri-vate sector opportunities to step in and work in conjunction with the NHS to try and provide clean, professional and economic healthcare in the right place at the right time for the best price. Not unnaturally, pri-vate healthcare providers seek to expand their business and influence in the face of a declining national healthcare system.

In the acute care sector, organisational success and survival are now partly defined by the ability to form public private partnerships and to market services efficiently. As example, both the Nuffield Hospital Group and Capio UK are involved in a year-long project to reduce waiting lists for admission to NHS hospitals in line with the current Labour government policy (Audit Commission, 2003). Another initiative, the Spine Chain, consists of nine independent sector treatment centres working as a joint-venture between the public and private sector (Capio, 2004). These contracts illustrate endeavour to reduce the NHS waiting list for operations but equally raise questions concerning immediate access to investigation and treatment on a needs-related basis and not on a basis of affordability (Comptroller and Auditor General, 2004).

The challenge of addressing ethical dilemmas in healthcare is recognised and studies have been undertaken at the individual and organisational level in order 'to balance the need to serve with the need to survive' (Kilner *et al.*, 1998). Orr and Chay's (2000) case studies contemplated issues such as late abortions, bedside clinical ethics (i.e. to resuscitate or not) and organisational ethics including lying and financial conflicts of interest. Further, on an organisational basis, accountability has become a key concern of the medical profession, particularly in acute care, where decisions address often controversial issues such as abortion, cosmetic surgery, cloning and assisted suicide (Witkin, 2000).

In order to advance thinking and understanding, 'role theory' has been increasingly adopted as a fundamental methodology of ethical studies. Role theory originates from sociological research examining the roles individuals adopt and pursue such as, for example, Moreno's (1977) cathartic psychodrama and Merton's (1968) study of social structures' maintenance and deviant behaviours. In fact, the concept of role is being adopted to explore individuals' behaviours and its effect on other stakeholders across a number of intellectual domains. Although no single, all-embracing and comprehensive theory of roles exists, examination of the roles people hold and adopt, particularly within a multi-stakeholder context, provides insight on how individuals interact with one another and with their environment where meanings are, both, socially constructed and individually determined (Katz and Kahn, 1978). The focus is on how individuals influence and are influenced by one another and by the setting in which they operate. The 'role theory' lens thus allows accounting for the skill, experience and temperament of individuals and ponders on the extent to which individuals interpret and perform their roles strictly or are loosely defined beforehand by prevailing social structures. People are said to occupy social positions and hold expectations of behaviour, both, of themselves and of others (Biddle, 1979), expectations which form scripts for social conduct (Bates and Harvey, 1975; Zurcher, 1983). Role conflicts (i.e. when expectations linked to two or more different roles enacted by an

individual emerge as conflicting) and role ambiguity (i.e. when expectations are too loosely defined by the role senders for the role recipient to
know how to respond) are amongst the constructs which have been
examined to inform ethical dilemmas in management (Kahn *et al.*,
1964; Biddle and Thomas, 1966; Katz and Kahn, 1978). Mismatches
between expectations expressed by customers and service providers, for
example, are a likely source of tension. The 'desired expectation level' is
determined by the quality, availability and affordability of the service as
offered by the service provider (Parasuraman, *et al.*, 1988). From that
prospect, a study by Webb (2000: 1) concluded that 'customer "role
understanding" appears to act as a mediator in the expectation formation process', a finding that confirms earlier work by Webster (1991).

Employees' roles have also been scrutinised. At the management level,
studies have examined the relationship between work role fit and organisational effectiveness, and concluded that some degree of flexibility
and adaptability, from either the individual or the organisation, is necessary in order for either to function (Bassett and Carr, 1996). Such
thinking led Mintzberg (1971) to famously identify ten managerial roles
emerging from observation of managers' behaviours. Role-based studies
acknowledge that individuals and organisations are not intrinsically
stable as they evolve through constant and consistent interaction.
Socialisation provides individuals with scripts to behave accordingly in
certain contexts and situations, a phenomena which cultural anthro-
pologists call 'multiple selves' (Barrett, 1983). Therefore, one inherent
assumption of role theory is that assigned roles can powerfully influence
behaviour and that the values projected in cases of ethical dilemmas are
potentially more a reflection of the role enacted than of the individual's
moral system on the basis that people tend to conform to contextually
dominant moral norms (Schwartz, 1977). To this extent, role models
have been viewed as a strong influence on others which can inspire,
either, higher standards of behaviour and morally responsible corporate
culture or poor ethical performance (Trevino and Victor, 1992).

Study design

The research outlined in this chapter aims to investigate the extent to
which private acute healthcare providers uphold ethical and moral
standards of care and human dignity against objectives of profit-
maximisation. In particular, the study explored the emergence and effect
of two major ethical archetypes that appear to be key to health organisations: deontological (both duty and rule-based) and consequentialist

(i.e. results orientated) philosophical adoption. In doing so, the study adopted a social constructivist ontology (Habermas, 1970) and an interpretivist epistemology in that 'reality' is determined by people rather than by objective and external factors. The task was to focus on what people, individually and collectively thought and felt and to interpret experiences and actions that ensue from different situations. Social constructivism emphasises that the most important part of management involves making sense of ambiguous and complex situations through conversations and dialogue (Shotter, 1993; Pye, 1995; Weick, 1995). The interpretivist epistemology allows for the uniqueness of people and their organisations to shine through and encourages interpretation of collected material with no prior hypothesis formulation.

In accordance with the qualitative approach chosen, ideographic methodologies (Burrell and Morgan, 1979) were used in the study in order to emphasise the analysis of subjective accounts by 'getting inside' situations. In practice, the exploratory study design adopted attempted to ascertain whether and how consultant physicians, health service marketing/ business managers and recipients (i.e. the patients) considered ethical issues whilst involved in designing marketing strategies, making life changing decisions and requesting a level, quality and type of service which may, or may not, be in the individual's best interest.

Thus this study, based in the private acute healthcare sector in the United Kingdom (Hickson, 1988), adopted a multi-stakeholder perspective. It was assumed that various stakeholders enacting various roles hold different frames of reference and interests at different times. The study sample comprised 22 participants from each of the three groups of acute care consultant surgeons, marketing and business managers working within the acute healthcare industry and patients, all considered as key stakeholders in the decision-making process (66 study participants in total). The consultants interviewed were all working in the private sector (i.e. CHUK) and in the National Health Service (NHS). The marketing and business personnel all worked for the private health provider of acute services, CHUK, whilst the patients were users of both private (e.g. CHUK and other private providers) and NHS services.

Data collection was based on semi-structured interviews conducted in person or on the phone, later supplemented by semi-structured questionnaires distributed by hand, by post and by e-mail to healthcare providers, medical staff, marketing personnel and consumers. An accompanying letter describing the research was sent together with the questionnaire. Although the interviews adopted a pre-written protocol specific for each of the participant groups (Merriam, 1997), additional questions were included when the need arose. Each interview lasted between one to four hours. Notes during interviews were taken by hand. Participants were interviewed both within the hospital environment and in their own homes (at their request) in order to best ensure that they were in 'neutral time', reducing any insecurity or pressure that they may feel and thus improve the reliability of the material obtained (Yin, 2003).

During interviews, study participants were asked to review how they 'actually' made decisions regarding the promotion, practice or use of acute care services. More precisely, the interviews aimed to explore the participants' perception and/or evaluation of:

- the importance of ethical standards for acute healthcare professionals;
- the marketing behaviour of private healthcare service providers;
- the spread of services that private healthcare providers should be and are offering;
- the methods of promotion of private healthcare services;
- the degree to which stakeholders (patients, shareholders, suppliers) considered themselves as fairly treated beneficiaries of acute care services and
- the respondents' individual experience of private healthcare service provision.

The ordering of the priorities considered when making a decision, the process of advertising services and the availability and use of counselling during an acute care procedure were elements given particular attention. Codes of conduct, especially the usefulness and value of published codes or official acceptance of 'good conduct' guidelines, were also discussed in the interview.

All of the participants in this study were guaranteed anonymity and confidentiality. The chairman of the Medical Advisory Committee and the regional hospital manager granted permission for the research to be pursued. A number of consultants outside CHUK but working across public/private boundaries were also included to ensure that an equitable sample of appropriate consultants were interviewed.

Research results

Several themes emerged from both the interviews and questionnaires but the major finding was that the three stakeholder groups involved in the study adopted distinctive modes of ethical reasoning related to their 'status'.

Table 5.1   Critical decision themes

Stakeholder group	Sub-themes
Consultants approach to decision making	Duty of care to cure and relieve suffering Leadership/role model Care management Communication and training Professional standards and personal distance
Marketing and business managers approach to decision making	The law Discussion with peers Previous experience Assessment of 'right and wrong' Business/commercial opportunities Customer enquiry
Patients' approach to decision making	Honesty of the medical staff Professionalism and endeavour of medical staff Respect of the law and what is right Patients' own agenda Information collection

Source: Compiled by the authors.

Table 5.1 identifies the sub-themes and issues to emerge from the three participating stakeholder groups. Each of the above themes are explored and illustrated below:

Consultants' approach to decision making

Five sub-themes emerged regarding consultants' approach to decision making, based on how consultants perceived their role both intrinsically (i.e. how they enacted and interpreted the social and moral values attached to the role of medical practitioner) and extrinsically (i.e. how they accounted for the expectations of other stakeholders with whom they interacted).

Duty of care to cure and relieve suffering

The majority of consultant respondents expressed adherence to one principle, 'above all do no harm'.

> I base my decisions solely on clinical factors. I am influenced by my own moral values and would reflect on difficult ethical decisions based not only on my own past experience but also following discussion with my peers if I remained unsure.
>
> Consultant 13

I always give patients 'informed choice'. I still, however, give advice according to my clinical experience.

Consultant 8

To treat the patient knowing that the healthcare product is of the highest quality or else refer the patient elsewhere.

Consultant 20

As the representative of the health requirements of the patients as well as the health of the public.

Consultant 22

Certain respondents maintained the minimalist perspective of 'do no harm'. Others, for reasons of self-interest or driven by their deeply held beliefs, expressed they would go further in order to maintain a sound reputation in the community, and for some to equally become prosperous.

Leadership/role model

Conscious of the debates on abortion and euthanasia, the consultants reported that training on the consequences of actions taken would only be effective if supported by, 'leadership by example'. Thus, the study respondents emphasised the importance of senior/junior and peer-to-peer relationships as well as awareness of one's own moral standards.

My own values and morals are very important to me and I try to pass them on to my juniors.

Consultant 4

I wouldn't like to be thought of as 'second rate', devious or dishonest.

Consultant 15

Leadership, standard setting, educating, managing and communicating. I no longer believe that consultants can significantly influence healthcare policy, as consultants are now seen as employees.

Consultant 7

Collective thinking and others' experiences are invaluable.

Consultant 21

The areas that most consultants highlighted as being ethically challenging in determining the 'right' way forward related to major cancer cases, gynaecological issues including termination of pregnancy and cosmetic and plastic surgery.

Care management

Certain consultants reported that they discharged their responsibilities towards patients in terms of a multi-level relationship concerning the treatment and welfare of the person. In effect, the patient was seen as a 'whole person'. However, a significant number adopted different thinking stating that the way they 'manage' patients was driven by their view of the risk/benefit potential to the patient. Such an orientation was not viewed as cynical but rather a pragmatic way of determining action and prioritising activities.

> I am responsible, as a consultant, for the overall management of a patient, particularly diagnosis and treatment.
>
> Consultant 9

> Decisions need to be based on a realistic identification of risks, costs, effectiveness and benefits. I am considerably influenced by my own moral standards.
>
> Consultant 22

Communication and training

It is significant that out of 22 consultants interviewed, only one stated that he felt training on ethical issues in decision making per se would be beneficial. The remaining consultants claimed that most of their decisions were determined by their learning as a result of being challenged clinically, professionally and personally. Recognising that experience comes with practice, a number of them mentioned that specific training on ethical issues takes place only in the third year of medical training before they, as students, had any contact with patients. As such, training in ethical thinking had little impact on them, which for some led to the making of decisions they later regretted.

> I do believe that consultants would benefit from training in ethical decision-making in specific areas.
>
> Consultant 22

> Yes, clinical ethics committees would be useful.
>
> Consultant 20

> No, I do not believe in clinical management by committee.
>
> Consultant 4

Would be useful to have a body to help with difficult decisions.

Consultant 8

No, life is too full of these already [codes, ethical bodies/committees].

Consultant 19

Would be most useful in making some decisions, particularly when medical opinion is at odds with that of relatives. Arises when the patient is not capable of decision making.

Consultant 9

Professional standards and personal distance

Most consultants felt they demonstrated high levels of professionalism in the making of decisions in so far as they would not 'push' the patient into surgery if they did not think it would be in their best interest, even though that could mean 'losing a customer'. The consultants in this sample emerged with clear and shared standards of action for their everyday practice, based on their understanding and experience of their role and work as physicians. However, no clear pattern emerged concerning the degree to which consultants maintained a personal distance when making a critical decision. More precisely, when a possible action may have substantial consequences, certain of the respondents expressed adopting their own perspective, that is, 'what would I like to do if it were me?', whilst others stated they were not driven by feelings and made decisions as a consultant, not as a potential patient or relative.

I use guidelines, knowledge and experience. I often personalise and choose a treatment/management plan that I would want for my relatives.

Consultant 4

Individual decisions should be based on knowledge and not ignorance. Sometimes surgery would be clinically inappropriate unless action was taken by the patient to improve health. ... To lose weight or stop smoking prior to surgery.

Consultant 20

Deciding with the patient and colleagues that this patient with bilateral kidney cancer and significant co-morbidity would be too much at risk with surgery and we would offer no treatment.

Consultant 18

Two additional factors were reported as affecting consultants' decision making in acute care, namely, social trends within healthcare and the use and availability of counselling. First, consultants acknowledged the rapid advances in technology which have surfaced moral issues in the use and spread of medical techniques or medicines. The use of HRT, ovarian conservation, designer babies, sibling donation or methods and delays in pregnancy termination, are just a few examples of areas quoted by the consultant respondents where decision making is fraught with unwelcome consequences and deserving of more time and open discussion (*Daily Mail*, 2004). Further, it was recognised that technological progress in medical science is no secret as the Internet allows for rapid access to information. The consultants admitted that their patients are becoming better informed and more knowledgeable about the options available to them. Whilst many consultants interviewed believed that such phenomenon was a positive step and allowed them to start the consultation 'at a higher level', they also expressed strong concern over the lack of policing of the web as especially unsubstantiated claims could mislead patients to them being given unfounded hope.

Second, despite their claim that patients should be thoroughly briefed as to what are the procedures and available options, most consultant interviewees admitted that they would not refer patients for counselling to help them make a better 'informed' decision. One reason offered was that insufficient resources are available to offer systematic consultation to patients before an operation. Another reason was that many patients had already decided on their course of action and hence refused counselling or paid little attention to the counselling process. However, cosmetic surgeons did feel that a 'body image counsellor' would be of benefit to patients, either or both, prior to and post the operation.

Summary of consultants' views

Consultants' decisions emerged from the study as based on clinical knowledge, personal experience, conscience, patient's wishes, 'common sense' and logic. Overall, consultants seemed to use deontological (or Kantian) ethics in determining their outlook to decision making. Consultants tended to focus on the best option for their patients, irrespective of the individual's ability to pay. The expressed concern of consultants was that of commitment of care to patients, to do good and equally to do no harm. Although not reliant on explicit codes of conduct, the consultants framed their decisions more in terms of rational, deontologically driven factors. To a lesser extent, rights-based ethics were also evident in consultants' reasoning as they

Table 5.2 Summary of the sub-themes identified by consultants

Sub-themes	Explanation
Duty of care to cure and relieve suffering	Representing the patient – being responsible as an advocate of the patient – 'duty of care' and following the Hippocratic oath as well as curing or relieving the suffering of their patients.
Leadership/role model	Leadership – to promote best practice and to act as a positive role model to colleagues, junior physicians, patients and to the community.
Care management	Management – not only of their team of doctors but also of control of resources and benefit to patients. To represent to financial controllers, patients' needs and requests.
Communication and training	Communication – between their team and others, for example hospital management, patients and relatives.
Professional standards and personal distance	Advice – on the best available treatments or the most appropriate course of action to take.

Source: Compiled by the authors.

often stressed the patient's right to know and right to privacy (Table 5.2).

Marketing and business managers' approach to decision making

Interviews with marketing and business managers revealed six sub-themes, the law, discussion with peers, previous experience, assessment of 'right and wrong', evaluation of the business/commercial consequences of a course of action and perception of customer enquiries. The views expressed by marketing and business managers placed more emphasis on business-related factors than on the other stakeholders when confronted with a moral dilemma.

The law

Advertising in acute care, as in any other sector, has to conform to the rules of the Advertising Standards Authority (ASA). Most of the managers interviewed acknowledged that ASA rules influenced their decisions, although a number stated they did not always follow the statute of law. Additional to ASA, medical advertising has to comply with a variety of 'official guidelines' such as the National Care Standards Act (2000) or the recommendations of the General Medical Council. Yet from the comments made, despite legal and codified requirements acting as constraints, potential business prospects were given greater attention.

> You have to stay within legal guidelines.
>
> Manager 1
>
> Decisions on advertising must adhere to legal requirements. My decision on what to advertise is based on the business plan and where our future business opportunities lie.
>
> Manager 5
>
> I take legal requirements into account but I mostly base my decisions on whether I feel the campaign will be a success and that the mode of advertising is appropriate to the product and target audience.
>
> Manager 3
>
> Decisions on advertising are based on a need to advertise, the ads list, the services and the content. They make no claims about the treatment or procedure.
>
> Manager 20

Discussion with peers

Faced with a difficult decision, most of the managers interviewed said they would consider, or seek approval, from their peers about the choice to make. However, few considered seeking clinicians' opinion. The prospect of managers and clinicians working together, based on the evidence from interview, was low and not seen as a valued 'partnership'.

> Yes I am aware of the need to consult clinicians as well as marketing colleagues. However, what I do may be something different.
>
> Manager 6
>
> I value the experience and suggestions of my peers at all times and will do what I can to take them into consideration when making decisions.
>
> Manager 4
>
> I feel a consultative/democratic process is best. However, if I felt strongly enough, I wouldn't be scared of making a decision myself.
>
> Manager 14

Previous experience

Managers acknowledged that past experience enabled them to feel more comfortable about the decisions they made. However, it was not clear from the interviews how the respondents learned from past experiences other than not repeating their mistakes of the past.

I have made decisions that I have learnt from which have helped me make better decisions in the future.

> Manager 4

I'm sure that in life we have all made decisions we have later regretted.

> Manager 17

I've made mistakes hundreds of times.

> Manager 10

With regards to the promotion and marketing of hospital services – no, I have never made a mistake I later regretted.

> Manager 18

Assessment of 'right and wrong'

Certain of the managers described their standards of what constitutes the right thing to do, more in terms of 'what I would not do' rather than 'what I would do'. Emphasis was given to not exploiting people in need. Less attention was given to explaining to patients the alternative options to healthcare treatment.

> We are simply offering an option/alternative rather than exploiting anybody.
>
> Manager 8

> We should always be able to justify why we have done something and should be proud to be associated with the work that we produce. I feel that unsubstantiated claims are dangerous and highly unethical. Patients should be able to trust the hospital. Transparent pricing (i.e. no hidden costs) is very important. Realistic outcomes are also important e.g. having a flat stomach will not cure depression. We should not make claims that even suggest that this will be the case.
>
> Manager 2

Business/commercial opportunities

A considerable number of the managers interviewed became defensive when the topic of conversation veered towards taking advantage of patients. However, quite a few concurred that they pursued opportunities even if that was not to be the most moral thing to do. The managers seemed willing to show they do their best to meet their organisation's profit-oriented demands, but also displayed certain pragmatism, even cynicism, concerning business and marketing, particularly in healthcare.

> When, for instance patients who require cancer-related breast surgery might not need to pay as the waiting time from the local trust hospital is only two weeks. I would inform them that from us receiving their enquiry, they may only save a matter of days for surgery but that they would receive a named surgeon of their choice undertaking the surgery and not, maybe, a registrar operating on them.
>
> Manager 5
>
> I cannot control society or affluence and we are simply offering an option to those 'fortunate' enough to be able to 'self pay'.
>
> Manager 14
>
> The most important ethical standard is good taste and non-exploitation. Obviously in marketing terminology we have to 'exploit' opportunities.
>
> Manager 8

Customer enquiry

The majority of managers interviewed stated that they adopted the principle of the 'customer is king'. They considered their job as providing information relevant to each customer's enquiry within the limits of the law and in accordance with the business objectives of their healthcare organisation.

> No, I believe that we provide the information and service. It is then up to the individual to finance their treatment if they wish to. It is all about providing a choice to the patient and then giving them enough information to make the financial decision.
>
> Manager 3

Summary of marketing and business managers' views

For most of the marketing and business managers interviewed, ethical concerns were viewed from the prospective of legal requirements as determined by relevant bodies such as the ASA. Not that such referral is unusual, as Kallman and Grillo (1996: 73) suggest 'that when we are confronted with an ethical decision, we should first research the law'. From there onwards, marketing and business managers displayed less concern than consultants over the ethical aspects of certain decisions reached. In fact, bottom-line criteria were given a strong emphasis. An act-utilitarian interpretation seems to have been adopted whereby utility-maximisation was defined in corporate terms but failed to distinguish patients as individuals.

Patient's approach to decision making

The participating patients were chosen according to their personal exposure and experience of infertility treatment, cosmetic surgery and termination of pregnancy. These emotive topics were judged as having strong ethical implications in terms of decision making. Five distinct sub-themes emerged from interview, namely honesty of the medical staff, doctors' professionalism and endeavour, respect for the law and 'what is right', one's own agenda and information collection.

Honesty of the medical staff

Patients expected honesty to be a core value of medical staff. They (patients) expressed a clear willingness to be treated fairly and to be provided with open and honest explanation of the nature of their situation.

> To be honest, to do the best they can.
>
> Patient 21

> To give me an honest opinion and honest advice.
>
> Patient 3

Professionalism and endeavour of medical staff

Similarly, patients expressed their expectation of high standards of care from doctors. In situations where life or death decisions needed to be made, patients demanded that staff be at their most professional and 'do their best'!

> To be professional, to do what they are supposed to do.
>
> Patient 18

> I know when people are dying they give extra injections. Yes I think they would do the best for me.
>
> Patient 7

Respect of the law and what is right

Patients expected their medical practitioner to act according to the law which was viewed as tantamount to doing good and providing the best of care. It was not clear whether patients would privilege doctors 'doing their best' for them against 'abiding by the law' if certain actions conflicted with each other.

> Wouldn't that be the same relationship if he was working properly, meaning abiding by the letter of the law.
>
> Patient 14

> To abide by the law.
>
> Patient 11

> To do what is right for me.
>
> Patient 17

Patients' own agenda

Patients expressed strong and distinct opinion concerning what they wanted and expected from consultants in terms of advice. The patients also stated that they expected consultants to ultimately accept their (the patients) decisions. This emergent finding contradicts the study participants expressed expectation that doctors do what is right for the patient. One patient described a willingness to have an operation despite it being too dangerous or unjustified with regard to the medical condition. The patient recognised that the right thing to do was for the doctor to refuse to perform the operation. Yet, a number of the study respondents stated that if they, as the patient, had set their mind to have the operation, they would not accept a doctor's refusal and would require their wish to be exercised.

> This is the surgery they do. If they do not want to do it I will go somewhere else.
>
> Patient 14

> I had to have an abortion. I would have gone abroad if I had to.
>
> Patient 1

> If they found something bad like cancer, then I suppose they would have to stop.
>
> Patient 18

> The consultant told me that the implants I wanted were too big. He put in smaller ones but I went back and had them changed.
>
> Patient 11

> The doctor told me everything that could go wrong but I still wanted it done.
>
> Patient 21

I needed to have an abortion. The timing was not right. I had been with my partner only a short while and he already had two children and did not want anymore. I had to decide between him and the baby. I chose him. I have subsequently been unable to conceive with him and regret having the abortion but it seemed the right decision at the time.

Patient 1

If the surgeon refused I would have gone somewhere different. I had decided and it's my money.

Patient 18

Information collection

The approach patients adopted to the gathering of information on available procedures varied enormously. Recommendation from significant others seemed a popular source for informing decisions, especially in cases involving plastic surgery. Decision making did not rely on official credentials but more on a personal assessment of the reputation of the practitioner. Of the patients interviewed, few had searched the Internet to find a surgeon and even fewer checked to see if the doctor concerned was a qualified specialist. However, most interviewees stated that they researched the actual operation that they wanted and what the procedures entailed.

I went to a surgeon who was recommended by word of mouth. No, I did not check his qualifications.

Patient 12

I am on television a lot and need to look my best to stay in demand as a presenter; I had my eyes and breasts improved. It cost a lot of money, I went on the recommendation of a friend as I think that is the best.

Patient 14

My friend had had it done so I asked her.

Patient 15

My client is a nurse and knows everyone, so I asked her.

Patient 16

One issue raised concern, namely the quality of information given to patients and the extent to which patients felt they gathered sufficient information to reach an informed choice. The emerging view is that patients relied little on information once their decision concerning appropriate healthcare was made.

> I was given a lot of info but I only glanced at it, I knew what I wanted.
>
> Patient 18
>
> Yes, I was given masses of literature which I skimmed through.
>
> Patient 7

A further concern to emerge was the offer and use of counselling, both, prior to and post the operation. Patients indicated that they attached greater importance to their own judgement than the arguments offered by counsellors. Whilst certain respondents acknowledged the value of counselling, most concluded they did not trust the counselling process sufficiently to re-evaluate their 'plans', thus backing consultants' perceptions of the limited value of counselling.

> No, I was not offered counselling but if I had been I would not have gone, I had made my decision.
>
> Patient 4
>
> I wanted cosmetic surgery. I had discussed it with my friends. No, not family, and decided to have breast enhancement and liposuction to my thighs. It was a clinic not a hospital, in London. When I had problems I had to go back daily which was inconvenient. I liked it at the time but ten years on the benefits are gone and I still have bad scars on my thighs. Counselling on long term effects would have been helpful but maybe I'm just saying that now.
>
> Patient 2
>
> More specific counselling would have been helpful. The specialist nurse was more concerned with me worrying about dying and I was more concerned that my husband would have an affair or leave me because I only had one breast. I was very concerned with body image.
>
> Patient 14

The greater majority of patients declared taking responsibility for their medical care, admitting that they would need to fend for themselves on certain aspects of care. Yet, when balancing concern for their own health against the availability of surgery, patients, despite declaring under-standing of prioritisation for operations, did not readily accept post-ponement of their own operation even when good reason was offered.

> I can understand that if other people need it more and you smoke a lot, they should come first and you should stop before they operate.
>
> Patient 15

My dad was told he had to stop smoking before they would operate, I suppose that is right although I would have been very upset if anything had happened to him before he had had his surgery performed because of the delay.

Patient 7

It would be very embarrassing if they said no because I'm too fat.

Patient 18

I'd go to another doctor.

Patient 21

Summary of patients' views

Overall, patients' decision making emerged as comparable to that of an egoistic philosophy. Greater emphasis was placed on their own interests, informed from various sources including word-of-mouth from friends or relatives and the Internet but essentially nourished by their own priorities. It was striking that the vast majority of the patients interviewed had made the decision to pursue surgery before seeking serious consultation or relevant advice.

In effect, patients emerged as seeking solutions and outcomes that they desired rather than those they needed. For the majority of those interviewed, when a consultant did not comply with their wishes, they went, or said they would go, elsewhere to a more 'understanding' surgeon. Information on medical procedures and their potential complications were formally provided to patients but most reported that they rarely paid attention to such documents, having already set their mind on a course of action.

Discussion

One of the more striking conclusions to emerge from this study is the degree to which the acute healthcare sector has become a consumer-aware market. Patients are identified as knowledgeable about their condition and medical procedures, have gathered information less via the Internet and more from a variety of indirect sources and have formed distinct views prior to formal consultation. However, this trend is not to be accompanied by a proportional strengthening of personal responsibility and liability. Whilst patients gain greater formal and informal knowledge of their medical condition and available treatment, the study findings suggest that they become less open to consultants' advice and recommendations. Yet to a large extent, the diffusion of information on medical procedures, providing it is accurate, is viewed as a positive step, improving transparency of medical procedures, enhancing trust towards medical staff and overall appreciating 'informed consent'. In turn, most consultants interviewed stated that they welcomed in-depth discussion with better informed patients. However, to the consultants' frustration, certain patients' greater acquired knowledge nurtured unreasonable demands so that, despite contradictory advice, the individual would proceed with life-endangering surgical procedure on the basis of desire not need.

The study results also highlight that the notion of 'informed consent' had been considerably reversed. Patients receive relevant information about medical procedures and risks but they demand, rather than consent, to have an operation or to receive a given treatment. In turn, the consultants are the ones upon whom the consent bears, as they ultimately decide whether they will act in accordance with their patients' wishes but against their professional assessment of 'what is in the best interest of the individual'.

Additionally, complementary services of counselling are identified by consultants as an available service in acute care. A minority of consultants considered that patients would benefit from counselling even more than from surgery but patients usually declined such an opportunity. Thus, the question of responsibility towards patient care becomes complex as the medical faculty emerge as having genuinely tendered to the care and interests of the patient despite contending with contrary wishes.

Conclusion

The study findings show that the three stakeholder groups employed distinct and contrasting patterns of moral theory. Overall, consultants adopted a more deontological approach to morally significant issues, whereas managers used of more a utilitarian framework with which to make their decisions and patients followed a rather egoistic mode of reasoning (Table 5.3).

Consultants, although referring to formal obligations, emerged as being driven by their moral imperative, namely 'duty of care' which is determined by professional standards, but conscious of the utilitarian-inspired concept of cost/benefit of a given treatment to a given patient. Many consultants also seemed conscious of the need to provide a positive example, emphasising the importance of training and acting as exemplars for the up and coming younger generation of doctors. Consultants also indicated that they reflected on their experience and

Table 5.3   Moral imperative in decision making

	Deontology	Utilitarianism	Egoism	Virtue ethics
Consultants	Duty of care Professional standards	Care management		Leadership/role model Communication and training
Managers	The law	Assessment of 'right and wrong' Business opportunities Customer enquiry Previous experience		Discussion with peers
Patients	Professionalism of medical staff Honesty of the medical staff Respect of the law and what is right		Patients' own agenda Information collection	

Source: Compiled by authors.

personal values and, as a result of past errors of judgement, attempted to improve their practice and decision-making ability. They, nonetheless, ensured that commitment to duty of care takes precedence when deciding on an ethically sensitive case.

Marketing and business managers, on the other hand, referred to mainly utilitarian concepts, notably the way they drew the line between what is right and wrong and how to set priorities in accordance with customer's agendas. However, they also underlined their respect for the law in their decisions and acknowledged the significance of a community of practice to help inform their decisions and reflect on their past experience, a factor considered by virtue ethicists as essential. Managers attended to ethical considerations on a case-by-case basis as well as focusing on short-term profitability. Ultimately, their success as managers was viewed as dependent on the financial performance of their organisation.

Finally, patients demonstrated a clear inclination to favour their personal interests over alternative moral reasoning. Patients' interpretation of the role of consultants seemed related to how the medical process, decision and action would eventually benefit them. Patients' benchmark emerged as their own definition of well-being, even though that may be to their medical disadvantage. Yet, despite a strong egoistic orientation, patients also demonstrated a significant attachment to formal rules and to the law. They praised honesty as if it were a categorical imperative, expecting medical staff to be fair and act appropriately no matter the circumstances. Patients seemed concerned to have a concise view of alternatives but displayed their displeasure to have their views and decisions challenged, despite obvious risks.

The study has found that decision making on medical issues which have a moral connotation is not a straightforward process. The various stakeholder groups under scrutiny place emphasis on differing moral frameworks. Also to emerge is the that individual stakeholder groups do not analyse an ethical dilemma purely in terms of one prevailing moral framework, but rather mix and match various moral aspirations and expectations. The critical issue to emerge from this study is the conflict between the marketing of image in contrast to meeting the best interests of the patients. The study results indicate that the pivotal point between two conflicting demands is the consultant who can, at best, only respond in a passive manner by refusing to proceed with surgery despite patients' protestations. The inquiry highlights that the focus of moral responsibility in the acute health sector lies at the level of management and the organisation and not at the level of the medical practitioner. As consultants are identified as more passive in terms of ethical decision making in terms of what they will not do, the pro-active projection of an ethical position is evident through the marketing of image for the purposes of 'attracting customers'. Such practice essentially conflicts with consultants' views concerning what is in the best interest of the patient.

In essence, this study on the ethical concerns of decision making in the acute sector concludes by seriously questioning the marketing and privatisation of healthcare. Not that any single manager behaves immorally but more that the very foundation of private acute care distracts from what is in the best interest of the individual. Relying on the Hippocratic oath, in effect, on the individual medical practitioner for ethical determination and guidance is insufficient in today's healthcare structures. The healthcare organisation is identified as the more dominant influence, which regrettably emerges as promoting the interests of the corporation, namely its shareholders, rather than the individual interests of its customers, the patients.

References

Abratt, R. and Sacks, D. (1988), 'The marketing challenge: Towards being profitable and socially responsible', *Journal of Business Ethics*, 7(7): 497–507.

Audit Commission. (2003), 'Achieving the NHS plan: Assessment of current performance, likely future progress and capacity to improve', available at http://www.audit-commission.gov.uk/reports/AC-REPORT.asp?CatID= ENGLISH%5EHEALTH%5ESUBJECT%5EH-CROSS-CUT&ProdID= 3BB3CA40–94D5–11d7-B2EE-0060085F8572 (accessed: 20.10.05).

Aupperle, K.E., Carroll, A.B. and Hatfield, J.D. (1985), 'An empirical examination of the relationship between corporate social responsibility and profitability', *Academy of Management Journal*, 28(2): 446–463.

Barrett, R.A. (1983), *Culture and Conduct: Excursion in Anthropology*, London: Wadsworth.

Bassett, G. and Carr, A. (1996), 'Role sets and organization structure', *Leadership and Organization Development Journal*, 17(4): 37.

Bates, F.L. and Harvey, C.C. (1975), *The Structure of Social Systems*, Chichester: John Wiley & Sons Inc.

Bentham, J. (1789/1970), *An Introduction to the Principles of Morals and Legislation*, by J.H. Burns and H.L.A. Hart (Eds), London: The Athlone Press.

Bevan, A. (1948), 'National Health Service Act', Minister for Health, Speech in the House of Commons, available at: http://www.spartacus.schoolnet.co.uk/ TUbevan.htm (accessed: 29.02.06).

Biddle, B.J. (1979), *Role Theory: Expectations, Identities and Behaviours*, London: Academic Press Inc. (London) Ltd.

Biddle, B.J. and Thomas, E.J. (1966), *Role Theory; Concepts and Research*, New York: John Wiley & Sons Inc.

Burrell, G. and Morgan, G. (1979), *Sociological Paradigms and Organisational Analysis*, Hampshire: Ashgate.

Capio, A.B. (2004), 'Press release: Capio appointed preferred bidder in final negotiations for UK's largest care contract', available at http://www.capio.com/ News/934738.htm (accessed 07.03.06).

Cavanagh, G.F. (2000), 'Executives' code of business conduct: Prospects for the Caux Principles', in O.F. Williams (Ed.), *Global Codes of Conduct: An Idea Whose Time Has Come*, Notre Dame, Chicago, IL: University of Notre Dame Press.

Comptroller and Auditor General. (2004), 'Improving patient care by reducing the risk of hospital acquired infection: A progress report', available at http://www.nao.org.uk/publications/nao_reports/03-04/0304876es.pdf (accessed 10.12.05).

Daily Mail. (2004), 'Straying into a moral minefield', July 22, available at http://www.dailymail.co.uk/pages/live/articles/news/newscomment.html?in_ article_id=311225&in_page_id=1787 (accessed: 20.02.06).

DOH (Department of Health. (2000), 'The NHS Plan: A plan for investment, a plan for reform', available at http://www.dh.gov.uk/ PublicationsAndStatistics/ Publications/PublicationsPolicyAndGuidance/PublicationsPolicyAndGuidance Article/fs/en?CONTENT_ID=4002960&chk=07GL5R (accessed: 20.02.06).

DOH (Department of Health. (2006), 'About NHS lift', available at http://www.dh.gov.uk/ ProcurementAndProposals/PublicPrivatePartnership/ NHSLIFT/AboutNHSLIFT/fs/en?CONTENT_ID=4000519&chk=D3TGGB (accessed 20.02.06).

Evans, R. (1991), 'Business ethics and changes in society', *Journal of Business Ethics*, 10(11): 871–879.

GMC (General Medical Council) (2001), 'Good medical practice', available at http://www.gmc-uk.org/guidance/good_medical_practice/index.asp (accessed: 20.02.06).

Gould, D. (1975), 'Some lives cost too dear', *New Statesman*, 90(2331): 633–634.

Habermas, J. (1970), 'Knowledge and interest', in D. Emmet and A. MacIntyre (Eds), *Sociological Theory and Philosophical Analysis*, London: Macmillan.

Hickson, D.J. (1988), 'Ruminations on munificence and scarcity in research', in A. Bryman (Ed.), *Doing Research in Organizations*, London: Routledge.

HMR (Healthcare Marketing report). (2000), 'Branding and marketing the primary care practice a key challenge for hospitals and health systems', available at http://www.hmrpublicationsgroup.com/Healthcare_Marketing_Report/ hmr_back_issues_2000.html (accessed: 19.10.05).

Kahn, R.L., Wolfe, D.M., Quinn, R.P., Snoek, J.D. and Rosenthal, R.A. (1964), *Organisational Stress: Studies in Role Conflict and Ambiguity*, New York: John Wiley & Sons.

Kakabadse, N.K. and Rozuel, C. (2006), 'Meaning of corporate social responsibility in a local French hospital: a case study', *Society and Business Review*, 1(1): 77–96.

Kallman, E.A. and Grillo, J.P. (1996), *Ethical Decision Making and Information Technology: An Introduction with Cases*, New York: McGraw-Hill.

Kant, I. (1990), *Critique of Pure Reason* (Reprint Edition), J.M.D. Meiklejohn (Trans), New York: Prometheus Books.

Katz, D. and Kahn, R.L. (1978), *The Social Psychology of Organizations* (2nd Edition), Chichester: John Wiley & Sons Inc.

Kilner, J.F., Orr, R.D. and Shelly, J.A. (1998), *The Changing Face of Healthcare*, USA: Wm B Eerdmans Publishing Co.

Machiavelli, N. (1532/1961), *Il principe (The Prince)*, G. Bull (Trans.), Harmondsworth: Penguin.

Medrise. (2004), 'Managed Care', available at http://www.medrise. mediwire.com/main/Default.aspx?P=managed_care (accessed on 20.04.04).

Merriam, S.B. (1997), *Qualitative Research and Case Study Applications in Education* (Revised Edition), Chichester: Jossey Bass Wiley.

Merton, R.K. (1968), *Social Theory and Social Structure*, London: Macmillan USA.

Meznar, M.B., Chrisman, J.J. and Carroll, A.B. (1991), 'Social responsibility and strategic management: Toward an enterprise strategy classification', *Business and Professional Ethics Journal*, 10(1): 47–66.

Mill, J.S. (1998), *On Liberty and Other Essays*, Oxford: Oxford University Press.

Mintzberg, H. (1971), 'Managerial work: analysis from observation', *Management Science*, 18(2): B97–B110.

Moreno, J.L. (1977), *Psychodrama Volume 1* (4th Edition), New York: Beacon House.

National Care Standards Act. (2000), 'Care Standards 2000 chapter 14', available at http://www.opsi.gov.uk/acts/acts2000/20000014.htm (accessed: 20.02.06).

NMC (Nursing and Midwifery Council). (2004), 'The NMC code of professional conduct: standards for conduct, performance and ethics', available at http://www.nmc-uk.org/aDisplayDocument.aspx?DocumentID=201 (accessed: 20.02.06).

Orlitzky, M., Schmidt, F.L. and Rynes, S.L. (2003), 'Corporate social and financial performance: A meta-analysis', *Organization Studies*, 24(3): 403.

Orr, R.D. and Chay, F. (2000), *Medical Ethics: A Primer for Students*, Bristol: Christian Medical and Dental Associations.

Parasuraman, A., Zeithaml, V.A. and Berry, L.L. (1988), 'Servqual: A multiple-item scale For measuring consumer perceptions of service', *Journal of Retailing*, 64(1): 12–40.

Polanyi, M. (1966), *The Tacit Dimension*, Garden City, New York: Doubleday & Co.

Pye, A. (1995), 'Strategy through dialogue and doing: A game of "Mornington Crescent?" ' *Management Learning*, 26(4): 445–462.

Rawls, J. (1971), *A Theory of Justice*, London: Harvard University Press.

Schwartz, S.H. (1977), 'Normative influences on altruism advances', in L. Berkowitz (Ed.), *Advances in Experimental Social Psychology*, New York: Academic Press.

Shotter, J. (1993), *Conversational Realities: Constructing Life Through Language*, London: Sage Publications Ltd.

Skinner, B.F. (1971), *Beyond Freedom and Dignity*, Westminster, MD: Random House Inc.

Solomon, R.C. (2002), 'Business ethics and virtue', in R.E. Frederick (Ed.), *A Companion to Business Ethics*, Oxford: Blackwell Publishers Ltd.

The Economist. (1990), 'Good takes on greed', 314: 71–74.

Trevino, L.K. and Victor, B. (1992), 'Peer reporting of unethical behaviour: A social context perspective', *Academy of Management Journal*, 35(1): 38–64.

Vardy, P. and Grosch, P. (1999), *The Puzzle of Ethics* (2nd Edition), London: Fount.

Waddock, S.A. and Graves, S.B. (1997), 'The corporate social performance-financial performance link', *Strategic Management Journal*, 18(4): 303–319.

Warburton, N. (1995), *Philosophy: The Basics* (2nd Edition), London: Routledge.

Watson Wyatt Worldwide (2001), 'Healthcare market review: Healthcare statistics', available at http://www.watsonwyatt.com/europe/pubs/healthcare/articles/render_oct.asp?ID=8894 (accessed: 24.06.04).

Webb, D. (2000), 'Understanding customer role and its importance in the formation of service quality expectations', *The Service Industries Journal*, 20(1): 1–21.

Webley, S. and More, E. (2003), *Does Business Ethics Pay? Ethics and Financial Performance*, London: Institute of Business Ethics.

Webster, C. (1991), 'Influences upon consumer expectations of services', *The Journal of Services Marketing*, 5(1): 5–17.

Weick, K.E. (1995), *Sensemaking in Organizations*, Thousand Oaks, CA: Sage Publications (USA).

WHO (World Health Organization) (2004), 'The world health report 2004 – changing history', available at http://www.who.int/whr/en/ (accessed: 20.07.05).

Witkin, S.L. (2000), 'Ethics-r-us', *Social Work*, 45(3): 197–200.
Yin, R.K. (2003), *Case Study Research: Design and Methods* (3rd Edition), London: Sage Publications Ltd.
Zurcher, L.A. (1983), *Social Roles: Conformity, Conflict and Creativity*, London: Sage Publications.

6

Insider Trading – So What's Wrong with It? Examination of the Vienna, London and New York Stock Exchanges

Andrew P. Kakabadse, Nada K. Kakabadse and Antje Kaspurz

Introduction

With globalisation and the growing importance of capital markets, the subject of insider trading has become a highly debated topic. The past decade of scandals involving Enron, WorldCom, Parmalat or Martha Stuart and the mistrust of shareholders towards board members, traders and investment banks, has increased awareness of insider trading regulation not only in the United States but also in Europe. Despite the increase of regulation to prevent misappropriation of public funds, economists and academics as well as investment professionals hold different views as to whether insider trading has any impact on market efficiency and market confidence and therefore whether its practice should be restricted by regulation. Questioning the contribution of regulation motivated the authors to initiate a study of the Vienna, London and New York Stock Exchanges in order to examine the effect of insider trading. Particular attention was given to exploring whether or not insider trading has an influence on the performance of the three Stock Exchanges. Preceding reporting the study, a literature overview outlines the nature of insider trading and its influence on market efficiency. Next is a description of the study pursued, followed by an analysis of findings. As a result of the inquiry, the authors conclude that insider trading is an insignificant consideration when comparing the volume of shares traded and the level of insider knowledge utilised. The issue is not of insider trading, but more how can traders become better informed so as to enhance their trading capacity.

Insider trading

Insider trading and/or the obtaining of inside information has been subject to scrutiny and contrasting interpretation (Harris, 2002). Generally insider trading is understood as the buying and selling of securities on the basis of non-public, or privileged information (Bettis *et al.*, 1998). Information is material that a reasonable investor is likely to consider as significant in making an investment decision which, in turn, may have a substantial impact on the market price of a company's securities. Non-public information refers to information that has not been disclosed to the market-place and investors have not had the opportunity to consider. To become public, information must be disseminated so that it is reasonably available to a broad array of investors. The disclosure of information by a corporate insider to a select group, for example analysts, is not sufficient to make that information public (AIMR, 1996).

Adequately defining the phenomenon of insider trading has not been easy. The very term 'insider trading' is misleading for two reasons. First, 'outsiders' may engage in insider trading and act on the basis of privileged information. Second, insider trading refers to trades made by insiders on the basis of privileged versus non-privileged information. Therefore, more appropriate terminology may be 'trading on the basis of inside information' (Irvine, 1986). But even such characterisation fails to provide clarity, as no distinction is made between trading on the basis of privileged information or trading on only some form of privileged data. The view offered by Zekos (1999), of insider trading including the buying and selling of securities relating to a company by a person connected with that company and who is in possession of specific or privileged information which, if made public, could have a significant effect on the determination of market price, goes further than other authors as the concept of the information stakeholder is introduced. The Zekos (1999) perspective raises the question of who utilises information stakeholders as well as the nature of the trade itself.

Insider information stakeholders are distinguished between two different types, primary and secondary. Primary information stakeholders are individuals who have willingly assumed an obligation to defend the interests of shareholders (Shaw, 1988). This includes not only employees and directors of the company but also people who have a privileged contract with that enterprise, such as consultants or other professionals. Secondary information stakeholders are those who have not voluntarily assumed an obligation to look out for the interests of the shareholders (Shaw, 1988), such as customers or managers of enterprises who form an element of the company's supply chain.

Insider trading – effect on market efficiency

Examining the nature of the 'insider trader' has been balanced by inquiry into the nature of privileged and unprivileged information in the financial markets (Zekos, 1999). In the stewardship of their funds, shareholders are likely to invest in what they consider to be the most profitable of investments. Investment efficiency requires the acquisition of information on the basis that its incremental benefits exceed its incremental costs (Parkman *et al.*, 1988). As the primary role of the capital market is to determine the allocation of ownership of that economy's capital, then the ideal is a market where price provides accurate signals for resource allocation, so that investors can purchase shares on the assumption that the price for securities at any one time reflects all available information; in effect, a truly efficient market (Zekos, 1999). On this basis, accuracy, timeliness and availability of information are important concerns. Should an event occur that unexpectedly changes interest rates or the characteristics of a company, the market price of stock can temporarily diverge from its present considered value. When market traders determine that a stock is undervalued they will purchase the stock, thus driving up price. Conversely, when market traders determine that a stock is overvalued, they will likely sell that stock, resulting in a price decline. Therefore, the factors that impact on market efficiency determination are the degree to which financial security prices adjust to news and the degree and speed with which stock prices reflect information about the firm and factors that affect firm value (Saunders and Cornett, 2002). According to Frankel and Li (2004) the information asymmetry between managers and investors is a fundamental consideration for investors and market observers on the basis that privileged information is viewed as benefiting the few who have such access but harming other investors and in this way undermining market efficiency.

Fama (1970) agrees and takes the view that insider trading decreases market efficiency, undermines strong markets and allows for abnormal returns to be earned. Other than the study of stocks on the relatively small Oslo Stock Exchange by Eckbo and Smith (1998), research suggests that insiders earn positive abnormal returns (Jaffe, 1974; Seyhun, 1986; Lakonishok and Lee, 2001). Although Saunders (2001) concurs, he also comments that once insider information becomes publicly available, abnormal returns are unlikely. Thus, the question arises – who gets what information when? According to strong market efficiency theory, the market has already reacted to insider information and adjusted the firm's stock price to a new equilibrium (Blake, 1999; Spencer, 2000; O'Hara, 2001).

However, an alternative view exists. Abdolmohammadi and Sultan (2002) postulate that through insider trading share price determination is more efficient as markets integrate insider information into the price of stocks faster and more efficiently than would otherwise have been the case. The argument put forward is that markets quickly respond to new information undermining any benefit for insiders (Laird, 1995).

Thus, on the one hand insider trading has been viewed as having an effect on market efficiency from two sides. According to Pope *et al.* (1990: 359) one of the 'cornerstones of a fair, open and transparent market is the prohibition of use of non-public information'. Government regulation and corporate governance application allows the market to perform efficiently by encouraging fairness and liquidity. Harris (2002) agrees with this statement and points out that traders stay away from markets they do not believe are fair. From the fairness perspective, it is therefore assumed that restrictions against insider trading benefit the markets by increasing investor confidence. As a result, greater investor confidence increases the funds that investors will invest in stocks, thus raising prices and thereby lowering the corporate costs of capital. To allow for insider trading would decrease market efficiency, thus emphasising the need for external preventive regulation (Ronen, 2000).

On the other hand, it has been argued that insider trading increases market efficiency since insiders are well-informed traders who, by their actions, push prices towards their fundamental value. The free flow of action in the market, albeit through a substitute for substantive information, provides the stimulus upon which others act (O'Hara, 2001). Manne (1992: 418) argues that:

> If there were effective enforcement of laws against Insider Trading, all corrections of price would have to come from individuals who received the information more slowly than insiders and who generally could not evaluate new developments as expertly. Certainly

the stock market would be less efficient than it is with no insider trading.

The contrasting argument emphasises that restriction on insider trading removes insiders and their information from the market, therefore making determining price less informative. Since informative-based price is essential to efficient decision allocation in market-based economies, insider trading makes markets more efficient. The value of having informative-based prices sooner rather than later depends on how much longer it would take prices to adjust to new information. If insiders accelerate the flow of information by months or years, restricting insider trading may be harmful (Harris, 2002). Treynor and LeBaron (2004) agree and argue that by eliminating insiders, markets are less informed and market prices no longer reflect the combined knowledge of all participants. Further, the pro insider trading lobby emphasise that blatant 'unfair' or misuse of information is relatively evident and can be dealt with (Pope *et al.*, 1990). However, it is the grey area that is problematic. Someone who already owns shares in a company and who has prior knowledge of 'good news' would almost certainly delay selling until after such information is released to the market. Similarly, someone with prior information of 'bad news' would be unlikely to buy until after that news has been revealed. In both cases the absence of trading activity until after news is released, and the consequent incremental profits that arise, results directly from having access to privileged, price sensitive information (Tomasic, 1991). Regulating hard price sensitive information, such as foreknowledge of a takeover bid is distinctly less challenging than doing likewise with soft price sensitive information, such as internal profit forecasts, especially if no trade takes place. As a result, insider trading regulation application is liable to be random and inequitable as it will likely be applied in extreme cases of hard information usage, and unlikely to deter less obvious dealings by insiders who are generally better informed than the market (Pope *et al.*, 1990).

Stock exchange background

The Vienna (VSE) and London Stock Exchange (LSE) have a substantial difference in terms of the number of listed companies on their exchange but they do share a 250 year history. However, what the LSE and the New York Stock Exchange (NYSE) share is comparability in terms of companies listed on each exchange with the LSE as leader displaying 2837 companies listed in December 2004, followed by the NYSE with just

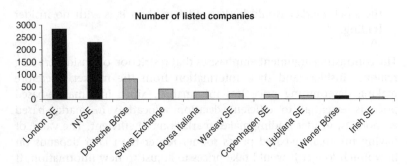

Figure 6.1 Listed companies in December 2004.
Source: Compiled from World Federation of Exchanges (2005).

over 2800 companies listed (Figure 6.1; World Federation of Exchanges, 2005). NYSE, however, is leader in terms of market capitalisation displaying US$12,708 trillion by the end of 2004 (World Federation of Exchanges, 2005).

The Vienna Stock Exchange (VSE) was established by Maria Theresia, Duchess of Austria, in 1771. Originally, the exchange performed as a market-place for trading bonds, bills of exchange and foreign currencies. Shares were traded for the first time in 1818. The new Stock Exchange Act, 1989, allowed for the introduction of electronic trading. An important highlight in the history of the exchange was the introduction of the German trading system, Xetra, in 1999. In 2000 the largest stock market transaction in the history of Austria was undertaken involving Telekom Austria AG, trading to a volume of approximately Austrian Schilling 14 billion (Wienerbörse, 2004).

The VSE's market capitalisation in December 2004 was €64,557 million an increase of 55 per cent compared to December 2003. The total value of shares traded in 2004 amounted €29,426 million, an increase of 6.7 per cent in relation to 2003, with the share capital of VSE € 5,089,000 that is divided into 700,000 no-par value shares allocated to 61 current shareholders (World Federation of Exchanges, 2005). The current top five shareholders of the VSE are listed in Table 6.1.

The London Stock Exchange (LSE) obtained its formal constitution and its own building at the beginning of the nineteenth century, but by that time organised dealing in stocks and shares had been pursued for well over a hundred years. Starting life in the coffee houses of seventeenth century London, the Exchange quickly grew to become the City's most important financial institution. In 1986 the deregulation of the market, known as 'Big Bang', took place. Trading moved from being

Table 6.1 Major shareholders of VSE

Name	Percentage of issued share capital (%)
Bank Austria Creditanstalt AG	11.71
Unternehmens Invest AG	10.41
Erste Bank der österreichischen Sparkassen AG	9.44
Raiffeisen Zentralbank Österreich AG	6.11
Österreichische Kontrollbank AG	5.86

Source: Wienerbörse (2004).

Table 6.2 Major shareholders of LSE

Name	Percentage of issued share capital (%)
Threadneedle Investments	7.43
Fidelity International Limited	5.99
UBS AG	3.89
Barclays PLC	3.72
Legal & General Group Plc	3.29
Deutsche Bank AG	3.01

Source: London Stock Exchange (2004).

conducted face-to-face on the market floor to being performed via computer and telephone from separate dealing rooms. Further, LSE ownership of member firms by outside corporations was also allowed. Additionally, the LSE became a private limited company under the Companies Act 1985 (London Stock Exchange, 2004).

The market capitalisation of the LSE in December 2004 stood at £1,466 trillion representing an increase of 16 per cent compared to December 2003. The total value of shares traded in 2004 amounted to £2,815 trillion, a decrease of 14.5 per cent compared to 2003 (World Federation of Exchanges, 2005). The major six shareholders of LSE are listed in Table 6.2.

The New York Stock Exchange (NYSE) is the largest stock exchange in the world. Its origins can be traced back to 1792 when 24 New York City 'brokers of stocks' together with certain rich merchants signed the so called Buttonwood agreement. The first listed company to emerge from this agreement was the Bank of New York. In 1817, through a redraft of the constitution, the New York Stock & Exchange Board emerged later to be incorporated in 1971 as the New York Stock Exchange Inc., a not-for-profit corporation. The NYSE has 1366 members, a number that has remained constant since 1953. Owning a seat (membership) entitles one to buy and sell securities on the floor, as an agent for others or for one's own account. However, being able to afford a seat is, by itself, not enough to gain membership. Candidates are reviewed by the NYSE Membership Department and must meet high standards of personal and financial integrity, demonstrating their knowledge of the securities business. The price of seat membership tripled in 2005 to US$3 million due to the acquisition of Archipelago, a deal that brought the NYSE into public ownership (New York Stock Exchange, 2004).

Market capitalisation of the NYSE in December 2004 stood at US$12,707,578.3 million, an increase of 12.2 per cent compared to December 2003. The total value of shares traded in 2004 stood at US$11,618,150.5 million, an increase of 19.9 per cent compared to 2003 (International Federation of Stock Exchanges, 2004; World Federation of Exchanges, 2005).

Study

The authors' past experience as consultants in the financial services arena allowed for access to the Vienna (VSE), London (LSE) and New York Stock Exchanges (NYSE). First, known contacts in Vienna were approached outlining the nature of the study concerning the respondents' views and orientation towards insider trading. The majority of those approached responded positively to being interviewed. In addition, a random sample of managers in registered Austrian financial institutions were approached requesting interview on the theme of insider trading. All respondents declined to be interviewed highlighting:

> [I]n Austria you don't talk about insider trading.
> we are sorry to inform you that we can't take a position on this topic. It is against our discretionary duty.
> we cannot help you as we cannot handle all study requests, especially, in your case, we have to deny because of the problematical topic.

Gaining access to the LSE was more challenging. The authors initially contacted 80 companies. Less than 20 per cent responded and of those 85 per cent declined to participate in the study. However, contact was first made through those Austrians who agreed to be interviewed.

Table 6.3   Participants and research sites

Research sites	Number of participants
Vienna (VSE)	14
London (LSE)	20
New York (NYSE)	20
Total	54

Source: Compiled by the authors.

See Appendix 1 for further analysis of study design.

Through their network in London and through the lead author's consultancy contacts in the investment industry, this led to further contact with US-based financial institutions. Table 6.3 identifies the sites and number of participants involved in the study. Finally, access to the NYSE was achieved through known contacts in financial institutions who hold seat membership to the exchange.

Certain participants in Austria, the United Kingdom and the United States requested access to the interview questions prior to participating in the study. These were duly provided. Before commencing with the interview, each participant was informed of the nature and objectives of the research and the approximate one-hour duration it would likely take to complete the interview. Certain interviews were conducted at the interviewee's work location and others outside the office over drinks or lunch. No difference was discerned between the respondents' openness and the location of their interview. In addition two telephone interviews were conducted.

Study results

Four themes concerning insider trading emerged from the interviews (Table 6.4).

Interpretations of insider trading

Parallel to the contrast of views concerning insider trading identified in the literature, the study participants equally offered a range of interpretations of insider trading. Differences of view of insider trading did not vary according to stock exchange location but more according to individual opinion.

Table 6.4   Insider trading: emerging themes

Themes	Sub-themes
Interpretations of insider trading	Formal interpretation of insider trading
	Informal interpretaton of insider trading
Inside Information	Grapevine versus inside information
	Uncertainty about maket sensitivity
	Professional prerogative: research
Motivators for insider trading	Power
	Money
	Excitement of deal
Market efficiency: Impact of insider trading	Positive impact
	Negative impact
	No impact

Thirty out of the 34 Austrian and British participants initially presented insider trading in a legalistic manner. Similarly, all 20 US participants initially presented insider trading in a legalistic manner.

> Insider trading means you get information and use it against orders. If the information is not published yet, then it is insider trading.
>
> (Interviewee 15, LSE)

> Insiders are people whose job gives them access to confidential market-sensitive information and if they trade on it, it is insider trading.
>
> (Interviewee 4, VSE)

> It is about who has access to privileged information. It is not only certain class of people within financial institutions, their hierarchical position or role but much broader. It is also about social connections and networks such as personal connections, circle of family, friends and acquaintances.
>
> (Interviewee 39, NYSE)

However, as a result of further probing, contrasting views of insider trading were expressed. The majority of participants viewed insider trading as the 'grey area' of finance.

> To be honest, it is such a grey area you can't draw a line and say this is insider trading and this is not. I don't think you can define insider trading. If someone wants to buy shares and does not buy them on account of insider information, such as bad news, in reality, although he did not do anything, he is still insider trading. He used inside

information which was only accessible to a certain number of people, in a certain position, to not buy shares.

(Interviewee 9, VSE)

Everyone tries to find a firm definition and when you look closely at it there are many questions open in these definitions. If I would always check every requirement given in this definition before I trade ... it would be impossible. You don't have the time!

(Interviewee 20, LSE)

In the trading business, insider trading is considered illegal but not immoral or illegitimate. What is legal is defined by regulators but what is moral or legitimate is determined by community norms and culture. Defending what is insider trading is culture specific.

(Interviewee 49, NYSE)

Interviewee 49 captured the sentiments of traders at the NYSE who felt that insider trading was defined by the regulatory bodies. However a number also commented that the industry is over regulated.

SEC, NYSE and SOX Act have tightened regulatory rules and imposed heavy penalties for all kinds of misbehaviour including insider trading. There is now a Chinese wall between analysts and traders, but whenever an industry is overregulated as it is the case now, there is also the Chinese whisper ... the pendulum needs to swing back.

(Interviewee 40, NYSE)

Further, certain of the US participants felt that due to their sheer size financial institutions have become markets in themselves, and through so doing insider trading has emerged as unintentionally institutionalised.

Since the mid-1980s, the financial services industry has been going through ever greater consolidations and now we have under one roof all kinds of financial professionals, from traders and analysts to investment bankers, security broker-dealers, fund-mangers and investment consultants, of which many have insider information ... now instead of occasional rogue individuals, we have a culture of institutionalised insider trading. SEC, NYSE and other regulators are aware of this, but the clock cannot be turned back.

(Interviewee 43, NYSE)

In contrast, interviewee 11 (VSE) believed that insider trading can be defined according to the level of trading risk involved.

> For me, insider trading is if somebody knows FOR SURE he has relevant information ... I think the term 'for sure' in this case is very important; otherwise it is difficult to draw a line to the grapevine. Furthermore, I think, if the one who trades has an economic risk beyond this trade, you certainly can't say it is insider trading. And in most of the cases you have an economic risk.
>
> (Interviewee 11, VSE)

Others felt that attempting to define insider trading was a worthless exercise, as proving insider trading was a legal requirement for debate in court, which in many cases would be impossible to replicate in every day working life.

> It does not matter how you define insider trading. The legal definition was introduced to make information more available. But that's not going to work for a very simple reason: companies don't want that because of competition. The key thing about it is that there will always be people who have insider information and use this for their personal gain. There is no way of stopping these people.
>
> (Interviewee 17, LSE)

As the emerging views concerning the nature of insider trading varied according to participant, source and type of information and circumstance, a contextualist interpretation of insider information rather than the trade itself, became the focus of inquiry.

Insider information

According to Bettis *et al.*, (1998) as well as the AIMR (1996), insider information refers to information that is material but not public. However, the study respondents disputed such distinction as they drew a difference between inside information and 'the grapevine' both of which could be an equally powerful stimulus for trade (or not). Although all of the study participants recognised it as illegal to trade on insider information, most held the view that it is impossible to draw a clear line between these two sources of information.

> The differentiation between the grapevine and insider information is so difficult that I do not dare to draw a line.
>
> (Interviewee 14, VSE)

The Stock Exchange lives on gossip and information. It is impossible in most of the cases to get to the source of information, which would make it easier to classify this info. Hence it is impossible to decide if it was gossip or insider information.

(Interviewee 15, LSE)

Quality of information is key for our business and individual-centric revenue growth and pay potential. Obviously word of mouth is a key. There is also a pecking order of who get's to know what first.

(Interviewee 49, NYSE)

Equally, the participants questioned whether obtaining material that was non-public could be classified as insider information. In their view, the only relevant, non-public material is that which is of a market sensitive nature. No clear view emerged concerning what constituted market sensitive information.

not all information you get is market sensitive, most of the time you don't know beforehand, all you can do is guess.

(Interviewee 30, LSE)

which means market price influencing information and the person uses this information. But you have to consider that information may not be price influencing even if you think so, but you don't know in most of the cases.

(Interviewee 7, VSE)

All information is time sensitive. Whether you are trading on insider's information depends when and how you use, what you consider to be, sensitive information.

(Interviewee 42, NYSE)

A critical aspect of a professional market trader's job is research. Interviewees believed that if they uncovered information through their own research endeavour, no matter its source, such information cannot be seen in the legal sense as insider information.

Every trader has the right to use information he is able to access. His job is to collect information, put it together and draw his conclusions out of it – to make decisions.

(Interviewee 15, LSE)

It is my job to investigate. I have to find out what is going on in the market to make the right decisions. If I find something out because of

my investigation, no one else, apart from me knows. I don't believe
that's insider information – that is my job.

(Interviewee 3, VSE)

Interviewee 38 presented a more traditional perspective.

Whenever research is based on publicly unavailable information you
are in possession of insider information.

(Interviewee 38, NYSE)

Motivators for insider trading

Even though no shared view emerged concerning the nature of insider
trading, the survey participants discussed the motivation for pursuing
what could be 'blatantly agreed' as insider trading. Three main motivators
for insider trading emerged:

- Power
- Money
- Excitement of the deal

Power was considered as a particularly pertinent motivator for insider
trading by the participants at both the LSE and VSE.

First of all, through the entanglements between the board of directors, the supervisory board and the banks, it is easier to get to information. That's because of the smallness of the market. There are not
so many companies in Austria, therefore people at these levels know
each other. Have a look in the different reports of the companies, you
will always find the same names in different firms. This goes up to the
highest political spheres. This network gives them power.

(Interviewee 14, VSE)

These people are in positions where they have the highest power in a
company. No one is above them. So they think who can ever get me?
I am the boss.

(Interviewee 22, LSE)

Participants of the NYSE also pointed to power as a particularly
pertinent motivator for insider trading, irrelevant of whether the individuals are personally powerful in their own right or have access to an

influential network.

> One can be in a powerful position without being powerful. Relationships in this business are key. That's where you get the information. I used to tell my wife what is going on in the business and she used to chat to her life-style coach, who used to trade on this information ... only after SEC's investigators asked me whether I know this guy and I said, yes I am writing to Roger monthly cheques for services rendered on behalf of my wife, I become aware of this situation.
>
> (Interviewee 50, NYSE)

The power perspective to emerge is that of an individual overcoming resistance on the part of others in order to exert their will and, in so doing, produce results consistent with their views and objectives (Buchanan and Huczynski, 2003: 828). Such degrees of personal influence were considered as placing the 'powerful person' above the law and infallible to prosecution. Even if suspected of having committed an 'insider trading offence', certain investigations were considered by the interviewees as smothered or not initiated.

Further, the majority of respondents considered money as an equally powerful motivator for insider trading.

> If you think that people who are in positions where they earn a lot of money, like senior executives, are less greedy, then you are very wrong. Especially these people are very tight-fisted and stingy. An example: one customer I traded for, he experienced the heights and unfortunately also the depths of the stock market in the past. He ended up with €8 million and about four houses and he laments about existence fears.
>
> (Interviewee 8, VSE)

> I would say a motivator for an insider's trade is the most natural human quality, avarice. Especially people who work in this business, it is all about money, otherwise we would not do it.
>
> (Interviewee 31, LSE)

> In Austria I believe it is also a question of money. If you compare managing directors' salaries to managing directors' salaries in Germany, you will recognise that they get a fraction of their colleagues in Germany. Therefore they give themselves a bonus.
>
> (Interviewee 4, VSE)

It is a part of human nature to take advantage of situations. It is also reinforced by the pay structure. We are paid based on a percentage allocation of the commission earned off every deal. The average annual package of investment professionals in America is about US$170,000. However bonuses can vary substantially depending on what you do. If you are successful in M&A, your bonus may be US$2 million plus, in hedge funds about US$4 million plus and in the private equities they may start at US$2 million.

(Interviewee 53, NYSE)

Whilst LSE, NYSE and VSE participants perceive that money is a key motivator, VSE participants expressed a view that corporate board members are also motivated to undertake insider trading in order to rebalance their perceived 'under reward', in this case, in comparison to their German counterparts.

Although power and money were identified by the majority of participants as motivators for insider trading, for certain of the participants the excitement of the deal emerged as an additional motivator.

insider information in the sense that I define it, may be rather exciting. People with insider knowledge, being human beings, quite often want to boast about how they have access to insider knowledge secrets.

(Interviewee 17, LSE)

The motivation is winning with the risk you are running, doing the deal!!

(Interviewee 34, LSE)

The penalties are very high but there are always individuals who are prepared to take that risk and push the envelope further.

(Interviewee 44, NYSE)

Impact of insider trading: market efficiency

Similar to the range of arguments put forward by the academic community (Manne, 1966), the study participants held equally contrasting positions regarding the effect of insider trading on market efficiency.

The minority of interviewees believed that insider trading has a positive impact on market efficiency. Similar to Manne (1966), one emerging view emphasises that insider trading maintains the real value of the market. Interviewee 10 (VSE) goes further by stating that information asymmetry exists in markets with or without insider trading and therefore questions why insider trading is viewed as harmful.

> On balance I think its effect is good. I mean, if you allow insider trading, and some of it goes on, the effect is simply to drive share prices sooner to the level that they ought to be.
>
> (Interviewee 21, LSE)

> I truly believe that insider trading has positive impact on market efficiency simply because of the fact that information is quicker processed in market price. Furthermore I think that you always have people who know more than others.
>
> (Interviewee 10, VSE)

> It depends on the perspective one takes. From the legal compliance perspective, I think that it always has negative impact. It takes trust away from the market and from wider ownership.
>
> (Interviewee 47, NYSE)

A shared view expressed by LSE and VSE participants highlighted liquidity as well as insider trading as an important influence on market efficiency. In contrast, NYSE participants placed emphasis on market size.

> If a lot of insider trading is going on, of course it influences market efficiency, if you want, in a positive way. However, you also have to consider the liquidity of a market. In illiquid markets like VSE, insider trading will have much more impact than in a liquid market like London.
>
> (Interviewee 15, LSE)

> It is important to consider market size for any kind of financial trading. Think of the recent incident that upset the European bond market and the impact one large player had on a number of small national banks ... size matters!
>
> (Interviewee 48, NYSE)

Interviewee 15 (LSE) argued that insider trading investigations should be selectively pursued according to its effects (i.e. liquid versus non-liquid markets) and not universally applied.

However, the majority of study participants considered that insider trading has a negative effect on market efficiency. While most agreed that market price is more realistically determined if insiders trade, the importance of trust in capital markets and its effect on efficiency, was also emphasised. The point being made is that insider trading under-mines investor trust which, in turn, harms market efficiency.

> The discussion about insider trading and its positive impact on market efficiency has for sure its justification ... however, I believe that if a lot of insider trading is going on, the majority of investors would restrain and leave the market. As a result no one except insid-ers buy and sell, that would not lead to a more efficient market.
>
> (Interviewee 14, VSE)

> I think market efficiency suffers if insider trading is going on because trust of shareholders disappears. Let's take VSE as an exam-ple. It was always called the 'Insider Stock Exchange' and if you look at the performance of VSE at this time you can see that insider trading has a very negative impact on market efficiency.
>
> (Interviewee 11, VSE)

> Market confidence can be undermined by a variety of forces and actions of which insider trading is only one.
>
> (Interviewee 39, NYSE)

Additional to the range of views concerning the nature of insider trading and its effect on the market, the participants did not emerge with a shared view concerning for whom were trust and risk relevant concerns? The study respondents reported that a certain amount of insider trading goes on with minimal risk to themselves. Tomasic (1991) supports this view and therefore, for whom is market confidence an issue? For the private investor – emerged as the predominant view! Interviewee 16 (LSE), in particular, emphasises that if private investors were enlightened about the reality of insider trading in capital markets and came to terms with the phenomena, then the problems of mistrust and loss of confidence would be dissipated.

> If everybody knew that there were insiders about, and that you shouldn't assume that what you know is all that anybody else knows, then perhaps you'd be more careful when you are trading. I mean, with that general warning you could allow the markets to operate and there would be no problem.
>
> (Interviewee 16, LSE)

> The Market Abuse Directive is an EU wide initiative for preventing and detecting financial malpractice such as insider dealings and sus-picious transactions, which includes the creation of insiders' lists and

reports on managers as well as on directors' dealings. But that is a crude way to control the flow of sensitive information.

(Interviewee 21, LSE)

Certainly, one question raised by certain of the study participants is, why are Eastern European stock markets attractive for investors? The infrastructure of the Russian market, for example, is underdeveloped when compared to western European stock markets and that of the United States. No meaningful regulations exist regarding insider trading or market abuse for a number of the Eastern markets, Russia included. Nevertheless, the respondents reported that Austrian as well as English banks trade in these markets knowing insider trading is active. It is these markets that study participants drew on as examples of lack of regulation presence and its indeterminate effect on market efficiency.

A minority of interviewees even queried the supposed interrelationship between trust, risk and market efficiency. Interviewee 11 (VSE) suggested that markets are only efficient in the long run and on this basis insider trading has an inconsequential effect.

Basically yes; it is right that insider trading has a positive impact on market efficiency, but only in the short run, not in the long run. In the long run, the curve is smooth. Hence insider trading has, in my opinion, no impact on market efficiency.

(Interviewee 11, VSE)

This view is supported by certain of the NYSE based participants.

Markets are very dynamic and any individual action produces only a blip!

(Interviewee 36, NYSE)

A further minority of interviewees questioned the validity of the concept of market efficiency. Interviewee 3 (VSE) and interviewee 14 (VSE) point to the psychological motive, which they consider undermines the universalistic economic models of market efficiency.

Market prices are not just driven by information. I would say that for about 20% market prices reflect pure psychological reasons. During terror attacks, for example, market prices decrease, but a company is not worth less because one country bombs another country. For this reason the theory of market efficiency for me is not valid.

(Interviewee 3, VSE)

Interviewee 30 (LSE) goes further, emerging with a more extreme perspective, questioning the concept of belief in market efficiency.

> At the end of the day markets are not efficient. Hence, if something is not present it can also not be influenced by insider trading.
> (Interviewee 30, LSE)

Perhaps one of the more extreme views questioning market efficiency emerged from interviewee 43 (NYSE) who suggested that:

> This industry has a very aggressive culture and a growing complexity due to sheer number and scope of financial transactions where conflict of interest within the same institution is a norm. Market efficiency usually refers to market liquidity and if you follow the Warren Buffet principle to invest into what you know, then the more intimate information you have the more effective is your investment.
> (Interviewee 43, NYSE)

Insider trading: a contradiction?

The contrast of views offered by the study participants parallels the literature concerning the insider trading effect on market efficiency, market confidence and insider trading regulation influence (Manne, 1992; Harris, 2002).

However, in contrast to the literature, the study participants raise doubt as to the meaning and definition of insider trading. Distinguishing insider trader from insider information, the study participants emphasise that gaining information through research and through their personal networks is a key aspect of their job. Clear distinction between research gathered information and insider information does not emerge. The study participants question the validity of so-called clear cut cases such as a director's wife purchasing shares due to privileged information access, who, if caught, would be penalised, compared to not prosecuting someone for not trading as they are in possession of privileged 'bad news'. The lack of equitable definition has led most of the study participants to conclude that the concept of insider trading exists for political reasons and does little to remove privileged insiders from trading in markets. The study participants consider that by creating an atmosphere of 'political correctness', Western governments simply look good!

On the basis that legal, ethical and cultural arguments are considered suspect, it is postulated that eliminating the cause for insider trading could be achieved through appropriate systems of remuneration and reward. The findings of this study attribute insider information pursuit to reasons of power, money and 'excitement of the deal'. Yet, if a practice of remuneration were to be introduced allowing insiders to utilise their 'exclusive' information publicly through stock option plans, or special salary agreements, their motives for insider trading would be undermined. An 'insider like deal' would therefore be made legal but whilst preserving the excitement of the deal. Further, markets could operate freely, as share prices would reflect all relevant information, thereby more likely increasing market efficiency (Treynor and LeBaron, 2004). In parallel with Treynor and LeBaron's (2004) view, it is asserted that more transparent means be created whereby insiders could identify market opportunities which other market participants could judge.

Yet, despite the recommendation concerning transparent rewarding for usage of insider information and generally all the attention given, is insider trading such a big deal?

Considering the volume and value of shares traded per day, the study participants and other commentators concur that the contribution of insider trading to market distortions is small. One insider or small groups of insiders are not considered as driving up share price to the point of generating dissonance in the market. Thus, at best, market performance is viewed as being only marginally impacted. Considering the market abuse tactics adopted by large organisations to drive share price artificially in the 'right' direction, insider trading, in comparison, is concluded to have little effect on the volumes traded. Werhane's (1989) position that some traders know more than others and that information affects their decision making and the trading behaviour of others should they become privy to that information, is concluded as factually true. However, the significance of that statement is challenged, as markets are competitive by nature and in order to be successful in a competitive market, one needs to be better informed than other parties. In order to minimise the mistrust and suspicion involved in being better informed, the view offered is that appropriate reward whilst simultaneously making that information transparent, benefits all. Rather than looking to regulate or limit the individual who has access to privileged information, this paper concludes that attention should now focus on making more information available rather than increasing prosecutions. At the end of the day, which is the bigger problem? – The insider trader or the large, transnational corporations who have the capacity to sway markets which, in turn, potentially harm market efficiency?

References

Abdolmohammadi, M. and Sultan, J. (2002), 'Ethical reasoning and the use of insider information in stock trading', *Journal of Business Ethics*, 37(2): 165–173.

AIMR. (1996), *Standard of Practice Handbook* (7th Edition), Virginia: Association for Investment Management and Research.

Bettis, J.C., Duncan, W.A. and Harmon, W.K. (1998), 'The effectiveness of insider trading regulations', *Journal of Applied Business Research*, 14(4): 53–70.

Blaikie, N. (1993), *Approaches to Social Enquiry*, Oxford: Polity Press.

Blake, D. (1999), *Financial Market Analysis* (2nd Edition), Chichester: John Wiley & Sons.

Buchanan, D. and Huczynski, A. (2003), *Organizational Behaviour: An Introductory Text* (5th Edition), Herts: Prentice Hall International Ltd.

Denzin, N.K. and Lincoln, Y.S. (1994), *Handbook of Qualitative Research*, Thousand Oaks, CA: Sage Publications.

Eckbo, B.E. and Smith, D.C. (1998), 'The conditional performance of insider trades', *The Journal of Finance*, 53(2): 467–498.

Fama, E.F. (1970), 'Efficient capital markets: A review of theory and empirical work', *Journal of Finance*, 25: 383–417.

Frankel, R. and Li, X. (2004), 'Characteristics of a firm's information environment and the information asymmetry between insiders and outsiders', *Journal of Accounting and Economics*, 37(2): 229.

Gillham, B. (2000), *Case Study Research Methods*, London: Continuum International Publishing.

Harris, L. (2002), *Trading and Exchanges: Market Microstructure for Practitioners*, Oxford: Oxford University Press.

International Federation of Stock Exchanges. (2004), 'Market capitalization', available at http://www.fibv.com (accessed: 03.04.05).

Irvine, W.B. (1986), 'Insider trading: An ethical appraisal', *Business and Professional Ethics Journal*, 6(4): 3–33.

Jaffe, J.F. (1974), 'Special information and insider trading', *The Journal of Business*, 47(3): 410.

Laird, M.J. (1995), 'Insider trading', *Managerial Auditing Journal*, 10(5): 16–26.

Lakonishok, J. and Lee, I. (2001), 'Are insider trades informative?', *The Review of Financial Studies*, 14(1): 79–111.

Leavy, B. (1994), 'The craft of case-based qualitative research', *Irish Business and Administrative Research*, 15: 105–118.

London Stock Exchange. (2004), 'Market reports', available at http://www.londonstockexchange.com (accessed: 24.10.04).

Manne, H.G. (1966), *Insider Trading and the Stock Market*, New York: The Free Press.

———. (1992), 'Insider trading', *The New Palgrave Dictionary of Money and Finance*, 2: 416–419.

Miles, M.B. and Huberman, A.M. (1994), *Qualitative Data Analysis: An Expanded Sourcebook (2nd Edition)*, Thousand Oaks, CA: Sage Publications.

New York Stock Exchange (2004), 'About the NYSE', available at http://www.nyse.com (accessed: 29.08.05).

O'Hara, P.A. (2001), 'Insider trading in financial markets: Legality, ethics, efficiency', *International Journal of Social Economics*, 28(10–12): 1046–1062.

Parkman, A.M., George, B.C. and Boss, M. (1988), 'Owners or traders: Who are the real victims of insider trading?', *Journal of Business Ethics*, 7(12): 965–971.

Pope, P.F., Morris, R.C. and Peel, D.A. (1990), 'Insider trading: Some evidence on market efficiency and directors' share dealings in Great Britain', *Journal of Business Finance and Accounting*, 17(3): 359–380.

Ronen, J. (2000), 'Insider Trading regulation in an efficient market: A contradiction', *Critical Perspectives on Accounting*, 11(1): 97–103.

Saunders, A. (2001), *Financial Markets and Institutions: A Modern Perspective*, Berkshire: McGraw-Hill Publishing.

Saunders, A. and Cornett, M.M. (2002), *Financial Markets and Institutions: A Modern Perspective*, Berkshire: McGraw-Hill College.

Saunders, M.N.K., Lewis, P. and Thornhill, A. (2002), *Research Methods for Business Students* (3rd Edition), Herts: FT Prentice Hall.

Seyhun, H.N. (1986), 'Insiders' profits, costs of trading, and market efficiency', *Journal of Financial Economics*, 16(2): 189–212.

Shaw, B. (1988), 'Should insider trading be outside the law?', *Business and Society Review*, 66: 34–37.

Spencer, P.D. (2000), *The Structure and Regulation of Financial Markets*, Oxford: Oxford University Press.

Tomasic, R. (1991), *Casino Capitalism? Insider Trading in Australia: Australian Studies in Law. Crime and Justice*, Canberra: Australian Institute of Criminology.

Treynor, J.L. and LeBaron, D. (2004), 'Insider trading: two comments', *Financial Analysts Journal*, 60(3): 10–12.

Van Maanen, J. (1979), 'The fact of fiction in organizational ethnography', *Administrative Science Quarterly*, 24(4): 539.

Werhane, P.H. (1989), 'The ethics of insider trading', *Journal of Business Ethics*, 8(11): 841–845.

Wienerbörse. (2004), 'The listed companies of Wienerbörse', available at http://www.wienerborse.at (accessed: 24.10.04).

World Federation of Exchanges. (2005), available at http://www.fibv.com/WFE/home.asp?action=document&menu=28 (accessed: 12.01.05).

Yin, R.K. (2003), *Case Study Research: Design and Methods* (3rd Edition), London: Sage Publications.

Zekos, G.I. (1999), 'Insider trading under the EU, USA and English laws: A well recognised necessity or a distraction', *Managerial Law*, 41(5): 1–32.

7
CSR in the Boardroom: Myth or Mindfulness

Andrew P. Kakabadse and Nada K. Kakabadse

Introduction

The Anglo-American model of business practice, concerned with maximising shareholder wealth, has, as highlighted in previous chapters, experienced considerable crisis through its tendency to allow less than scrupulous corporate management to pursue their personal agendas. Charkham (1995) emphasised the point highlighting short-termism as a fundamental concern of capital markets. Equally, Kay and Silberston (1995) argued that the majority of publicly quoted companies are dominated by board directors that function as self-perpetuating oligarchies and, as such, are unlikely to diligently pursue their governance obligations. Equally, there is increasing recognition by international institutions such as the European Commission, the World Bank, the United Nations and the Organisation for Economic and Corporate Development (OECD) that profit serves private interests and its blind pursuit is likely to prove harmful (*The Economist*, 2005b: 12).

Bearing in mind concerns over shareholder value, this chapter presents a study exploring how board members of Anglo-American companies perceive CSR and its significance in terms of their pursuit of their board roles. To begin with, current responsibility practice and the cases for and against CSR from the literature are presented in order to provide a roadmap for better understanding the role and responsibility of board directors towards social responsibility. Attention is given to a review of literature concerning corporate practices, the different interpretations of corporate and social responsibility and emerging findings on CSR thinking and application at strategic levels, particularly in the boardroom. Highlighted are cases of corruption that have come to light over the past two decades, considered as substantially responsible for the ever greater number of corporate governance requirements placed on boards. One key point is that little has changed in the Anglo-American world in terms of the focus on shareholder value. If anything, the marketisation of the private and public sphere and the push of the Anglo-American economies to have their philosophy predominate over all others in the world is now increasingly evident despite the defence of the stakeholder philosophy by Continental European companies and agencies. Further, the literature review also highlights the range of meanings concerning corporate and social responsibility, ranging from responsibility to people and communities, sustainable development and concerns for the environment.

It is with such a background that attention is given to the varying roles, functions and processes found on boards in order to understand how CSR is viewed from this strategic perspective. The results of an international comparative study of boards and board directors and their views of the relevance of CSR to board functioning and contribution, is outlined. The chapter concludes that CSR has not captured the imagination of board directors and that risk management is the language and concern of boards.

Corporate practices

The impatience for realising short-term value in UK and USA corporate boardrooms, which first became evident in the 1980s in the form of corporate raiding by self-interested financiers such as James Goldsmith, Michael Milken, Ivan Boesky, Robert Maxwell and Alan Bond who respectively asset-stripped, downsized, delayered and re-engineered the companies they ran, became recognised as processes which ultimately damaged value with the failure of companies as BCCI and Polly Peck. Equally, unwelcome practices within firms as Enron, WorldCom, Global Crossing, ImClone, Tyco International, Arthur Anderson, Harris Scarfe and HIH (Australia), induced a flood of protests from investors and media drawing attention to alleged widespread improper business conduct, corporate wrongdoing and corporate collapse through the actions (or inactions) by external/non-executive directors and executive officers. Identified as the most tumultuous financial period in America since the 1930s, these scandals spawned legislation notably that of the Sarbanes-Oxley Act, 2002, and corporate governance reforms required by the New York and London Stock Exchanges. The United States experienced five of its ten biggest corporate collapses in this short period of time which resulted in a record US$880 billion of corporate bonds and loans being in a distressed or default state (Thornton *et al.*, 2002).

As example, in 2001, WorldCom paid its auditor, Arthur Andersen, a total of US$16.8 million in fees, of which only US$4.4 million related to annual audit services (Kirchgaessner *et al.*, 2002). That in itself was not unusual as Arthur Andersen partners were partially performance measured by their ability to cross-sell services across the firm (Ryan, 2002). Such practice was on the increase, for in 1976, audit fees made up 70 per cent of accounting firms' revenues but by 1998 audit fees fell to 31 per cent of total revenue (Ryan, 2002). By the year 2000, S & P 500 companies paid their auditors US$3.7 billion for non-audit services in contrast to the sum of US$1.2 billion in audit fees (Levitt and Dwyer, 2002; Levitt and Dwyer, 2003). Moreover, bankruptcies in the 1980s and 1990s also revealed so called 'institutionalised greed' amongst investment bank 'analysts', who are reported to have worked in a manner designed to generate investment banking business rather than produce expert and informed stock appraisal for the total benefit of the client (Levitt and Dwyer, 2002). Bank 'analysts', supposedly primarily responsible to their clients, have been viewed by certain writers as subverted by incentive payments to support the more profitable task of selling investment services through allegedly (Thornton *et al.*, 2002);

- lending despite high default risk and passing this risk on to others through securitisation in order to gain investment banking business,
- allocating IPO shares to favoured executives in exchange for investment banking business rather than 'selling' them to the highest bidders, and
- earning large sums by disguising debt through off-balance sheet partnerships, then selling these partnerships on to institutional investors.

Further, the two housing finance giants, Freddie Mac and Fannie Mae, the worlds largest insurer, AIG (American International Group), and General Re (unit of Warren Buffett's Berkshire Hathaway) have stood accused of using illicit accounting to smooth profits and to boost executive pay inappropriately whilst investment banks such as J.P. Morgan, Morgan Stanley and CSFB face regulatory attention (*The Economist*, 2005c).

Additional to scandal has been the recent downturn in the economy whereby investors and shareholders have become increasingly uneasy about 'excessive' executive remuneration when corporate performance and share price are in decline. The CEO's of the United Kingdom's top FTSE 200 companies have benefited from an average 77 per cent rise in remuneration over the last five years whilst the value of shares have dropped 33 per cent (*The Economist*, 2005a). In fact, the average UK CEO's pay is reported as almost 100 times higher than that of the average employee (Conyon and Sadler, 2005; *The Economist*, 2005a). A study of 476 of the world's largest private and public corporations, spanning 25 countries, revealed that nearly half of all current CEOs have held their job for less than three years emphasising the pressure for profitability and the need to visibly justify their substantial rewards (DBM, 2000). For example, in the United Kingdom, the average tenure of a FTSE 100 (or Fortune 500 in the United States) CEO is now under four years, down from ten years a decade ago (Behr, 2003). The CEO therefore has little incentive to consider the long-term consequences of the actions of the corporation, particularly on internal stakeholders such as employees and external stakeholders such as local communities. Recent examples are provided by Avon UK who moved their manufacturing from the underemployed town of Northampton to cheaper labour sites in Poland and James Dyson's decision to switch production of vacuum cleaners away from the UK market town of Malmesbury in Wiltshire to Malaysia. Similar actions have been noted by Ford, BMW, Barclays Bank, British Telecom who are pressurised to control costs as a key step to ensuring ever rising share prices that has given precedence to alternative sourcing of operations at the expense of local needs.

In a survey of more than 600 leading UK companies, Geroski and Gregg (1997) found that, even in times of recession, relatively few companies cutback on dividends but engage in considerable reductions of the workforce. Considering that in the past a typical recession in the United Kingdom lasted approximately ten months, Geroski and Gregg's (1997) study illustrates that firms are prepared to sacrifice the knowledge and skills of their employees in order to maintain shareholder return. According to the UK's Trade Union Congress (TUC, 1999), the primacy accorded to shareholder interest in the Anglo-American model of corporate governance weakens the economic performance of British companies and places a disproportionate burden of challenge on employees who, unlike shareholders, cannot hedge against risks. Shareholders have been perceived as the risk bearers and, as a result, the beneficiaries of legislative protection entitling them to see the company run in their interests (Kay and Silberston, 1995). Operating within an essentially principal–agent governance model in which the management are agents to the shareholder principals, executives are required to primarily consider shareholders when making operational and strategic decisions (Kay and Silberston, 1995). Within such an operating environment, the question remains, to whom then is the corporation responsible?

To whom is the corporation responsible?

Over the past 200 years, corporations have grown enormously in scale and importance whereby the invisible hand of Adam Smith has given way to the visible hand of the corporation or what Chandler (1977) called the 'managerial revolution'. Some even argue that certain corporations now govern societies to an even greater extent than governments (Bakan, 2005). Yet, and as shown in previous chapters, in support of the firm, proponents of free-market economics, such as Milton Friedman (1962; 1970), forcibly argue that the only purpose of a firm is to make profit for its shareholders. According to Friedman (1962: 133), there is 'one and only one social reasonability of business to use its resource and engage in activities designed to increase its profits so long as it ... engages in open and free competition without deception or fraud'. From the point of view of the social responsibilities of the corporation, Friedman (1994: 10) argues that CSR undermines the basic economic mission of business emphasising that shareholders are the only significant stakeholder group that corporate managers should consider when making decisions. Similarly, Arrow (1972; 1997: 138–139) proposes that 'firms ought to maximise profits ... there is practically a social obligation to do so', since business profit represents the 'next contribution that the firm makes to the social good and profit should therefore be made as large as possible'. Arrow (1997: 143–144) tempers that view by indicating that profit-maximisation should be limited according to local and international laws or ethical codes. Jensen and Meckling (1976) also promote a shareholder philosophy by viewing the firm as a legal fiction which, in reality, serves as a nexus of contracts for agreements between parties within the firm, or doing business with the firm, and, as such, relies on the rational behaviour of self-interested economic agents who understand the incentives of all contracting parties and equally protect themselves from exploitation from these parties. Windsor (2001: 227) argues that Adam Smith's proposition that 'wealth creation is the best path to social welfare' is a view that has gained extensive support amongst the Anglo-American as well as elements of the international business community. In effect, the neoclassical economic paradigm holds that profit-maximisation is perfectly reasonable and 'does not merely ignore the moral dimension but actively opposes its inclusion' (Etzioni, 1989: 12).

In contrast, the Continental European social obligation perspective requires companies to bear their communal responsibility by paying a greater level of taxation to the state so that government is enabled to meet its obligations to its citizens. The counter to state communal provision is the United States where philanthropy has a long tradition through charitable donation balanced by tax relief. Continental European communitarians take a different stance regarding corporate responsibility as inclusive of social and environment concerns as well as that of shareholder benefit. A study carried out by PricewaterhouseCoopers in 2001 (PWC, 2001: 42) concluded that the Anglo-American 'business model will not win an outright victory in Europe. Instead, a distinctively European style of capitalism will emerge drawing on many facets of the Anglo-American approach but preserving an eclectic European identity'. The Anglo-American 'concessionarian' model, based on the principal–agent relationship, is becoming increasingly compromised as in reality there is no 'ownership' concern with respect to the corporation except through contractual claims on assets and liabilities. European financial institutions, such as pension funds having substantial shareholdings in corporations, have been viewed by some as unlikely to behave as direct owners but fiduciaries which reinforce the communitarian perspective that large public corporations are owned by the community (Panapanaan *et al.*, 2001). In support, others note that the myopic nature of the free market paradigm systematically undervalues long-term investment, such as capital investment and research and development spending (Charkham, 1995). The Continental European 'communitarian' model identifies the corporation as a constitutional creation of the State, a status that considers the firm to have an existence beyond a 'nexus of contracts' thereby bearing responsibilities to stakeholders such as the workforce, the broader society in which the firm operates and future generations. Not that the European perspective is isolated for American writers such as Dahl (1972: 17) argued that 'every large corporation should be thought of as a social enterprise, that is an entity whose existence and decisions can be justified insofar as they serve public or social purposes', emphasising that companies hold a moral responsibility to community. In their review of UK company law, the Pensions and Investment Research Consultants Ltd (PIRC) (2000: 4) comment that it 'should be recognised that companies are social as well as economic entities and their activities have profound impacts on the community and the environment in a variety of ways and particularly through the externalisation of their costs'. Thus, 'since companies wield power and influence, it is clearly in society's interests that there is an effective system of corporate accountability' (PIRC, 2000: 4). Such has been the perspective in Continental Europe where the welfare society orientation obliges the firm to participate in the maintenance of society, not by providing chartable benefit but principally through paying taxes (Carroll, 1999; Panapanaan *et al.*, 2001).

CSR, governance and the boardroom

Even within predominantly shareholder economies, adopting the mantle of social responsibility has shown positive business effect. In a study over an 11-year period of 172 companies in 19 industries, Kotter and Heskett (1992) found that large US companies which gave equal priority to employees, customers and shareholders delivered a sales growth four times higher and an employment growth eight times higher when compared to 'shareholder first' companies. Buchholz (1982: 413), as well as Collins and Porras (2000) study of 'visionary' companies, concluded that adopting a CSR philosophy in the management of the enterprise offers, in the long run, higher levels of corporate performance. It has equally been argued that evident corporate responsibility practice improves the public image of the organisation through repositioning its traditional business mission (Davis, 1967; Carroll, 1989). A survey, carried out jointly by McKinsey Consulting and Institutional Investor Inc, found that investors pursuing a value strategy paid premium price for well-governed companies on the basis that companies displaying sound governance performed better, reduced risk and overtime became attractive to other investors who recognised the value of good governance (Agrawal *et al.*, 1996; IRB 2000a; 2000b; IBE, 2003). Their findings illustrate that sound corporate governance can serve as a tool for attracting socially conscious investors as well as influencing stock price with investors paying an additional premium of between 11 per cent and 16 per cent for a well-governed company (Agrawal *et al.*, 1996). Socially concerned shareholder activism has swept through America, the United Kingdom and even countries such as Venezuela and Indonesia, where institutional investors have shown themselves as prepared to pay an above average premium for well-governed companies (IRB, 2000b). Additionally, in Europe and Japan, partly through movements such as the International Corporate Governance Program of 1996 (SpencerStuart, 1999), external stakeholders are beginning to place pressure on corporate boards to think and act responsibly. The social responsibility of publicly owned enterprises are reported as increasingly on the twenty-first century agenda where media attention to globalisation is active in monitoring multinational capitalism (Panapanaan *et al.*, 2001). The emerging phenomenon of global activism and the growing number of special interest groups provide particular challenges for corporate public relations practitioners to the point where some suggest that, in the future, organisations will be judged more by their social policies than just by their delivery of products and services (Clarke, 1998; Daugherty, 2001).

Turning from a broader governance and societal perspective to the contribution of boards of corporations, despite considerable attention, no central all-embracing theme concerning the purpose and functioning of boards has emerged due to contrasting perspectives over board role and performance (Table 7.1). The concept of principal and agent itself has spawned three interrelated interpretations of board role in terms of guardian (Harris, 1994), that of compliance (Berle and Means, 1932/1968), control and conformance (Fama and Jensen, 1983). Equally, in terms of institutional shape and orientation, again differences of view have emerged (Domhoff, 1967; Friedland and Alford, 1991) ranging from partnership (Lorsch and MacIver, 1989), cross institutional and societal resource orientation (Pfeffer and Salancik, 1978; Freeman, 1983) to that of adopting a pluralistic/societal overview (Robson *et al.*, 1997). Such breadth of interpretation has been further stretched by the identification of three critical board roles, namely those of control, service and strategy (Zahra and Pearce, 1989; Johnson *et al.*, 1996; Maassen, 1999; Kakabadse and Kakabadse, 2001).

In the separation of ownership from the daily control of the enterprise (basis of agency theory), many view that the board's primary role is that of controlling and monitoring management (Berle and Means, 1932/1968; Eisenhardt, 1989). From this central role, a number of writers consider that activities such as enhancing company reputation, establishing contacts with external stakeholders and offering counsel and advice to executives are of sufficient importance to merit clustering under the banner of the board's service role (Lorsch and MacIver, 1989; Baxt, 2002). A third role is also identified as that of providing access to resources whether in the form of information (e.g. industry or competitor data) and/or physical resources (investors to support an IPO, extending lines of credit, bank loans) which Zahra and Pearce (1989) term as strategising, sometimes subsumed under the 'advising' role (Zald, 1969; Pfeffer, 1972; 1973; Preffer and Salancik, 1978). Certain scholars have argued that the strategising role now holds equal status to that of control and monitoring due to the performance pressures being applied by

Table 7.1 Board role and contribution: spread of interpretations

Theory	Influential authors	Board role	Performance criteria
Agency principle (trust law model)	Blackstone (1979); Harris (1994)	Guardian: Safeguards owners' interests Oversees management	Furthering of owners'/beneficiaries' interests
Agency principle (case law model)	Berle and Means (1932/1968); Williamson (1974); Blackstone (1979); Cieri *et al.* (1994)	Compliance: Monitor compliance and conformance Oversee management Safeguard owners' interests	Furthering of owners'/beneficiaries' interests Social (responsiveness to society)
Principal agency or agency theory (financial model)	Jensen and Meckling (1976); Fama and Jensen (1983)	Control/conformance: Control over management Safeguard and further owners' interests Audit compliance and conformance	Financial (Low operating cost, profitability) Systemic (survival, growth)
Managerial hegemony theory	Berle and Means (1932/1968); Wright Mills (1956); Domhoff (1967)	Symbolic (rubber-stamp): Ratify decisions Give legitimacy Service – support management	Financial (profitability) Systemic (oligopolistic, market power)
Institutional theory	Meyer and Rowan (1977); Friedland and Alford (1991)	Instrumental: Maintain legitimacy – order, stability and effectiveness Strategy/policy design Oversee conformance	Strategic contribution Board role Work norms Financial efficiency
Resource dependency theory	Pfeffer (1972; 1973); Pfeffer and Salancik (1978)	Boundary spanning/legitimising (co-option of external influences): Secure resources Promote networks/links Maintain stakeholder relations Provide external perspective Control management	Financial (profitability) Systemic (survival, growth, goal driven, competitive, market position) Social – CSR
Stewardship theory	Mace (1972); Lorsch and MacIver (1989); Donaldson (1990)	Partnership: Performance improvement Value adding Strategic partnering Support management	Value adding (strategic growth of resources, goal achievement) CSR

Continued

Table 7.1   Continued

Theory	Influential authors	Board role	Performance criteria
Stakeholder theory	Rhenman (1968); Freeman (1983); Blair (1995)	Balancing: Stakeholder interests Strategy/policy design/balance Control of management	Financial (profitability) Systemic (survival, growth) Social – CSR
Democratic theory (political model)	Teubner (1993); Robson *et al.* (1997)	Political (pluralistic): Promote mission Strategy/policy formulation Negotiate/balance plurality of needs and interests Probity/accountability	CSR Financial accountability and/or satiability Probity/transparency Systemic – survival

Source: Adapted from Kakabadse and Kakabadse (2001).

institutional investors (Tricker, 1984; Black, 1992; Kiel and Nicholson, 2002).

Yet despite guidelines and voluntary codes of best practice in the United Kingdom in particular, it is commonly accepted that each board determines its own practice (Kakabadse *et al.*, 2006). Certain boards view their role as developing the strategic questions for management to answer. Others see the board as setting the broad objectives for management to implement, whilst yet others combine elements of the three roles of control, service and strategic, certain focusing more on control and co-ordination with others principally attending to corporate reputation. In this myriad of applications, certain writers consider that boards increasingly need to play a more active role in orchestrating the CSR path to follow and/or be more active in examining the effectiveness of CSR application by management (Lawrence and Lorsch, 1967; Gordy, 1993).

The study

The call for boards to play a more active CSR role acted as the reason to pursue the study outlined in this chapter. Explored are how US, UK and Continental European board members perceive CSR and how adoption of CSR policy effects boards and corporate performance. For the purposes of this inquiry, it was assumed that CSR relevance and effect on board performance are best judged by individual board members (Mangham and Pye, 1991). It was also equally assumed that the differences of role of CEO, chairman and non-executive/independent directors (NEDs) are likely to induce differences of experience and perspective towards corporate responsibility, corporate social performance and sustainable development. Being an exploratory study, privileged inside information, which some refer to as the 'black-box of boardroom deliberation' (Daily *et al.*, 2003), was obtained in part by observation over a period of 26 months on how the boards of four corporations functioned and in part from one-to-one in-depth interviews with 42 board members who separately held the roles of chairman, CEO and NED.

Study participants were asked to reflect on how their boards operated in terms of effectiveness and to describe events or incidents in the boardroom relating to discussions concerning how CSR is understood and lived at the board level. The study participants were also asked to reflect on their personal role and contribution to the board in terms of CSR as well as on the role and contribution of other board members. The intention was to access relational level thinking in order to lead into relationship narratives. Previous studies (Baumeister *et al.*, 1990; Harvey and Orbuch, 1990; Baumeister and Newmann, 1994; Kramer, 1996) have shown how personal narratives provide rich sources of data highlighting how individuals frame social experiences and justify decisions made. Thus, it is considered that narrative methods of data gathering are useful in organisational inquiry from the point of view of better understanding socially constructed organisational processes (Pentland, 1999; Ng and de Cock, 2002). Given the networked nature of boards, each participant was able to draw on their experiences from a variety of role perspectives such as chairman, CEO and NED. Half of the participants were members of boards of multinational corporations, whilst 30 per cent were members of boards of companies whose shares were traded only on a local Stock Exchange in either the United States, the United Kingdom, France or Germany. Finally, a further 20 per cent of the participants held positions on the board of UK public authorities. Although 42 individuals participated in the study, a considerable number occupied two or more director roles on a number of boards, such as CEO on one board and NED on another, leading to an aggregate experience of 67 board roles. Certain of the participants held a director role on the board of a public company and also on the board of a public agency. Participant's personal, educational and professional backgrounds were of a significant diversity but no discerning trend could be determined concerning personal demographics and their effect on CSR pursuit in the boardroom.

All interviews were tape-recorded and transcribed. Narratives scripts were subsequently analysed and coded adopting a grounded theory approach, allowing for emerging themes and frameworks to be amended in the light of ensuing transcriptions (Guba and Lincoln, 1994; Miles and Huberman, 1994).

Study results

Four themes emerged concerning participants' experience of CSR considerations, discussions and pursuits in the boardroom, namely:

- CSR interpretations: spread of meanings, consistency of behaviour,
- CSR benefit: risk management,
- CSR policy: whose job is it? and
- CSR in the boardroom

  - not part of boardroom language in the United Kingdom and the United States
  - more a strategy for stakeholder engagement for board members of Continental European companies and the boards of UK public agencies.

CSR interpretations

Study participants expressed a plethora of CSR interpretations, supporting the Kakabadse *et al.* (2006) view that CSR represents a nearly endless range of perspectives and definitions, or as Frankental (2001: 20) states; a 'vague and intangible term which can mean anything to anybody'. Despite such variance, a particular theme did emerge, namely, the visibility of CSR-oriented behaviours at the level of enterprise and their potential positive or negative effect on personal and enterprise-wide reputation.

> I think it's more about an underlying culture in a business than necessarily coming up and filling in the 120 pages of the BiE (Business in the Community) corporate social responsibility questionnaire. In fact I've actually moved away from even calling it corporate social responsibility because I think it's much wider than that. I think it is corporate responsibility and it's more about the whole behaviour and ethos of the organisation. It's about behaviours and behaviours are not easily checked by check lists.
>
> CEO, Service Industry, UK board

A ghastly term, because it's become shorthand, but it does mean different things to different people. It's like that dreadful word, sustainability, which could mean anything but … no, I do not think that it is a fad and I suspect it'll keep evolving. … However, this is a business not a charity and as long as you do not break the law, you are behaving responsibly.

NED (External) Director, Service Industry, US Board

It is a complex language. Some of the complexity has been introduced deliberately by academics and promoted by consultants and some evolved intentionally. Call it as you will, for me it is about integrity. It represents integrity or lack of it of people who run the enterprise. In short, it is individual and organisational behaviour.

Non-Executive Director, Food industry, UK Board.

CSR benefits: risk management

The study participants further expressed the view that discussion of CSR was instrumental in enhancing awareness of risk management or what Jackson (2001) terms the new 'fashion' in business management. The perception put forward is that pursuit of CSR minimises the emergence of a negative reputation for the organisation (Aula and Heinonen, 2002). The adoption of CSR within the strategic portfolio of the enterprise is, in fact, positive image promotion, or in Lewis's (2001) terms, that of being recognised as one of the 'good' companies building a positive relationship with the 'public' and other stakeholders (e.g. media). The majority of the participants identified CSR initiatives as that of enlightened self-interest for the purpose of threat reduction and effective risk management.

We are a large corporation and you may say we have a bit of a past. But that has all changed in the last few years and we now have membership of the World Business Council for Sustainable Development, and we perform well in a variety of sustainable indices such as Dow Jones and FTSE 4 good and Storebrand. Our stock is included in a number of funds specialising in suitability and ethical performance including the BG Investment fund and Robur's ethical fund. We have built a strong reputation and we work hard on building relations with our customers, NGOs and our critics.

Non-Executive Director, Food Industry, UK Board

I think that we have given charitably. But now, of course with the environment and sustainability that's another game. I'm worried to some extent that the agenda has been hijacked. ... I'm nervous of corporate social responsibility becoming a box ticking exercise and where the rating agencies are not very responsible in the way they do it. Look at this listing, you've got McDonald's at the top of the list of most corporate responsibility tables. It does start to worry you.

> CEO, Retail Industry, US Board

It is all about balancing risk of reputation and we now have a responsibility committee. Since I'm the chair of that committee, the agenda is driven by the risks and particularly the non-financial risks to the company. A lot of them are licensed to operate reputation risk and so on, some of them are more immediate risks. So safety will be the number one.

> NED (External Director), Infrastructure, US Board

Participants also expressed concern that CSR governance and audit across countries and sectors is not differentiating those responsible from those irresponsible companies. Many commented that whilst some companies pursue genuinely well-intended CSR policies, promoted by enlightened business leaders, others use CSR as a marketing tool on behalf of the firm or as a self-serving promotion of personality. These insights support McDonnell's (1995) comment that the effect of corporate responsibility application, whether of a CSR or corporate philanthropy nature, is observable but the motivation for such action is much harder to ascertain. The view being put forward is that what is positioned to be in the public domain does not portray the reality of CSR practice.

Every listed company nowadays produces glossy CSR reports. It is taken as a norm. However, we are no more or less responsible as a result of it nor has our share price been affected in any significant way by it. Our shareholders know we produce it but they don't read it. All they want to know is how our shares trade.

> CEO, Infrastructure Company, UK Board

Enron, Parmalat and many others all had exemplary CSR reports and that makes many people cynical. Many see it as a marketing tool and in a way it is. Companies use reports to communicate to the market their good deeds whether it is a pollution prevention programme, environmental management, community outreach or employee volunteering initiative and corporate charity. However, I have seen companies that go beyond glossies. I also see my role as sharing good CSR and other practices with the board.

> Non-Executive Director, UK Board

CSR policy: whose job is it?

Participants expressed the view that CSR and environmental sustainability are sufficiently important issues that should not be left to the voluntary endeavour of directors of companies. The emergent view is that regulatory bodies need to play a more prominent role in crafting social policy, capturing the consensus of constituents and, in so doing, answer the question posed by Carmen and Lubelski (1997) of whose responsibility is CSR? The respondents acknowledge that commercial decisions weigh in favour of the financial aspects rather than the 'softer' people and ecological aspects of corporate strategy. It was surprising, therefore, that a considerable number of participants offered the view that regulatory pressure was important in terms of acting as a deterrent to the abuse of the environment and as a promoter of sustainability innovation.

> The business case for sustainability clearly has its limits under the prevailing economic and political conditions. Even with the best-case scenario, a company with a board of concerned self-reflective directors and enlightened ethical shareholders may spend, in some exception cases, up to 5% of overall turnover on social and environmental causes arguing that it will produce cost savings in the long run. The rest is maximising shareholder value. ... If I am to make a start today, where would I find these shareholders? Hence, I think that national and international regulators have to play a more responsible role. Environment is a societal issue and not an optional extra left to voluntary codes of conduct.
>
> CEO, Service Industry, UK Board

> The scandal of poverty and hunger is ultimately a political and ethical challenge to us all. And because businesses, large or small, are the major users of resources and to some extent are seen as ecologically the ones with a 'heavy footprint' or perpetrators of exploitation, we are involved in a complex web of moral issues. But no governing board, unless of a voluntary organisation, can afford to take on the burden of rectifying the ills of generations or of political failings. Business must make money and government must provide the legal framework of what is acceptable within which the market can be left to work. The initiative has to be a political one. Yes, corporations will lobby governments but they will also fall in line and implement as most of them do.
>
> Chairman, Legal Services, UK

Questions of any business's future sustainability needs to be answered in the context of debate over the ethics and consequence of what is generally called 'development'. What kind of development should we choose as a society and why? I think that sustainability is a big question that should not be left alone to politicians, or businessmen, or any one group of people but be deliberated by all. The issue spans beyond national borders and requires political influence to mediate among different interests and ensure social justice.

President, Financial Services, French Board

The views expressed resemble Bowen's (1953) argument that it is industry's obligation to pursue policies and to follow lines of action that enhance societal values, thus implying that CSR is the responsibility of industry regulatory bodies and the national political process rather than individual organisations. Equally, other scholars (Preston and Post, 1975; Sethi, 1975; Carroll, 1979) argue that social responsibility comprises economic, legal, ethical and discretionary obligations whereby economic responsibilities are expressed as the products and services that society wants for-profit, legal responsibilities as the formal contract with society and ethical or discretionary responsibilities representing society's expectations of business that venture beyond basic legal obligations.

Sustainability is not voluntary corporate behaviour. However, the excessive influence of international corporate lobby groups over EU (European Union) policy making has muted EU efforts. Multinationals lobbied governments affecting the markets within which they operate. They seek to influence the debate on a broad range of public concerns – such as the adoption of genetic modification or environmental pollution. They also often support political parties or politicians financially, with an expectation in some places of heightened access to that politician when it counts. ... It is a greedy corruptionism.

Non-Executive Director, Service Industry, French Board

Certain of the participants felt that powerful lobby groups have unduly influenced the European Commission's CSR policy exposing CSR as a voluntary or discretionary activity of enterprises, namely that CSR is a 'concept whereby companies integrate social and environmental concerns in their business operations and in their interactions with their stakeholders on a voluntary basis' (EC, 2001: 1). The view to emerge more from the Continental European directors is that CSR, exposed to discretionary action, nurtures a platform of substantially varying standards of responsible practice which, from a longer-term perspective, is unsustainable.

CSR in the boardroom

Two distinct views emerged concerning the role of CSR in the boardroom. One strongly held perspective of UK and US participants is that CSR has no place in boardroom discussions (Fitzpatrick, 2000). In contrast, CSR as a strategy for stakeholder engagement was considered crucial by French and German board directors as well as board members of UK public agencies (e.g. housing and health trusts). Such views capture the Kakabadse and Kakabadse (2001) assumption that societal structures and governance philosophies are a significant determinant of boardroom behaviour.

Predominantly, UK and US board directors consider that the role of the board is to assess strategic initiatives in terms of 'sound' return on investment. The terminologies of 'risk', 'reputation', 'brand management' and 'investment' are accepted boardroom lexicon (Fombrun and Shanley, 1990). Corporate responsibility pursuit was expressed as that of enhancing shareholder value and minimising the dilution of profits. CSR initiatives presented to the board in terms of risk and reputation were more likely to receive approval especially if a rise in profit margins was pending.

> Listed companies live by their quarterly performance. To make the case for intangible expenses with shareholder funds is difficult as it has to be part of strategy. Boards do not craft strategy. They assess and approve management strategy. In some cases, the argument can be made for less tangible costs such as reputation, brand image, industry peer pressure and social factors to be considered if you have operations in deprived areas of the world. But when stock prices dive, all of these will not help and therefore are easily put aside as you concentrate on the bottom line. Remember that cost-effectiveness, profit-optimisation, profit-maximisation and risk management are the lingua franca of the board.
>
> Non-Executive Director, Service Industry, UK Board

> Do not believe when people tell you that they deal with CSR issues in the boardroom. Because they do not. At least not in my experience and I currently sit on four boards. Secondly, CSR is not a boardroom issue. It is a management issue. It is a daily grind concerning how you go about managing your business. External directors do not have

day-to-day knowledge of operations. The board is concerned with macro issues in terms of risk and market position.

Non-Executive Director, numerous UK Board positions

A typical board agenda here has a strong emphasis on safety which is the culture that runs right through the business. Then the focus is on the performance of the business, both financial and other issues which may or may not have financial impact but may have a reputation impact of one sort or another.

CEO, Infrastructure Company, UK Board

As an independent director, my role is to oversee the maximisation of shareholder wealth and that is also the most important goal of US corporate law. Corporate internal affairs are governed by the law of the State where the company is incorporated. Until laws change, there is no way that management should be spending shareholder money on anything that does not generate value for shareholders. If you do not break the law, by employing illegal labour or violate tax or security laws you are behaving responsibly. The moment you break the law, it displays irresponsible behaviour and you are using shareholders money to fix the problem. The role of the board is to oversee that management behave responsibly, efficiently and create shareholder value.

External Board Director, Service Industry, US Board

Social responsibility here is acting within the law. We are not in a polluting industry in the same way as the oil and chemical industry or some bits of the minerals industry. But we think in terms of risk management. The boardroom discussion is about managing risks.

President, Infrastructure Company, US Board

In contrast, members of Continental European boards strongly indicated that sustainable development is a key consideration in the enterprise strategy formulation process. Continental European board members emphasised that boards of EU companies are intensely involved in stakeholder dialogue and the embedding of CSR in the strategic debate, thus pro-actively exercising their resource and strategic role in addition to their oversight (control) and service role.

We are a French enterprise and we are constitutionally bound to protect the environment and social rights. France is the first country in the world that has put the right to live in a healthy environment on the same legal footing as human rights. Environmental protection and social cohesion underpin everything we do. We spend a considerable time at our meetings devoted to strategy and how it may impact or be integrated with environmental and social issues.

President, Service Industry, France

In France the language of CSR is new but the ideas of 'social cohesion', 'social dialogue', 'solidarity' and 'ecology' are norms irrelevant of one's political persuasion. We have the shortest working week in all OECD countries, higher productivity than both US and UK and our government supports the idea of an international solidarity levy on international transactions.

NED, Food Industry, France

We operate within 'Rhenish capitalism' or corporate law of co-determination which gives considerable importance to the interests of employees as well as those of shareholders and other stakeholders. Our managing board (Vorstand) has introduced a reward system encouraging people to operate in ways that are innovative but also in ways that fit with how they believe the rest of society should be operating. We are concerned with our next generation.

Director, Supervisory Board (Aufsichtsrat), Germany

Directors of UK public agency boards expressed views resonant with Continental European board members. Social and environmental issues were deemed as being at the centre of public agency strategy.

I guess the reason I joined a board of a public agency is because its fundamental value is social responsibility. That makes this board so completely rewarding to work for. You know that corporate social responsibility is not exercised here as a marketing tool.

Chairperson, Public Housing, UK Board

You can read an ancient inscription in the main hallway of the foundation hospital which says quite a lot about CSR, I think it pretty much sums up this hospital, something about honesty and integrity enshrined within the organisation right down to its foundations. I believe it is so fundamental in a public sector organisation and that is what makes the NHS so wonderful to work for. You know what CSR is here as it's almost inbuilt in the sense of providing public service.

Chairperson, National Health Services, UK Board

Board directors of companies who adopted a stakeholder philosophy toward governance consistently pronounced the promotion of core values concerned with service to community, their active involvement with stakeholders on key strategic issues and the evaluation and re-evaluation of sustainable performance.

> Here we are all partners and shareholders. This structure has been introduced by our founders. It also means that all decisions are made by consensus and although parts of our shares are public, no one can buy us without partners' consensus. It is written in our constitution. ... Social and environmental well-being is at the heart of our core values and are fundamental to our Quaker philosophy.
>
> Chairman, Components Industry (Stakeholder Structured Enterprise), UK Board

It is worth noting that all the UK companies in our sample that pursued a stakeholder philosophy, shared a common thread whereby core values were enshrined in the company's constitution. Such realisation adds weight to the Collins and Porras (2000) finding that company pursuit of socially progressive policies results in long-term success with higher benefits for shareholders, the carrying of less debt and demonstratably better treatment of stakeholders.

Conclusion

Similar to the analysis of the literature on corporate and social responsibility thinking and practice, a substantial divergence of thinking and application was expressed by the study respondents. However, one consistent theme is identified. Directors of boards of Continental European companies, UK public agency boards and UK companies who explicitly pursued a stakeholder orientation to corporate governance considered sustainable development (including that of CSR) as a core responsibility of the board of directors. It is concluded, therefore, that the fundamental model of corporate governance of the organisation is a decisive factor for embedding sustainability into the firm's strategy.

The study results also revealed that CSR, sustainability or other 'soft' social issues did not emerge as part of the language of the majority of the US and UK boards examined. Rather the language of effective risk management, compliance, internal controls and reputation management emerged as critical to the pursuit of accountability and the reduction of risk to shareholders. Moreover, the assessment of business risks were focused on financial matters and, in some cases, overlooked risks such as those related to environment, health and, at times, even safety matters.

Moreover, the prevailing view was that of 'not breaking the law' such as not paying taxes. In effect, Anglo-American social contribution to society practice emerged as limited.

Concerns were expressed that the label of CSR was not delivering on the promise of added value. Certain firms were seen to misuse CSR as a PR exercise, promoting image and reputation without substance. Members of US/UK national and multinational boards expressed views that both executive and non-executive directors considered the role of boards as primarily that of oversight (control), only then followed by service and strategic development. Participants from Continental European boards offered a different picture emphasising service, and only then the strategy and oversight roles thus positioning CSR as an exercise of substance and not just one of communication management.

Overall, US/UK board members observed that they were not opposed to the idea of and the benefit to be gained from CSR. What they expressed was that the pursuit of profit (or cost management) was so important for organisational survival that such thinking dominated the board's concern in terms of responsibility to its shareholders. For the Anglo-American enterprise, until a change of political scenario occurs, little else will change concerning CSR in the boardroom.

References

Agrawal, R., Findley, S., Greene, S., Huang, K., Jeddy, A., Lewis, W.W. and Petry, M. (1996), 'Capital productivity: Why the US leads and why it matters', *The McKinsey Quarterly*: 38–55.

Arrow, K.J. (1972), 'Some models of race in the labor market', in A.H. Pascal (Ed.), *Racial Discrimination in Economic Life*, Lexington, MA, USA: Lexington Books.

———. (1997), 'Intergenerational equity and the rate of discount in long-term social investment', *Working Paper 97005*, Stanford, CA: Stanford University Department of Economics.

Aula, P. and Heinonen, J. (2002), *Reputation: A Business Driver (Maine: menestystekijä, in Finnish)*, Helsinki: WSOY.

Bakan, J. (2005), *The Corporation: The Pathological Pursuit of Profit and Power*, New York, USA: Free Press.

Baumeister, R. and Newmann, L. (1994), 'How stories make sense of personal experiences: Motives that shape autobiographical narratives', *Personality and Social Psychology Bulletin*, 20: 676–690.

Baumeister, R.F., Stillwell, A. and Wotman, S.R. (1990), 'Victim and perpetrator accounts of interpersonal conflict: autobiographical narratives about anger', *Journal of Personality and Social Psychology*, 59(5): 994.

Baxt, R. (2002), *Duties and Responsibilities of Directors and Officers* (17th Edition), Sydney: Australian Institute of Company Directors (AICD).

Behr, R. (2003), 'Boarding school to boardroom', *BBC News Online*, available at http://news.bbc.co.uk/1/hi/business/3244277.stm (accessed: 04.04.05).

Berle, A.A. and Means, G.C. (1932/1968), *The Modern Corporation and Private Property* (Revised Edition), New Brunswick, USA: Transaction Publishers.

Black, B.S. (1992), 'Agents watching agents: the promise of institutional investor voice', *UCLA Law Review*, 39(4): 811–893 New Brunswick.

Blackstone, W. (1979), *Commentaries on the Laws of England: A Facsimile of the First Edition of 1765–1769* (Vols 1–4), Introduction by S.N. Katz, A.W.B. Simpson, J.H. Langbein and T.A. Green, Chicago, IL: University of Chicago Press.

Blair, M.M. (1995), *Ownership and Control: Rethinking Corporate Governance for the Twenty-first Century*, Washington DC: Brookings Institution Press.

Bowen, H.R. (1953), *Social Responsibilities of the Businessman*, New York: Harper & Row.

Buchholz, R.A. (1982), *Business Environment and Public Policy: Implications For Management*, Englewood Cliffs, NJ: Prentice-Hall.

Carmen, R. and Lubelski, M. (1997), 'Whose business is it anyway? – The question of sustainability', in P.W.F. Davies (Ed.), *Current Issues in Business Ethics*, London: Routeledge, pp. 27–38.

Carroll, A.B. (1979), 'A three-dimensional conceptual model of corporate performance', *Academy of Management. The Academy of Management Review*, 4(4): 497–505.

———. (1989), *Business and Society: Ethics and Stakeholder Management*, London: South Western College Publishing.

———. (1999), 'Corporate social responsibility: Evolution of a definitional construct', *Business and Society*, 38(3): 268–295.

Chandler, A.D. (1977), *The Visible Hand: Managerial Revolution in American Business*, London: Harvard University Press.

Charkham, J.P. (1995), *Keeping Good Company: A Study of Corporate Governance in Five Countries*, Oxford: Oxford Paperbacks.

Cieri, R.M., Sullivan, P.F. and Lennox, H. (1994), 'The fiduciary duties of directors of financially troubled companies', *Journal of Bankruptcy Law and Practice*, 3(4): 405–422.

Clarke, T. (1998), 'Research on corporate governance', *Corporate Governance: An International Review*, 6(1): 57–66.

Collins, J. and Porras, J. (2000), *Built to Last: Successful Habits of Visionary Companies* (3rd Edition), London: Random House Business Books.

Conyon, M. and Sadler, G. (2005), 'Rewards to UK chief executives start to match those of american bosses', The Royal Economic Society Annual Conference, Nottingham: University of Nottingham, March 21–23.

Dahl, R. (1972), 'A prelude to corporate reform', *Business and Society Review*, 1(1): 17.

Daily, C.M., Dalton, D.R. and Cannella, A.A. (2003), 'Corporate governance: Decades of dialogue and data', *Academy of Management. The Academy of Management Review*, 28(3), p. 371.

Daugherty, E.L. (2001), 'Public Relations and Social Responsibility', in R.L. Heath (Ed.), *Handbook of Public Relations*, London: Sage Publications Ltd, pp. 389–401.

Davis, K. (1967), 'Understanding the social responsibility puzzle: What does the businessman owe to society?', *Business Horizons*, 10, pp. 45–50.

DBM (Drake Beam Morin). (2000), 'CEO tenure at risk worldwide, reports Drake Beam Morin', DBM, available at hhtp://www.amgr.com/pdf/0200.pdf (accessed: 04.04.05).

Domhoff, G.W. (1967), *Who Rules America?*, Englewood Cliffs, USA: Prentice Hall.

Donaldson, L. (1990), 'The ethereal hand: Organizational economics and management theory', *Academy of Management. The Academy of Management Review*, 15(3): 369–381.

EC (European Commission). (2001), 'Promoting a European framework for corporate social responsibility', *Green Paper*, Brussels: EC.

Eisenhardt, K.M. (1989), 'Agency theory: An assessment and review', *Academy of Management. The Academy of Management Review*, 14(1): 57–74.

Etzioni, A. (1989), *The Moral Dimension: Towards a New Economics*, London: Macmillian.

Fama, E.F. and Jensen, M.C. (1983), 'Separation of ownership and control', *Journal of Law and Economics*, 26(2): 301–325.

Fitzpatrick, K. (2000), 'CEO views on corporate social responsibility', *Corporate Reputation Review*, 3(4): 292–302.

Fombrun, C.J. and Shanley, M. (1990), 'What's in a name? Reputation building and corporate strategy', *Academy of Management Journal*, 33(2): 233–258.

Frankental, P. (2001), 'Corporate social responsibility – A PR invention?', *Corporate Communications*, 6(1): 18.

Freeman, R.E. (1983), *Strategic Management: A Stakeholder Approach*, London: Financial Times Prentice Hall.

Friedland, R. and Alford, R.R. (1991), 'Bringing society back in: Symbols, practices, and institutional contradictions', in W.W. Powell and P. DiMaggio (Eds), *The New Institutionalism in Organizational Analysis*, Chicago, IL: University of Chicago Press.

Friedman, M. (1962), *Capitalism and Freedom*, Chicago, IL: University of Chicago Press.

———. (1970), 'The social responsibility of business is to increase its profits', *The New York Times Magazine*.

———. (1994), *Money Mischief: Episodes in Monetary History*, Australia: Harcourt Australia.

Geroski, P.A. and Gregg, P. (1997), *Coping with Recession: UK Company Performance in Adversity*, Cambridge: Cambridge University Press.

Gordy, M. (1993), 'Thinking about corporate legitimacy', in B. Sutton (Ed.), *The Legitimate Corporation: Essential Readings in Business Ethics and Corporate Governance*, Cambridge: Basil Blackwell, pp. 82–101.

Guba, E.G. and Lincoln, Y.S. (1994), 'Competing paradigms in qualitative research', in N.K. Denzin and Y.S. Lincoln (Eds), *Handbook of Qualitative Research*, Thousand Oaks, CA: Sage Publications, pp. 105–117.

Harris, M. (1994), 'The power of boards in service providing agencies: Three models', *Administration in Social Work*, 18(2): 1–15.

Harvey, J.H. and Orbuch, T.L. (1990), *Interpersonal Accounts: A Social Psychological Perspective*, Oxford: Blackwell Publishers.

IBE (Institute of Business Ethics) (2003), 'Does business ethics pay?', *Press Release*, available at http://www.ibe.org.uk/DBEPpr.htm

IRB (Investors Relations Business). (2000a), 'News features: global firms win awards for best corporate governance', *Staff Reports*, Institutional Shareholders Services Inc, March 6, pp. 1–2.

———. (2000b), 'Good governance pays off: institutions will pay a premium for an independent board', *Staff Reports*, Institutional Shareholders Services, July 10: 1–3.

Jackson, B. (2001), *Management Gurus and Management Fashions*, London: Routledge.

Jensen, M.C. and Meckling, W.H. (1976), 'Theory of the firm: Managerial behavior, agency costs and ownership structure', *Journal of Financial Economics*, 3(4): 305–360.

Johnson, J.L., Daily, C.M. and Ellstrand, A.E. (1996), 'Boards of directors: A review and research agenda', *Journal of Management*, 22(3): 409–438.

Kakabadse, A. and Kakabadse, N. (2001), *The Geopolitics Of Governance: The Impact Of Contrasting Philosophies*, New York: Palgrave Macmillan.

Kakabadse, A., Kakabadse, N.K. and Barratt, R. (2006), 'Chairman and chief executive officer (CEO): that sacred and secret relationship', *Journal of Management Development*, 25(2): 134–150.

Kay, J. and Silberston, A. (1995), 'Corporate governance', *National Institute Economic Review*, 153: 84–97.

Kiel, G. and Nicholson, G. (2002), *Boards That Work: A New Guide for Directors*, Berkshire: McGraw–Hill Education.

Kirchgaessner, S., Chaffin, J. and Walters, R. (2002), 'The scandal that nobody saw coming', *FT. com*, June 26, London.

Kotter, J.P. and Heskett, J.L. (1992), *Corporate Culture and Performance*, London: Free Press.

Kramer, R.M. (1996), 'Divergent realities and convergent disappointments in the hierarchic relation: Trust and the intuitive auditor at work', in R.M. Kramer and T.R. Tyler (Eds), *Trust in organizations: Frontiers of Theory And Research*, Thousand Oaks, CA: Sage Publications, pp. 216–245.

Lawrence, P.R. and Lorsch, J.W. (1967), 'Environmental demands and organizational states', in *Organization and Environment: Managing Differentiation and Integration*, Boston, MA: Harvard University Press, pp. 250–264.

Levitt, A. and Dwyer, P. (2002), 'Arthur Levitt's crusade', *BusinessWeek*, September 30.

——. (2003), *Take on the Street: What Wall Street and Corporate America Don't Want You to Know: What You Can Do to Fight Back*, Thorndike, ME, USA: Thorndike Press.

Lewis, S. (2001), 'Measuring corporate reputation', *Corporate Communications*, 6(1): 31.

Lorsch, J.W. and MacIver, E. (1989), *Pawns or Potentates: Reality of America's Corporate Boards*, Boston, MA: Harvard Business School Press.

Maassen, G.F. (1999), *An International Comparison of Corporate Governance Models*, Amsterdam: SpencerStuart.

Mace, M.L. (1972), *Directors: Myth and Reality*, Boston, MA: Harvard Business School Press.

Mangham, I.L. and Pye, A. (1991), *The Doing of Managing*, Oxford: Blackwell Publishers.

McDonnell, C. (1995), 'Does big business have a big heart?', in M.L. Stackhouse, D.P. McCann, S.J. Roels and P.N. Williams (Eds), *On Moral Business: Classical and Contemporary Resources for Ethics in Economic Life*, Grand Rapids, Michigan, USA: Wm B Eerdmans Publishing Co, pp. 726–732.

Meyer, J.W. and Rowan, B. (1977), 'Institutionalized organizations: Formal structure as myth and ceremony', *American Journal of Sociology*, 83(2): 340–363.

Miles, M.B and Huberman, A.M. (1994), *Qualitative Data Analysis: An Expanded Sourcebook* (2nd Edition), Thousand Oaks, CA: Sage Publications.

Ng, W. and de Cock, C. (2002), 'Battle in the boardroom: A discursive perspective', *The Journal of Management Studies*, 39(1): 23.

Panapanaan, V.M., Linnanen, L., Karvonen, M-M. and Phan, V.T. (2001), *Roadmapping Corporate Social Responsibility in Finnish Companies*, Finland: Helsinki University of Technology.

Pentland, B.T. (1999), 'Building process theory with narrative: From description to explanation', *Academy of Management. The Academy of Management Review*, 24(4): 711–724.

Pfeffer, J. (1972), 'Size and composition of corporate boards of directors: The organization and its environment', *Administrative Science Quarterly*, 17(2): 218.

———. (1973), 'Size, composition, and function of hospital boards of directors: a study of organization-environment linkage', *Administrative Science Quarterly*, 18(3), p. 349.

Pfeffer, J. and Salancik, G.R. (1978), *The External Control of Organizations: A Resource Dependence Perspective*, Harlow: Longman Higher Education.

PIRC (Pensions and Investment Research Consultants Ltd). (2000), 'Companies fail to report on their most important asset – People, PIRC Press Release, available at http://www.pirc.co.uk/pr17feb.htm (accessed: 20.03.02).

Preston, L.E. and Post, J.E. (1975), *Private Management and Public Policy: Principle of Public Responsibility*, Englewood Cliffs, USA: Prentice Hall.

PWC (PricewaterhouseCoopers). (2001), 'Corporate reputation: Global risk management', available at http://www.pwcglobal.com/extweb/newcolth.nsf/docid/019d1cd3a2905dbd85256a450063549d (accessed: 20.03.02).

Rhenman, E. (1968), *Industrial Democracy and Industrial Management*, London: Tavistock Publishing.

Robson, P., Locke, M. and Dawson, J. (1997), *Consumerism or Democracy? User Involvement in the Control of Voluntary Organisations*, Bristol: The Policy Press.

Ryan, C. (2002), 'Andersen's impartiality "not an issue" ', *The Australian Financial Review*, October 29, p. 3.

Sethi, S.P. (1975), 'Dimensions of corporate social performance: An analytical framework', *California Management Review*, 17(3): 58–64.

SpencerStuart, (1999), *European Board Index: Current Board Trends and Practices at Major European Corporations*, Amsterdam: SpencerStuart.

Teubner, G. (1993), *Law as an Autopoietic System*, Oxford: Blackwell Publishers.

The Economist. (2005a), 'Britain: Compensation culture; Boardroom pay: Compensation culture', 374(8419), p. 31.

———. (2005b), 'The good company: A survey of corporate social responsibility', 374(8410), pp. 1–18.

———. (2005c), 'Finance and economic: Knocked off their pedestals; Wall Street', 375(8420): 71–72.

Thornton, E., Coy, P. and Timmons, H. (2002), 'The breakdown in banking. Trust is eroding and profits may follow as business models falter', *Business Week*, October 7, p. 40.

Tricker, R.I. (1984), *Corporate Governance: Practices, Procedures and Powers in British Companies and Their Boards of Directors*, Hampshire: Ashgate.

TUC (Trade Union Congress). (1999), *Modern Company Law for a Competitive Economy – The Strategic Framework, A Consultation: A TUC Response*, London: TUC.

Williamson, O.E. (1974), *Economics of Discretionary Behaviour*, London, UK: Kershaw Pub. Co.

Windsor, D. (2001), 'The future of corporate social responsibility', *International Journal of Organizational Analysis*, 9(3): 225–256.

Wright Mills, C. (1956), *The Power Elite*, Oxford: Oxford University Press.

Zahra, S.A. and Pearce, J. A. II (1989), 'Boards of Directors and corporate financial performance: A Review and Integrative Model', *Journal of Management*, 15(2): 291–334.

Zald, M.N. (1969), 'The power and functions of Boards of Directors: A theoretical synthesis', *American Journal of Sociology*, 75(1): 97–111.

Index